Frontline Solution

The best solution for agricultural examination time

RAEO, RHEO, ICAR AIEEA, JRF/SRF, IBPS AFO, NABARD, FCI, ASRB NET, SAUs CET

RAVINDRA DOHLEY

(Ph.D. Research Scholar)

RAVI YADAV

(M.Sc. Horticulture)

NOTION PRESS

NOTION PRESS

India. Singapore. Malaysia.

ISBN xxx-x-xxxxx-xx-x

To the earth's peasants and farmers whose hard work and perseverance will develop our world, and to the teachers and inquisitors who lead us wisely,

Thank you for their unwavering commitment to growth, knowledge, and sustainability.

Contents

Foreword

Agriculture is not just a business; It is the foundation of culture, a symbol of sustaining life, uplifting the economy and the resilience of people who work on the ground. This book tries to explore the breadth and depth of agriculture not only as a science but also as a way of life. By providing a comprehensive overview of crops, farming techniques, resource management, and plant health, this book will become an essential guide for growing and experienced readers in the field.

The book provides an invaluable foundation for those preparing for competitive audits in agriculture. These include careful evaluation of agricultural practices, a focus on horticultural cultivation, and significant innovations in pest and disease management, plant species, and nutritional deficiencies. The structural layout serves not only as a means of learning, but also as a sustainable resource that bridges the gap between textual knowledge and practical application.

Through well-planned maps, detailed descriptions, and fascinating examples, this book showcases the dedication of scientists, farmers, and educators who have shaped agriculture. It is a reminder of the enduring importance of innovation and tradition, at a time when sustainable practices are essential to the future of food security and environmental protection.

This book will inspire our readers to step forward, challenge existing examples, and come up with their own ideas in this ever-evolving field. The path of agriculture is a path of continuous development, and the journey of learning and discovery from this work is a step closer for every reader.

Name of the author of the Foreword

Credentials

Ravindra Dohley
Ravi Yadav
Date:03/11/2024

Preface

The journey of this book began with a simple goal: to provide an inclusive and accessible resource for those entering the agricultural field as students, scholars, or activists. Agriculture is as old as human culture and essential to the foundation of our society. It has evolved over centuries, adapting to new inventions, new technologies, and new challenges. Aimed at reflecting on both this rich history and recent developments, this book offers a comprehensive guide covering a wide range of topics, from crop management to resource conservation and pest control.

Focusing on preparing readers for competitions, the book summarizes important information about plant species, plant physiology, soil health, and climate resilience. The broad sections on gardening, standard practices, and post-harvest management not only understand how we grow our own food, but also how we care for and improve it.

During the writing process, I gained knowledge from reputable academic resources and experts in the field to create a text that balances scientific rigor and practical application. The structure of the book, which includes tables, example tables, and descriptive guides, is designed to facilitate effective teaching and memorization.

Whether it is a farmer, researcher or student, this book is dedicated to those who safeguard the values of agriculture daily. The book will contribute significantly to his journey and promote his unwavering commitment to the growth and sustainability of agriculture.

Author name

Ravindra Dohley
Ravi Yadav

Date:03/11/2024

Acknowledgments

This book would not have been possible without the collective support and contribution of many individuals and organizations dedicated to the advancement of agriculture.

First, I would like to sincerely thank the valued teachers and mentors who have guided me in my journey towards agricultural science. His expertise and encouragement in developing the direction and content of this book is invaluable. In particular, we have to thank the agricultural companies that provide the research and resources that provide an encyclopaedia that will enrich this work.

I greatly appreciate those whose experience and knowledge of agricultural challenges have made this book truly relevant. Their commitment to innovative and sustainable practices inspires everyone working in the field.

I would like to thank my colleagues for their valuable contributions, whose opinions and shared knowledge have helped me improve this course. Their results have greatly improved the breadth and clarity of the topics discussed.

Finally, thank you to my family and friends for their unwavering support and patience during this project. His encouragement provided strength and inspiration.

I am very happy to support this book as a collaboration and the people who have contributed to its success. It will be a resource and inspiration for those who are passionate about agriculture.

Prologue

Agriculture was the first enterprise of humanity that was closely linked to the structure of cultures. From the beginning, land management has not only supported lives, but shaped societies, economies, and cultures around the world. This book explores many aspects of agriculture and gives an in-depth review of all the foundations of the complex ecosystem of modern agriculture – plant science, plant genetics, soil health and pest control.

Agricultural science has made significant progress in recent decades. Global challenges in food security, climate change and sustainable practices have highlighted the need for innovation and knowledge sharing. Combining fundamental and cutting-edge developments, this book provides readers with an understanding of responsible resource use issues, the complexities of increasingly resilient plants, and how to address plant health and environmental protection.

The lessons featured on these pages are designed for students, scholars, and those who want to improve their knowledge of agriculture. This book provides important information that will serve as a powerful tool by guiding people preparing for competitions through basic concepts and practical applications. Through a detailed table of chapters and examples, readers are invited to explore policies that support one of the most important parts of the world.

As you read these pages, you will see both inspiration and wisdom that motivate you to contribute to the future of agriculture. There is a vision in this work – not only to understand agricultural science, but to respect the timeless relationship between people and land.

Important Table

Important Table		
Glossary of English, Botanical and Hindi Names of Important Crops		
English	**Botanical**	**Hindi**
Cereals		
Bara(Bulrush or spiked millet)	*Pennisetum Typhoides*	Bajra
Barley	*Hordeum vulgare*	Jau
Barnyard millet	*Echinochloa frumentacea*	Kutki
Cholam(Great Millet)	*Sorghum bicolour*	Jowar
Common Millet	*Panicum milliaceum*	Cheena
Little Millet	*Penicum milliare*	Sawan
Italian foxtail Millet	*Setarisiaitalica*	Kangani
Kodo Millet	*Paspalum scrobiculatum*	Koden
Maize or Indian corn	*Zea mays*	Makka
Oat	*Avena sativa*	Jaie
Ragi	*Eleusine coracana*	Mundua
Paddy (Rice)	*Oryza sativa*	Dhan (Chawal)
Wheat	*Triticum acstivum*	Gehun
Pulses and Beans		
Black gram	*Vignamungo*	Urad
Chickpea (Bengal gram)	*Cicer arietinum*	Chana
Chicking vetch	*Lathyrus sativus*	Khesari
Cluster Bean	*Cyamopiss tetragonoloba*	Guar
Cowpea	*Vigna unguiculate*	Lobia
Green Gram	*Vigna radiata*	Mung
Horsegram	*Dilichos biflorus*	Kulthi
Kidney bean	*Vigna aconitifolia*	Moth
Lentil	*Lens culimaris*	Masur
Peas	*Pisum sativum vararvense*	Matar
Red gram (Pigion pea)	*Cajanus cajan*	Tur,Arhar
Soyabean	*Glucine max*	Soyabean
Sugarcane	*Saccharum Officinarum*	Ganna
Fruits		
Apple	*Malus sylvespris*	Seb
Apricot	*Prunus armeniaca*	Khoobani

Cashewnut	*Anaardium occidentale*	Kaju
Fig	*Ficus carica*	Anjeer
Grape	*Vitis vinifera*	Angur
Guvava	*Psidium guajava*	Amrood
Jackfruit	*Artocarpur heterophyllus*	Katahal
Lemon	*Citrus Lemon*	Nimbu
Lime	*Citrus Urantifolia*	Bara Nimbu
Litchi	*Litchi chinensis*	Litchi
Mango	*Magnifera indica*	Aam
Orange Mandar	*Citrus reticulata*	Santara, Narangi
Papaya	*Carica papaya*	Papeeta
Pear	*Pyrus communis*	Naspati
Pineapple	*Ananas comosus*	Ananas
Banana	*Musa paradisiaca*	Kela
Pomegranate	*Punica granatum*	Anaar
Sweet Orange	*Citrus sincensis*	Malta, Mosambi
	Vegetables	
English	Botanical	Hindi
(2)	(3)	(4)
Ash gourd	Benincasa hispida	Petha
Beet	Beta vulgaris	Chukandar
Bitter gourd	Momordica charantia	Karela
Bottle gourd	Lagenaria siceraria	Lauki
Brinjal	Lolanum melongena	Baingan
Cabbage	Brassica oleracca var,	Band gobi
	Capitata	
Carrot	Daucus carota	Gajar
Cauliflower	Brassica oleracca var	Phul gobi
	Botrytis	
Cowpea	Vigna unguiculate	Lobia
Cucumber	Cucumis satius	Kheera
French bean	Phaseolus vulgaris	Faras bean
Indian flat bean or sem	Dolichos lablab	Sem
Kaol Khol	Brassica oleracea var,	Ganth gobi
	Gongylodes	
Lady's finger	Abelmoschus esculentus	Bhindi
Little gourd	Cuccinia cordifolia	Kundur
Musk melon	Cucumis melo	Kharbooza
Onion	Allium cepa	Piyaz
Pointed gourd	Trichosanthes dioica	Parwal, Potal
Potato	Solanum tuberosum	Aaloo
Pumpkin	Curcurbita moschata	Sitaphal, Lal
		Kaddu, Kumbhra
Radish	Raphanus satius	Muli
Round gourd of	Citrullus vulgaris var,	Tinda

India		
	fistulosus	
Snap melon	Cucumis melovvar,	Phoot
	momordica	
Snake gourd	Trichosanthes anguina	Chachinda
Tomato	Lycopersicon escen lentum	Tamatar
Turnip	Brassica rapa	Shalgam
Water melon	Cirtrullus vulgaris	Tarbooz
	Drugs and Narcotics	
Betal Leave	Areca catechu	Paan
Betalnut(arecanut)	Cannabis sativa	Supari
Indian hemp	Papaver somniferum	Bhang
Opium	Nicotiana tabacum and	Afeem
Tobacco	Nicotiana rustica	Tambaku
Black pepper	Piper nigrum	Kalimirch
Cardamom, Cardamum	Elettaria cardamomum	Chhoti Ilaichi
(lesser)		
Chillies	Capsicum annuum	Lalmirch
	Seed Rate of Sowing for Important field crops	
Crop	Variety Seed Rate	Hybrid Seed Rate
(1)	(2)	(3)
Cereals		
Wheat	100-125	15-20 for normal planting, 5-7 under SRI planting, 100 for normal
Barley	100-125	planting, 125 for late planting & problematic soils, 100 for normal
		planting, 125 for late planting & problematic soils
Sorghum	Grain Rabi 8-10; Grain Kharif 10	7.5
Pearl Millet	4-5	4-5
Maize	Normal field corn 18-20; Fodder 30-40	20
Ragi	10-12.5	10-12.5
Pulses		
Pigeon pea	Early duration 17-19 Medium duration 15-17; Long duration 12-15	
Chickpea(Large	75-100	

seeded)		
Chickpea Desi (small seeded)	65-75	
Chickpea Kabuli	100-120	
Mungbean	Kharif-20, Rabi 25-30, Summer 20-30	
Urdbean	Kharif-20, Rabi 25-30, Summer 20-30	
Fieldpea	80-100	
Lentil	50-60	
Rajmash	75-100	
Mothbean	15-18	
Kulthi	22-30	
Oilseeds		
Groundnut	140-160	
Rapeseed & Mustard	3-5	3.5
Soybean	65-75	
Sunflower	5	5
Sesame	5	
Niger	5	
Safflower	7	
Linseed	25-30	
Castor	5	5

Crop	**Variety Seed Rate**	**Hybrid Seed Rate**
(1)	(2)	(3)
Forage crops		
Forage Sorghum	25 in small seeded varieties; 40 in bold seeded varieties	
Sorghum	Grain Rabi 8-10	7.5
	Grain Kharif 10	10
Maize	40-50	
Guar	20-30	
Pearl Millet	4-5	4-5
Oats	80(small), 100 (Bold)	
Berseem	20-25	
GobhiSarson	4	
Lucerne	15	
Fibre Crops		
Cotton	10-12	Bt. Cotton – 1.5-2.25 Non-Bt.

		Cotton 3-4
Jute	6 (olitorius), 7 (capsularis)	
Sunhemp	25	
Mesta	12 (Roselle), 15 (Kenaf)	
Sugar Crops		
Sugarcane	60 qtls., (45,000 sets of 3 buds in sub tropics), (25,000-30,000 sets of 3 buds in tropics)	
		-

Conversion Table (Length)	
1 kilometre (km)	1000 metres (m)
1 km	0.6214 miles
1 m	1.0936 yards
1 m	3.2808 feet
1 mile	1760 yards
1 mile	1.609 km
1 yard	0.9144 m
1 foot	0.3048 m
Area	
1 km^2	100 hectares (ha)
1 km^2	0.3861 square mile
1 km^2	247.105 acres
1 m^2	10.7639 square feet
1 ha	10,000 m^2
1 ha	2.4711 acres
1 square mile	2.591 km^2
1 acre	0.4047 ha
1 acre	4046.86 m^2
1 acre	4840 square yard
1 square yard	9 square feet
1 square yard	0.8361 m^2
1 square foot	0.0929 m^2
Weight	
1 tonne	1000 kg
1 tonne	1.1023 US ton
1 US ton	0.9072 tonnes
1 hg	100 gram
1 kg	2.2046 pounds (Ib)

1 kg	35.274 ounce (oz)
1 lb	0.4536 kg
1 oz	28.3495 gram
Units	
1 crore	10 million
1 million	10 lakh
1 lakh	100000
1 billion	1000 million

Agricultural Statistics at a Glance- All India				
S.No.	**Indicator**	**Year**	**Unit**	**Value**
	Land Use Indicators			
1	Geographical Area	2019-20	Million Hectare	328.75
2	Reported Area for Land Utilization Statistics	2019-20	Million Hectare	306.54
3	Area under Forest	2019-20	Million Hectare	71.75
4	Percentage of Area under Forest to Reported Area	2019-20	-	23.41%
5	Gross Cropped Area	2019-20	Million Hectare	211.36
6	Percentage of Gross Cropped Area to reported area	2019-20	-	68.95%
7	Net Area Sown	2019-20	Million Hectare	139.90
8	Percentage of Net Area Sown to Reported Area	2019-20	-	45.64%
9	Area sown more than once	2019-20	Million Hectare	71.46
10	Cropping Intensity (%)	2019-20	-	151.08
11	Net Irrigated Area	2019-20	Million Hectare	75.46
12	Gross Irrigated Area	2019-20	Million Hectare	112.23
	Production & Procurement Indicators			
14	Foodgrains Production (as per 4th Advance Estimates)	2021-22	Million Tonnes	285.71
	(a) Kharif	2021-22	Million Tonnes	141.03
	(b) Rabi	2021-22	Million Tonnes	144.68

15	Horticulture Production (as per 3rd Advance Estimates)	2021-22	Million Tonnes	342.33
16	Milk Production	2020-21	Million Tonnes	209.96
17	Meat Production	2020-21	Lakh Tonnes	87.98
18	Livestock Population as per 20th Livestock Census	2019	Million Numbers	536.76
19	Fish Production	2020-21	Lakh Tonnes	162.48
20	Procurement			
	(a) Rice- for Kharif Marketing Season 2022-23*	2022-23	Lakh Tonnes	478.27
	(b) Wheat- for Rabi Marketing Season 2022-23*	2022-23	Lakh Tonnes	187.92
	(c) Nutri/Coarse Grains*	2022-23	'000 Tonnes	263.00
	(d) Pulses Procurement under PSS *	2022-23	MT	120131.09
	(e) Oilseeds Procurement under PSS*	2022-23	MT	47926.50
	(f) Cotton	2021-22	Lakh Bales	15.00
	(h) Jute (as on 30.10.2022)	2022-23	Lakh Bales	0.76
	Macro-Economic Indicators			
22	Growth Rate of GVA in Agri and Allied sector at Constant	2022-23	-	3.3%

Crop	Origin	Colour Pigment Reason	Health Benefit	Aromatic Compounds	Optimum Temp (°C)
Mango	India, Southeast Asia	Beta-carotene (yellow-orange colour)	Rich in Vitamin A, antioxidant properties	Terpenes, Esters, Aldehydes	24-30
Papaya	Tropical Americas	Lycopene (orange-red colour)	High in Vitamin C, aids digestion	Limonene, Hexyl acetate	21-33
Pineapple	South America	Bromelain enzyme (for protein digestion)	Anti-inflammatory, aids digestion	Esters (ethyl hexanoate, acetate)	20-30
Banana	Southeast Asia	Carotenoids (yellow colour)	High in **Potassium**, aids in heart health	Isoamyl acetate	24-30
Avocado	Central	Chlorophyll	Rich in healthy	Terpenes	16-24

	Mexico	(green)	fats, good for heart		
Sapota (Chikoo)	Mexico, Central America	Carotenoids (yellow-brown colour)	Good for digestive health	Terpenoids	24-30
Guava	Central America, Mexico	Lycopene, Beta-carotene (pink flesh)	High in Vitamin C, improves immunity	Hexenal, Esters	23-28
Jackfruit	South India, Malaysia	Carotenoids (yellow colour)	High in dietary fiber, boosts immunity	Esters, Aldehydes	24-32
Tamarind	Africa	Tannins (brown colour)	High in antioxidants, aids digestion	Geraniol, Citral	25-30
Carambola	Southeast Asia	Oxalic acid (yellow-green colour)	Rich in Vitamin C, improves skin health	Esters, Linalool	20-30
Mangosteen	Southeast Asia	Anthocyanins (purple colour)	Anti-inflammatory, antioxidant properties	Terpenes	25-35
Passion Fruit	South America	Carotenoids, Anthocyanins (purple-yellow)	Rich in dietary fiber, boosts immunity	Ethyl butanoate, Hexyl butanoate	20-28
Bilimbi	Southeast Asia	Chlorophyll (green colour)	High in Vitamin C, antioxidant properties	Citric acid	20-30
Rambutan	Malay-Indonesian region	Anthocyanins (red colour)	Rich in iron, boosts blood health	Butyl acetate, Hexyl acetate	25-35
Longan	South Asia, India		Rich in Vitamin C, anti-aging properties	Dimethyl sulfide, Esters	22-32
Durian	Southeast Asia		High in energy, boosts immunity	Sulphur compounds, Esters	24-30
Citrus (Orange)	Southeast Asia	Beta-carotene (orange colour)	High in Vitamin C, boosts immune function	Limonene, Linalool	15-30
Grapes	Near East	Anthocyanins, Flavonoids (purple/green)	Rich in antioxidants, good for heart health	Terpenes, Esters	18-24

Pomegranate	Iran, Northern India	Anthocyanins (red colour)	High in antioxidants, improves heart health	Esters, Terpenes	15-30
Litchi	Southern China	Anthocyanins (red skin colour)	Rich in Vitamin C, improves digestion	Methyl butanoate, Esters	20-30
Apple	Central Asia	Anthocyanins (red colour), Chlorophyll (green)	Rich in dietary fiber, good for heart	Esters, Aldehydes	18-24
Pear	Europe, Asia	Flavonoids (green-yellow colour)	Rich in dietary fiber, aids digestion	Esters	16-22
Peach	Northwest China	Carotenoids (orange-red colour)	Rich in vitamins, boosts skin health	Aldehydes, Esters	20-30
Plum	Europe, Asia	Anthocyanins (purple/red colour)	Good for digestive health, antioxidant-rich	Esters	18-24
Apricot	China, Central Asia	Carotenoids (yellow-orange colour)	High in vitamins A & C, aids eye health	Terpenes, Esters	16-24
Cherries	Europe, Asia	Anthocyanins (red colour)	Rich in antioxidants, good for heart	Esters, Alcohols	18-22
Strawberry	Europe, North America	Anthocyanins (red colour)	High in Vitamin C, boosts immune function	Esters, Furas	15-20
Kiwifruit	China	Chlorophyll (green)	Rich in Vitamin C, aids digestion	Esters, Alcohols	10-18
Walnut	Central Asia, Europe		High in omega-3, good for brain health	Phenols	18-25
Almond	Middle East, South Asia		Rich in healthy fats, good for heart health	Phenolic compounds	16-24
Pecan Nut	North America		High in healthy fats, boosts heart health		18-24
Hazelnut	Europe, Asia		Rich in omega-9 fats, good for skin health		10-20
Chestnut	Europe,		High in		18-22

Asia	Vitamin C, boosts immune function

Vegetable Crop	Origin	Colour/Pigment Reason	Health Benefit	Temp (°C)
Tomato	South America (Peru)	Lycopene (red colour)	High in Vitamin A, C, boosts immunity	20-25
Brinjal (Eggplant)	India, Indo-Burma	Anthocyanins (purple)	Rich in **Potassium**, lowers cholesterol	22-30
Chilli	Central/South America	Capsaicin (red colour)	Boosts metabolism, rich in Vitamin C	24-30
Muskmelon	Africa, Southwest Asia	Beta-carotene (orange)	High in Vitamin A, good for skin and eyes	25-30
Watermelon	Africa	Lycopene (red)	Hydrating, rich in Vitamin C	20-30
Cucumber	India	Chlorophyll (green)	Hydrating, high in fiber	22-28
Bitter Gourd	South-East Asia	Chlorophyll (green)	Lowers blood sugar, good for diabetes	24-30
Pumpkin	North America	Beta-carotene (orange colour)	Rich in Vitamin A, supports vision and skin	20-30
Okra (Ladyfinger)	Ethiopia	Chlorophyll (green)	Rich in fiber, helps digestion	24-35
Cowpea	Africa		High in protein, improves digestive health	25-30
Sweet Potato	Tropical America	Beta-carotene (orange colour)	Rich in Vitamin A, supports eye health	20-28
Cluster Beans	India	Chlorophyll (green)	Good for heart health, rich in fiber	22-28
Amaranth	South America	Betalains (red pigments)	Rich in iron, boosts blood health	20-30
Basella	Tropical Asia	Betalains (red pigments)	Rich in vitamins, supports immunity	25-30
Moringa (Drumstick)	India	Chlorophyll (green leaves)	High in Vitamin C, supports overall immunity	25-30
Tapioca	South America		Good for energy, rich in carbohydrates	20-30
Carrot	Central Asia	Beta-carotene (orange colour)	Rich in Vitamin A, good for eye health	15-20
Radish	Southeast Asia	Anthocyanins (purple/red)	Rich in Vitamin C, supports digestion	18-25
Turnip	Europe, Central Asia	Anthocyanins (purple)	Rich in fiber, boosts digestion	15-20
Beetroot	Mediterranean region	Betalains (red pigments)	High in nitrates, lowers blood pressure	18-24
Cabbage	Europe	Anthocyanins (red varieties)	Rich in Vitamin C, boosts digestion	15-20

Cauliflower	Mediterranean region		High in Vitamin C, antioxidant properties	15-25
Knolkhol	Europe	Anthocyanins (purple varieties)	Rich in Vitamin C, helps digestion	15-20
Broccoli	Mediterranean region	Chlorophyll (green colour)	Rich in fiber, supports immune system	15-20
Brussels' Sprouts	Europe	Chlorophyll (green)	Rich in Vitamin K, supports bone health	15-18
Chinese Cabbage	East Asia	Chlorophyll (green)	Rich in fiber, supports digestive health	15-20
Pea	Mediterranean		Rich in protein, improves digestion	15-20
Potato	South America (Peru)		Rich in **Potassium**, supports heart health	12-18

Tuber Crop	Origin	Colour/Pigment Reason	Health Benefit	Optimum Temp. (°C)
Potato	South America		High in carbohydrates, good for energy	15-25
Sweet Potato	Central America	Beta-carotene (orange flesh)	Rich in Vitamin A, good for eye health	20-28
Arrowroot	South America		Easy to digest, good for stomach health	25-30
Cassava (Tapioca)	South America		High in starch, good for energy	20-30
Colocasia (Taro)	Southeast Asia	Anthocyanins (purple varieties)	Rich in dietary fiber, supports digestion	20-25
Amorphophallus (Elephant foot yam)	India		High in carbohydrates, good for digestion	25-30
Dioscorea (Yam)	Africa, South America		Rich in fiber, boosts digestive health	20-30
Jerusalem Artichoke	North America		Good for digestive health, contains inulin	18-22
Horse Radish	Europe, Western Asia		Antibacterial properties, boosts immunity	18-24
Coleus (Kenchur)	India, Southeast Asia		Used in traditional medicine, supports heart health	22-30
Yam Bean	Mexico, Central America		Rich in Vitamin C, supports skin health	18-30

Flower Crop	Origin	Colour/Pigment Reason	Health Benefit	Optimum Temp. (°C)
Rose	Asia, Europe, North America	Anthocyanins (varied colours)	Antioxidant properties, boosts mood	15-25
Jasmine	South Asia, Middle East	(White flowers)	Relieves stress, improves mood	18-25
Carnation	Mediterranean region	Anthocyanins (varied colours)	Anti-inflammatory, improves relaxation	15-18
Chrysanthemum	China, Europe, Asia	Carotenoids (yellow/white)	Improves mood, antioxidant properties	15-20
Gladiolus	South Africa	Anthocyanins (varied colours)	Decorative purposes, boosts emotional health	10-25
Marigold	Central and South America	Carotenoids (yellow/orange)	Antibacterial, improves skin health	15-30
Tuberose	Mexico	(white flowers)	Used in perfumes, improves relaxation	18-30
Gerbera	South Africa	Carotenoids (yellow/orange)	Air purifying, improves mood	15-25
Orchids	Asia, South America	Anthocyanins (varied colours)	Used in decor, boosts emotional wellness	18-25
Anthurium	South America, Caribbean	Anthocyanins (red, white)	Improves air quality, boosts mood	18-25
Lilium (Lily)	Europe, Asia, North America	Anthocyanins (varied colours)	Decorative purposes, boosts emotional health	10-20
Dahlia	Mexico, Central America	Anthocyanins (varied colours)	Used in decor, boosts emotional wellness	15-25
Gaillardia	North America	Carotenoids (yellow/red)	Ornamental, improves mood	18-28
Crossandra	South India, Sri Lanka	Carotenoids (orange)	Ornamental, improves mood	22-30
Aster	China, Europe	Anthocyanins (varied colours)	Ornamental, improves mental health	18-25
Petunia	South America	Anthocyanins (varied colours)	Ornamental, improves mood	15-25
Zinnia	South America, Mexico	Carotenoids, Anthocyanins	Ornamental, air purifying	20-25

Snapdragon	Mediterranean	Anthocyanins (varied colours)	Ornamental, boosts mood	15-25
Stock	Mediterranean	Anthocyanins (varied colours)	Used in decor, boosts emotional wellness	12-18
Pansy	Europe, Western Asia	Anthocyanins (varied colours)	Used in decor, ornamental	15-22
Calendula	Mediterranean, South Europe	Carotenoids (orange/yellow)	Antibacterial, used in skin care products	15-25
Balsam	Asia, North America	(varied colours)	Decorative purposes, used in medicine	20-28
Dianthus	Europe, Asia	Anthocyanins (varied colours)	Anti-inflammatory, ornamental	15-20

Medicinal Crop

Medicinal Crop	Origin	Health Benefit	Optimum Temperature (°C)
Ashwagandha		Reduces stress, boosts immunity	20-30
Costus (Saussurea)	Himalayas	Anti-inflammatory, supports digestion	15-25
Isabgol (Psyllium)	Mediterranean, West Asia	Improves digestion, relieves constipation	20-25
Mint	Mediterranean	Aids digestion, used in aromatherapy	20-30

Multi diseases resistance varieties

fruit Crop	Variety (with disease resistance)	Points
Mango	**Dasheri, Alphonso, Langra, Amrapali**	**Amrapali** shows good resistance to **powdery mildew** and **anthracnose**.
Papaya	**Red Lady, Taiwan 786, Pusa Nanha**	**Pusa Nanha** shows resistance to **papaya ring spot virus** and **mosaic virus**.
Pineapple	**Queen, Kew, Mauritius**	**Mauritius** is resistant to **mealybugs** and **wilt**.
Banana	**Grand Naine, G9, Robusta, Dwarf Cavendish**	**G9 variety** has resistance to **Panama disease** and **bunchy top virus**.
Avocado	**Fuerte, Hass, Pinkerton**	**Hass** shows some resistance to **root rot** caused by **Phytophthora**.
Sapota	**Kalipatti, Cricket Ball, PKM 1**	**Kalipatti** has tolerance to **fruit borer**.
Guava	**Allahabad Safeda, Lucknow 49, Arka Mridula**	**Lucknow 49** is known for its resistance to **wilt** and **nematodes**.
Jackfruit	**Singapore, Varikka, Thornless**	**Singapore** variety shows tolerance to **fruit rot**.

Tamarind	**Urigam, Prathisthan, PKM-1**	**Prathisthan** has some tolerance to **seed borer.**
Carambola	No known resistant varieties	Primarily grown for its ornamental value.
Mangosteen	No specific resistant varieties identified	Grows well in warm, humid climates, no widely recognized disease-resistant varieties.
Passion Fruit	**Purple Passion, Yellow Passion**	**Yellow passion fruit** shows resistance to **Fusarium wilt** and **root-knot nematode.**
Bilimbi	No specific resistant varieties identified	Primarily used in traditional medicine, low susceptibility to pests and diseases.
Rambutan	**Rongrien, Seematjan**	**Rongrien** variety shows resistance to **fruit rot.**
Longan	No specific resistant varieties identified	Grown primarily in Southeast Asia, some varieties tolerate **leaf blight.**
Durian	**Mon Thong, Chanee, Monthong**	**Mon Thong** has good tolerance to **fruit borer** and **stem canker.**
Fruit Crop	**Variety (with disease resistance)**	**Points**
Citrus	**Kinnow, Nagpur Orange, Sweet Lime**	**Nagpur Orange** is tolerant to **citrus canker** and **greening disease.**
Grapes	**Thompson Seedless, Anab-e-Shahi, Perlette**	**Thompson Seedless** has some resistance to **powdery mildew.**
Pomegranate	**Bhagwa, Ganesh, Ruby**	**Bhagwa** shows good resistance to **bacterial blight.**
Litchi	**Shahi, China, Bombai**	**Shahi** shows tolerance to **fruit cracking** and **sunburn.**
Loquat	**Tanaka, Advance**	**Tanaka** has some tolerance to **fire blight.**
Apple	**Red Delicious, Golden Delicious, Gala**	**Golden Delicious** shows resistance to **scab** and **powdery mildew.**
Pear	**Bartlett, Bosc, Anjou**	**Bartlett** has some resistance to **fire blight.**
Peach	**July Elberta, Florida Prince, Shan-e-Punjab**	**Florida Prince** is resistant to **leaf curl** and **root-knot nematode.**
Plum	**Santa Rosa, Green Gage, Early Golden**	**Santa Rosa** shows resistance to **brown rot.**
Apricot	**Moorpark, Newcastle**	**Moorpark** shows resistance to **brown rot** and **blight.**
Cherries	**Bing, Rainier, Montmorency**	**Montmorency** is resistant to **cherry leaf spot** and **powdery mildew.**
Berries	**Raspberry Heritage, Boysenberry, Blackberry Triple Crown**	**Heritage** raspberries show resistance to **root rot.**
Persimmon	**Hachiya, Fuyu**	**Fuyu** has moderate tolerance to **fruit drop** and **root rot.**

Kiwifruit	**Hayward, Monty, Bruno**	**Hayward** shows resistance to **root rot** and **bacterial canker**.
Walnut	**Chandler, Howard**	**Chandler** has resistance to **walnut blight**.
Almond	**Nonpareil, Carmel, Sonora**	**Nonpareil** is resistant to **blossom blight** and **leaf spot**.
Pecan Nut	**Mahan, Desirable, Western Schley**	**Desirable** variety is tolerant to **pecan scab**.
Hazelnut	**Barcelona, Tonda di Giffoni**	**Tonda di Giffoni** has resistance to **blight** and **canker**.
Chestnut	**Chinese Chestnut, Colossal**	**Chinese Chestnut** shows resistance to **chestnut blight**.
Strawberry	**Chandler, Camarosa, Albion**	**Albion** is resistant to **Verticillium wilt** and **powdery mildew**.
Vegetable Crop	**Variety (with disease resistance)**	**Points**
Tomato	**Pusa Ruby, Arka Rakshak, Arka Vikas**	**Arka Rakshak** is resistant to **bacterial wilt**, **early blight**, and **leaf curl virus**.
Brinjal (Eggplant)	**Pusa Purple Long, Arka Neelkanth, Pusa Kranti**	**Arka Neelkanth** is resistant to **bacterial wilt**.
Chilli	**Pusa Jwala, Arka Meghana, Bhut Jolokia**	**Arka Meghana** is resistant to **anthracnose** and **leaf curl virus**.
Muskmelon	**Arka Rajhans, Punjab Hybrid, Hara Madhu**	**Arka Rajhans** has resistance to **powdery mildew**.
Watermelon	**Arka Manik, Sugar Baby, Durgapura Lal**	**Arka Manik** is resistant to **Fusarium wilt**.
Cucumber	**Poinsett 76, Arka Sumeet, Kakdi Punjab Naveen**	**Arka Sumeet** has resistance to **downy mildew** and **powdery mildew**.
Bitter Gourd	**Pusa Vishal, Priya, CO-1**	**Pusa Vishal** is resistant to **downy mildew** and **powdery mildew**.
Pumpkin	**Arka Chandan, Punjab Samrat, CO-2**	**Arka Chandan** shows tolerance to **mosaic virus**.
Okra (Ladyfinger)	**Pusa Sawani, Arka Anamika, Parbhani Kranti**	**Parbhani Kranti** is resistant to **yellow vein mosaic virus**.
Cowpea	**Pusa Komal, Arka Garima, Kashi Kanchan**	**Pusa Komal** is resistant to **bacterial blight** and **yellow mosaic virus**.
Sweet Potato	**Sree Bhadra, Kiran, Hawaii-2**	**Sree Bhadra** is resistant to **sweet potato weevil**.
Cluster Beans	**Pusa Sadabahar, Rajasthan Guar, Himmat**	**Pusa Sadabahar** is resistant to **yellow mosaic virus**.
Amaranth	**Pusa Kiran, Arka Suguna**	**Arka Suguna** is resistant to **leaf blight**.
Basella	**Arka Upkar, Pusa Jyoti**	**Arka Upkar** has high yield potential and is less prone to pests.
Moringa	**PKM-1, Coimbatore-2**	**PKM-1** has tolerance to **leaf spot** and **fruit rot**.

Tapioca	**H165, Sree Sahya, Sree Jaya**	**Sree Jaya** is resistant to **cassava mosaic virus** and **cassava bacterial blight.**
Vegetable Crop	**Variety (with disease resistance)**	**Points**
Carrot	**Pusa Yamdagni, Nantes, Kuroda**	**Pusa Yamdagni** has resistance to **alternaria leaf blight.**
Radish	**Pusa Chetki, Pusa Himani, Japanese White**	**Pusa Himani** is resistant to **white rust** and **downy mildew.**
Turnip	**Purple Top White Globe, Snowball**	**Purple Top White Globe** shows resistance to **powdery mildew.**
Beetroot	**Detroit Dark Red, Crosby Egyptian**	**Detroit Dark Red** is resistant to **downy mildew** and **leaf spot.**
Cabbage	**Golden Acre, Pusa Mukta, Pride of India**	**Pusa Mukta** has resistance to **black rot** and **fusarium wilt.**
Cauliflower	**Pusa Snowball, Pusa Himjyoti, Pusa Shubra**	**Pusa Snowball** is resistant to **black rot** and **downy mildew.**
Knolkhol	**White Vienna, Purple Vienna**	**White Vienna** is tolerant to **root-knot nematode** and **club root.**
Broccoli	**Green Head, Calabrese, Pusa Broccoli KTS-1**	**Pusa Broccoli KTS-1** is resistant to **downy mildew.**
Brussels' Sprout	**Jade Cross, Long Island Improved**	**Jade Cross** is resistant to **black rot** and **fusarium wilt.**
Chinese Cabbage	**Hirayama, Tokyo Bekana, Granaat**	**Granaat** shows resistance to **fusarium wilt.**
Pea	**Arkel, Bonneville, Azad Pea-1**	**Arkel** is resistant to **powdery mildew** and **root-knot nematode.**
Potato	**Kufri Jyoti, Kufri Bahar, Kufri Anand**	**Kufri Jyoti** is resistant to **late blight** and **early blight.**
Tuber Crop	**Variety (with disease resistance)**	**Points**
Potato	**Kufri Jyoti, Kufri Bahar, Kufri Anand**	**Kufri Jyoti** is resistant to **late blight** and **early blight.**
Sweet Potato	**Sree Bhadra, Sree Vardhini, Gauri**	**Sree Bhadra** is resistant to **sweet potato weevil** and **leaf spot.**
Arrowroot	**Variety not widely recognized**	Arrowroot is mostly resistant to common pests due to its hardiness.
Cassava (Tapioca)	**Sree Jaya, H-165, Sree Sahya**	**Sree Jaya** is resistant to **cassava mosaic virus** and **cassava bacterial blight.**
Colocasia (Taro)	**Muktakeshi, Sree Rashmi**	**Muktakeshi** is resistant to **leaf blight** and **corm rot.**
Xanthosoma	**No specific variety known**	Grown for its tubers, generally hardy in tropical environments.
Amorphophallus	**GA-1, Sree Padma, BRS Vishal**	**GA-1** is resistant to **collar rot** and **soft rot.**
Dioscorea (Yam)	**Sree Roopa, Sree Keerthi, Orissa Elite**	**Sree Roopa** shows resistance to **anthracnose** and **rot.**

Jerusalem Artichoke	No specific variety recognized	Generally hardy, resistant to most common diseases due to its adaptability.
Horse Radish	No specific variety known	Grown for its pungent roots, generally resistant to common diseases.
Coleus	No specific variety recognized	Mostly used in herbal medicines, generally hardy and resistant to pests.
Yam Bean	No specific variety recognized	Grown for its edible tubers, with some varieties resistant to **root rot**.

Flower Crop	Variety (with disease resistance)	Points
Rose	Arka Swadesh, Arka Pride, Pusa Mohit	**Arka Swadesh** is resistant to **powdery mildew** and **black spot.**
Jasmine	CO-1, CO-2, Arka Surabhi	**Arka Surabhi** is resistant to **root rot** and **leaf blight.**
Carnation	Master, Pusa Aditya, Pusa Shalini	**Pusa Aditya** is resistant to **fusarium wilt** and **bacterial wilt.**
Chrysanthemum	Arka Chandrika, Arka Ravi, Pusa Centenary	**Pusa Centenary** is resistant to **powdery mildew** and **stem rot.**
Gladiolus	Pusa Suhagin, Punjab Glance, Snow Princess	**Pusa Suhagin** is resistant to **Fusarium wilt** and **spike rot.**
Marigold	Pusa Narangi Gainda, Arka Bangara, Pusa Basanti	**Pusa Narangi Gainda** is resistant to **blight** and **leaf spot.**
Tuberose	Prajwal, Shringar, Arka Nirantara	**Prajwal** is resistant to **stem rot** and **leaf spot.**
Cut Foliage Crops	Varieties depend on species (Ferns, Philodendrons, etc.)	Various cut foliage crops show resistance to **pests** and **leaf diseases** based on species.

Fower Crop	Variety (with disease resistance)	Points
Gerbera	Arka Ashwa, Arka Nesara, Arka Krishika	**Arka Ashwa** shows resistance to **powdery mildew** and **stem rot.**
Orchids	Dendrobium Sonia, Phalaenopsis Pink	**Dendrobium Sonia** shows tolerance to **bacterial blight.**
Anthurium	Tropical Red, Anthurium Acropolis	**Tropical Red** is resistant to **bacterial wilt** and **leaf blight.**
Lilium (Lily)	Asiatic Hybrid, Oriental Hybrid, Arka Naveen	**Arka Naveen** is resistant to **botrytis blight.**
Chrysanthemum	Arka Chandrika, Pusa Centenary, Arka Ravi	**Arka Chandrika** is resistant to **powdery mildew** and **stem rot.**
Carnation	Pusa Aditya, Master, Arka Flame	**Pusa Aditya** is resistant to **fusarium wilt** and **bacterial wilt.**
Dahlia	Violet Flame, Yellow Sun, Orange Glory	**Violet Flame** shows resistance to **powdery mildew.**
Gaillardia	Arka Kesar, Lorenziana	**Arka Kesar** shows resistance to **leaf blight.**

Crossandra	Arka Shravya, Arka Ambara	**Arka Shravya** is resistant to **leaf spot** and **root rot**.
Aster	Arka Kamini, Arka Shashank	**Arka Kamini** is resistant to **fusarium wilt** and **leaf blight**.
Petunia	Pusa Hybrid 1, Dream Series	**Pusa Hybrid 1** is resistant to **leaf blight**.
Zinnia	Dreamland Series, Pusa Zinnia 1	**Pusa Zinnia 1** shows resistance to **powdery mildew** and **blight**.
Snapdragon	Rocket Series, Solstice Series	**Rocket Series** is resistant to **rust** and **powdery mildew**.
Stock	Legacy Series, Iron Series	**Iron Series** is resistant to **rust** and **blight**.
Pansy	Cool Wave Series, Matrix Series	**Cool Wave Series** shows resistance to **root rot** and **leaf spot**.
Calendula	Arka Golden Yellow, Pacific Beauty	**Arka Golden Yellow** shows resistance to **powdery mildew**.
Balsam	Rose Balsam, Double Camellia	**Double Camellia** shows resistance to **downy mildew** and **blight**.
Dianthus	Super Parfait Series, Pusa Hybrid 1	**Super Parfait Series** shows resistance to **fusarium wilt**.

Disease/Host Plant	Causal Agent
Bacteria	
Citrus Canker	Xanthomonas citri
Black rot of crucifers	Xanthomonas campestris
Bacterial blight of rice	Xanthomonas oryzae
Angular leaf spot of Cotton (Black arm disease)	Xanthomonas malvacearum
Leaf spot of chili	Xanthomonas vesicatoria
Red stripe of sugarcane	Xanthomonas blushing
Bacterial wilt of plants	Pseudomonas
Solanaceous ring disease of Potato	Pseudomonas solanacearum
Fire blight of Apple and Pear	Erwinia amylovora
Soft rot of carrot	Erwinia crotovora
Scab disease	Streptomyces scabies
Mycoplasma	
Rice	Yellow dwarf disease
Safflower	Phyllody
Sesame	Phyllody
Brinjal (Egg Plant)	Little leaf
Citrus	Greening disease

Sugarcane	Grassy shoot, white leaf
Potato	Purple top, witches broom
Coconut	Lethal yellowing
Ufra disease of Rice	Ditylenchus angustus
Nematodes	
Ear cockle of wheat	Anguina tritici
Root lesion disease (Chilies, Coffee, Cotton, Tea & Rice)	Pratylenchus spp.
Golden nematode disease (Potato, Brinjal, Sugarbeet)	Heterodera rostochiensis
Burrowing nematode disease (banana, Rice, citrus)	Radopholus similes
Root knot disease (coffee)	Meloidogyne exigua
Virus	
Bajra	Mosaic
Banana	Bunchy top, mosaic, Banana streak
Barley	Mosaic, yellow dwarf
Bhindi	Yellow vein mosaic (YVM)
Chilli	Leaf curl, mosaic
Citrus	Tristeza and Quick decline
Groundnut	Clump disease, mosaic, chlorosis
Jowar	Yellowing
Maize	Mosaic, veination
Onion	Yellow dwarf
Papaya	Distortion ringspot, mosaic, leaf curl
Pigeon Pea	Sterility Mosaic
Potatoes	Potato Necrosis, Potato severe Mosaic, leaf roll
Rice	Tungro, grassy stunt
Sugarcane	RSD (Ratoon Stunting Disease)
Tobacco	Leaf curl, yellow net vein (YNV), Ring spot
Tomato	Leaf curl, mosaic, Black ring spot

Nutrient	**Deficiency Symptoms**	**Toxicity Symptoms**
Nitrogen (N)	Yellowing (chlorosis) of older leaves, stunted growth, pale green foliage.	Dark green, lush foliage, delayed maturity, increased susceptibility to pests and diseases, lodging (falling over).
Phosp	Dark green or purplish leaves, stunted	Can cause deficiencies of micronutrients

horus (P)	growth, delayed flowering and fruiting.	like iron, zinc, and copper, resulting in chlorosis in new leaves.
Potassium (K)	Yellowing or scorching of leaf edges, weak stems, poor root development, increased susceptibility to disease.	Causes **Magnesium** and **Calcium** deficiencies, leading to leaf curling, tip burn, and interveinal chlorosis.
Calcium (Ca)	Blossom end rot in tomato, tip burn in lettuce, brittle leaves, poor root growth, stunted growth.	Interferes with **Magnesium** and **Potassium** uptake, leading to chlorosis and growth deficiencies.
Magnesium (Mg)	Interveinal chlorosis in older leaves, leaf curling, premature leaf drop.	Rare, but excess can lead to **Calcium** deficiency, with stunted growth and leaf curling.
Sulphur (S)	Yellowing of younger leaves, stunted growth, pale foliage (similar to **Nitrogen** deficiency).	Leaf yellowing and necrosis (leaf edges die off) in severe cases; generally uncommon.
Iron (Fe)	Interveinal chlorosis in young leaves, pale or yellow leaves with green veins, particularly in alkaline soils.	Brown spots on leaves, especially older ones, and stunted root growth; common in waterlogged soils.
Manganese (Mn)	Interveinal chlorosis, brown or tan spots on leaves, poor leaf formation, crinkling or distortion in severe cases.	Brown spots, chlorosis, and necrosis along veins, crinkling or distortion of leaves.
Copper (Cu)	Leaf curling, chlorosis in young leaves, stunted growth, "dieback" in woody plants.	Stunted growth, dark roots, leaf chlorosis, necrosis, and inhibited root growth.
Zinc (Zn)	Shortened internodes, small leaves, interveinal chlorosis, bronzing of leaves, particularly in citrus and corn.	Chlorosis in younger leaves, interference with iron absorption, stunted growth, pale leaves.
Boron (B)	Brittle stems, poor root development, "corkiness" in apples, hollow stems in celery, internal necrosis in various fruits.	Yellowing or browning of leaf tips and edges, leaf scorch, and leaf tissue death (appears as "burnt" edges).
Molybdenum (Mo)	"Whiptail" in cauliflower, marginal chlorosis, poor growth, and poor seed development.	Rare in nature, but may cause interveinal chlorosis and leaf deformation in extreme cases.
Chlorine (Cl)	Wilting, bronzing of leaves, leaf curling, reduced root growth; deficiency is rare since chlorine is abundant.	Leaf burn or tip burn, yellowing of leaf margins, and reduced root growth; can resemble salt stress symptoms.
Sodium (Na)	Deficiency is generally not common as sodium is not an essential nutrient for most plants.	Leaf burn, chlorosis, and necrosis starting at leaf tips, reduced vigor and root growth.
Aluminum (Al)	Deficiency symptoms not generally observed in plants; aluminum toxicity is more common in acidic soils.	Stunted root growth, purple or brown discolouration in roots, which can lead to reduced water and nutrient uptake.

Category	Name	Details
Agricultural Milestone	Neolithic Revolution	Transition from hunting to farming in early civilization
Agricultural Policy	Common Agricultural Policy (CAP)	EU policy supporting sustainable agriculture

Influential Agronomist	Justus von Liebig	Father of Agricultural Chemistry; pioneered plant nutrition
Influential Agronomist	George Washington Carver	Promoted soil health and crop rotation in the US
Influential Figure in Plant Breeding	Gregor Johann Mendel	Father of Genetics; developed principles of heredity in plants
Influential Crop Toxin	Solanine	Found in green or sprouted potatoes, causes gastrointestinal issues
Nutrient Deficiency	**Nitrogen** Deficiency	Yellowing in older leaves, stunted growth
Agricultural Pest	Aphids	Sap-sucking pest causing stunted growth
Agricultural Disease	Late Blight	Caused by *Phytophthora infestans*, affects potatoes and tomatoes

Pest/Disease	Affected Crops	Symptoms/Effects
Aphids	Vegetables, fruits, ornamentals	Sap-sucking, stunted growth
Armyworms	Maize, rice, wheat	Leaf damage, defoliation
Cutworms	Vegetables, cotton, grains	Seedling cut-off at soil level
Leaf Miners	Vegetables (tomatoes, spinach)	Burrowing, reduced photosynthesis
Fruit Flies	Fruits (mango, citrus, guava)	Eggs in fruit, spoilage
Whiteflies	Vegetables, cotton, tomatoes	Sap-sucking, virus transmission
Root-Knot Nematodes	Tomatoes, potatoes, carrots	Root galls, stunted growth
Stem Borers	Maize, rice, sugarcane	Boring into stems, wilting
Spider Mites	Vegetables, fruits, cotton	Stippling, leaf drop
Cabbage Worms	Cabbage, cauliflower, broccoli	Leaf holes, reduced photosynthesis
Corn Earworm	Maize, tomatoes, cotton	Kernel damage, yield loss
Weevils (e.g., Boll Weevil)	Cotton, grains, beans	Seed damage, reduced storage quality
Leafhoppers	Rice, grapes, potatoes	Sap-sucking, virus transmission
Locusts	Various crops, cereals	Mass crop consumption
Japanese Beetles	Soybeans, maize, fruits	Leaf damage, skeletonization
Late Blight	Potatoes, tomatoes	Leaf and tuber rot
Rust Diseases	Wheat, barley, coffee	Pustules, reduced photosynthesis
Powdery Mildew	Grapes, apples, cucurbits	White powder spots
Rice Blast	Rice	Lesions, reduced yield

Anthracnose	Mango, beans, peppers	Dark spots, fruit rot
Downy Mildew	Cucumbers, grapes, spinach	Yellow spots, downy growth
Verticillium Wilt	Tomatoes, potatoes	Wilting, leaf discolouration
Bacterial Blight	Rice, beans, cotton	Leaf blighting
Fusarium Wilt	Bananas, tomatoes	Vascular discolouration
Clubroot	Cabbage, broccoli	Swollen roots, stunted growth
Grey Mold (Botrytis)	Strawberries, grapes, tomatoes	Soft rot on fruit
Citrus Canker	Citrus fruits	Leaf lesions, reduced yield
Apple Scab	Apples, pears	Dark spots on fruit
Black Sigatoka	Bananas	Leaf spots, reduced quality
Mosaic Viruses (e.g., Tobacco Mosaic Virus)	Tomatoes, cucumbers, peppers	Mottled leaves, stunted growth
Cercospora Leaf Spot	Beet, soybean, peanuts	Dark leaf spots
Root Rot	Beans, tomatoes, cucumbers	Root decay, stunted growth

Nutrient Deficiency	Disease/Symptom
Nitrogen (N)	Buttoning in cauliflower
Phosphorus (P)	Sickle leaf disease
Potassium (K)	Leaf scorching and burning of leaves, Litchi leaf burn
Calcium (Ca)	Blossom end rot in tomato and Ber, Tip hooking/burning in Cauliflower
Magnesium (Mg)	Sand-drawn disease of Tobacco
Sulphur (S)	Tea yellow disease
Iron (Fe)	White-eye of Paddy, Leaf bleaching in Sugarcane
Manganese (Mn)	Water core in Brassica and turnip, Marsh disease in Pea, Spotted yellow disease in Sugarbeet
Copper (Cu)	Dieback and little leaf in Citrus, Reclamation disease in cereals
Molybdenum (Mo)	Yellow spot disorder in Citrus, Whiptail disease in Cauliflower
Zinc (Zn)	Little leaf in Brinjal and Mango, Bronzing in Guava, White bud in Maize, Khaira disease in Paddy
Boron (Bo)	Internal necrosis in Aonla and Mango, Browning in Cauliflower, Rot in Sugarbeet, Hen and Chicken disorder in Grape, Millerandge in grapes, Tuberculosis in Jackfruit, Hollow Heart in Peanuts, Cotton little leaf
Water Core	Water core in Banana, snowflakes and Sorbitol deposits
Chloride Excess	Black vein disease in Mango due to SO2 gas
Fungal Deficiency	Tikka disease in groundnut (Cercospora personata), Charcoal rot in maize (Macrophomina fasciolae), Ergot and smut in millet, Red rot in sugarcane

Bacterial Deficiency	Black arm in cotton
HCN Poisoning	Poisoning in Sorghum (chari) due to HCN, Dhurin
Helminthosporium oryzae and Pyriculariya oryzae	Blast and Brown leaf spot in grains

Category	Plant
King of Arid and Semi-fruits	Ber
King of Cereals	Wheat
King of Flower Crops	Rose
King of Fodder Crops	Berseem
King of Fruits	Mango
King of Nut Crops	Walnut
King of Oilseeds	Groundnut
King of Pulses	Chickpea
King of Spices	Black Pepper
King of Temperate Fruits	Apple
King of Vegetables	Potato
Queen of Cereals	Maize
Queen of Flower Crops	Gladiolus
Queen of Fodder Crops	Lucerne
Queen of Fruits	Pineapple
Queen of Nut Crops	Peanut
Queen of Oilseeds	Sesame (Til)
Queen of Pulses	Pea
Queen of Spices	Cardamom
Queen of Vegetables	Okra

Name	crop
Coarsest of All Food Grains	Kodo (Paspulum scrobiculatum)
Wonder Crop	Soybean
National Fruit of India	Mango
Wonder Tree	Neem
Bioenergy Plant	Jatropha
Adams Fig	Banana
Oldest Tropical Fruit	Banana

Tree of Heaven	Coconut
White Gold of America	Cotton
Yellow Jewel of America	Soybean

Commission	Year
First Famine Commission	1880
First Irrigation Commission	1901
Royal Commission on Agriculture	1926
Central Water Commission	1945
Finance Commission	1951
Khadi and Village Industry Commission	1957
Central Forestry Commission	1965

Plant	Toxin
Cotton	Gossypol
Lathyrus	Neurotoxin (B-oxalyl-L-a,ÃŸ-diaminopropionic acid, ODAP)
Rapeseed & Mustard	Erucic acid (linked to myocardial fibrosis and lipidosis)
Soybean	Goitrogen
Lucerne/Alfalfa	Saponin and plant estrogen
Groundnut	Aflatoxin (high moisture, Aspergillus flavus & A. niger)
Potato	Steroidal alkaloid
Yam	Alkaloids
Cole crops	Sinigrin
Celery	Appin
Brinjal	Salasodine
Gooseberry	Tannins, ellagic acid, gallic acid, polyphenols
Vine	Marmelotsin
Almonds	Amyladin
Pepper	Olymposyn
Radish	Isocyanate (isothiocyanate)
Turnip	**Calcium** oxalate
Cabbage	Crispness (Raw: Allyl isothiocyanate, Cooked: Dimethyl)
Crop	Term
Banana	Propping, Mattocking (Cutting Pseudostem after harvesting)
Caster, Chick Pea, Cotton	Nipping

Cauliflower	Blanching, Scooping
Coffee	Stripping
Cotton	Ginning, Topping, Nipping
French bean, Tomato	Stalking
Groundnut	Pegging
Jute	Retting, Stripping
Jute, Linseed, Sunhemp	Retting
Lucerne	Lopping
Maize	De-tasseling
Oil palm	Stripping
Potato	Earthing up
Rice	Parboiling
Rubber	Tapping
Tomato	Staking
Sugarcane	Ratooning, Propping, Arrowing, Wrapping, Detrashing, Trashing
Sunhemp	Degumming
Tea	Pruning, Skiffing, Tipping
Tobacco & Tea	Curing
Tobacco	Desuckering, Topping, Rubbing, Priming

Event	Year
Indian Meteorological Department established	**1875**
First Department of Agriculture established	**1881**
Forest Research Institute at Dehradun	**1906**
First Irrigation Commission	**1901**
Sugarcane Breeding Institute at Coimbatore	**1912**
First Tractor bought for Agriculture use	**1914**
Destructive Insect and Pests Act passed	**1914**
First Livestock Census Conducted	**1919**
Central Cotton Committee	**1921**
Royal Commission on Agriculture	**1928**
Great Bengal famine caused by Helminthosporium oryzae	**1943**
Planning Commission Established	**1950**
Indian Institute of Sugarcane Established at Lucknow	**1952**
Central Soil Conservation Research Development	**1954**

National Extension Service	1953
Panchayati Raj started	1957
Doordarshan Services Inaugurated by the President	1959
First Agricultural University established at Pantnagar	1960
Food Corporation of India	1965
High yielding varieties Programme started	1966
Insecticides Act passed	1968
The Green Revolution started	1966
First KVK established in Tamilnadu Agri. University, Pondicherry	1974
National Seed Project	1974
ICRISAT (International Crops Research Institute) for the Semi-Arid Tropics	1974
NAARM (National Academy of Agricultural Research Management) established	1976
NBPGR (National Bureau of Plant Genetic Resources) established	1976
MANAGE (National Institute of Agricultural Extension Management) established at Hyderabad	1987
Plant Quarantine Regulations passed	1981
National Gene Bank established in New Delhi	1996
Kisan Credit Card Scheme started	1998
National Agriculture Insurance Scheme started	1999
Agricultural Technology Management Agency (ATMA)	2005
Biodiversity Act Passed	2002
National Floriculture Mission started	2006
National Bamboo Mission	2006
Rashtriya Krishi Vikas Yojana	2007
Mahatma Gandhi National Rural Employment Guarantee Act (MGNREGA)	2006
Paramparagat Krishi Vikas Yojana	2015

Day	Date
National Youth Day (Swami Vivekanand)	Jan-12
World Wetland Day	Feb-02
National Science Day	Feb-28
World Wildlife Day	Mar-03
World Forestry Day	Mar-21
World Meteorological Day	Mar-23

National Panchayati Raj Day	**Apr-22**
World Milk Day	**Jun-01**
International Yoga Day	**Jun-21**
NABARD Foundation Day	**Jul-12**
ICAR Foundation Day	**Jul-16**
National Agricultural Education Day	**Dec-03**
World Soil Day	**Dec-05**
Farmer's Day (Kisan Divas)	**Dec-23**

Instrument	Use
Albodometer	Measures solar radiation (Reflectivity)
Altimeter	Measures height above sea level
Aneroid Barometer	Measures atmospheric pressure
Beaufort scale	Measures wind speed
Crescograph	Measures growth of plant
Lactometer	Measures density of milk
Lysimeter	Measures percolation and leaching loss
Piezometer	Measures depth of water table
Psychrometer	Measures relative humidity
Pyranometer	Measures solar radiation

Policy	Country/Region	Description
Minimum Support Price (MSP) Policy	India	Provides a guaranteed price for certain crops to protect farmers from sharp price fluctuations
National Food Security Act (NFSA)	India	Subsidized food grains for approximately two-thirds of India's population for food security
Common Agricultural Policy (CAP)	European Union	EU policy supporting farmers through subsidies and programs for sustainable agriculture
Farm Bill (USA)	United States	Comprehensive bill addressing crop insurance, commodity subsidies, and food assistance
Pradhan Mantri Krishi Sinchai Yojana (PMKSY)	India	Irrigation coverage expansion for sustainable water use in agriculture
Integrated Pest Management (IPM) Policies	Various	Encourages sustainable pest control practices to reduce chemical dependency
Soil Health Card Scheme	India	Provides farmers with soil fertility information and nutrient recommendations

Agricultural Adjustment Act (AAA)	United States	New Deal program to stabilize agriculture by reducing crop surplus and raising prices
Organic Agriculture Policy	Various	Promotes organic farming through standards, incentives, and certification processes
Agricultural Policy Framework (Canada)	Canada	Canada's program supporting research, safety, environmental sustainability, and risk management
One District One Product (ODOP)	India	Promotes district-wise specific crop focus for diversification and export potential
Comprehensive Africa Agriculture Development Programme (CAADP)	Africa	Focuses on improving food security and agriculture-based economic growth in Africa
National Mission on Sustainable Agriculture (NMSA)	India	Part of India's climate plan, promoting sustainable practices and climate resilience
Crop Insurance Programs	Various	Provides insurance coverage to protect against natural disasters, pests, and diseases
Precision Agriculture Policies	Various	Promotes technology like GPS mapping, soil monitoring to improve agricultural practices
Incentives for Agroforestry	Various	Incentivizes tree integration with crops to enhance biodiversity and income options
Digital Agriculture Policy	India and other countries	Supports digital solutions in agriculture, including mobile apps and data analytics
New Agricultural Export Policy	India	Aims to double India's agricultural exports by focusing on infrastructure and markets
Smart Agriculture and Climate-Resilient Policies	Various	Adaptation strategies for climate resilience in agriculture through diversified practices
Global Food Security Act	United States	Aims to reduce hunger and improve global food security through agricultural support
Peri-Urban Agriculture Policies	Various	Encourages farming near urban areas to provide fresh produce and reduce transportation emissions
Agri-Environment Schemes	European Union, Various	Pays farmers to adopt eco-friendly practices exceeding conventional requirements
Subsidized Loans for Agricultural Machinery	Various	Offers low-interest loans to support mechanization and farm technology adoption
Direct Income Support for Farmers	European Union, USA	Provides direct payments based on land to support farmer incomes and sustainable land use
Integrated Horticulture Development Policy	India	Promotes high-value horticulture crops for both export and domestic markets
Agricultural Biosecurity Policies	Australia, USA	Aims to prevent pest and disease spread through monitoring and control measures
Zero Budget Natural Farming (ZBNF)	India	Supports natural farming with chemical-free practices and minimal external expenditure

Institute	Location
International	
International Irrigation Management Institute	Sri Lanka
International Livestock Research Institute	Nairobi, Kenya
International Plant Genetic Resources Institute	Rome, Italy
International Rice Research Institute	Los Banos, Philippines
World Meteorological Organization (WMO)	Geneva, Switzerland
ICAR Institute - Deemed Universities	
Indian Agricultural Research Institute	Pusa Campus, New Delhi
Indian Veterinary Research Institute	Izatnagar, Uttar Pradesh
National Dairy Research Institute	Karnal, Haryana
Central Institute of Fisheries Education	Mumbai, Maharashtra
National Institutes	
Central Arid Zone Research Institute	Jodhpur
Central Coastal Agricultural Research Institute	Old Goa
Central Institute for Arid Horticulture	Bikaner
Central Institute of Agricultural Engineering	Bhopal
Central Institute of Fisheries Technology	Cochin
Central Institute of Research on Cotton Technology	Mumbai
Central Institute of Sub Tropical Horticulture	Lucknow
Central Institute of Temperate Horticulture	Srinagar
Central Institute on Post-harvest Engineering and Technology	Ludhiana
Central Marine Fisheries Research Institute	Kochi
Central Plantation Crops Research Institute	Kerala
Central Potato Research Institute	Shimla
Central Research Institute of Dryland Agriculture	Hyderabad
Central Sheep and Wool Research Institute	Avikanagar, Rajasthan
Central Tobacco Research Institute	Rajahmundry
Central Tuber Crops Research Institute	Trivandrum
Indian Agricultural Statistics Research Institute	New Delhi
Indian Grassland and Fodder Research Institute	Jhansi
Indian Institute of Horticultural Research	Bengaluru
Indian Institute of Natural Resins and Gums	Ranchi
Indian Institute of Pulses Research	Kanpur

Indian Institute of Soil and Water Conservation	Dehradun
Indian Institute of Spices Research	Calicut
Indian Institute of Sugarcane Research	Lucknow
Indian Institute of Vegetable Research	Varanasi
Institute for Research on Buffaloes	Hissar
Institute for Research on Goats	Farah, Uttar Pradesh
Institute of Cotton Research	Nagpur
Institute of Freshwater Aquaculture	Bhubaneshwar
National Academy of Agricultural Research & Management	Hyderabad
National Institute of Abiotic Stress Management	Malegaon, Maharashtra
National Institute of Biotic Stresses Management	Baroda, Raipur
National Rice Research Institute	Cuttack
Sugarcane Breeding Institute	Coimbatore
Directorate of Cashew Research	Puttur, Karnataka
Directorate of Groundnut Research	Junagadh

Organization	Headquarters	Focus
Bill & Melinda Gates Foundation (BMGF)	Seattle, USA	Funds agricultural R&D in Africa and South Asia to improve food security
International Development Association (IDA)	Washington, D.C., USA	Provides low-interest loans and grants for enhancing agricultural productivity
United States Agency for International Development (USAID)	Washington, D.C., USA	Supports global agricultural development, focusing on food security and rural poverty
African Development Bank (AfDB)	Abidjan, CÃ´te d'Ivoire	Loans, grants, and assistance for agricultural development in Africa
European Union (EU)	Brussels, Belgium	Supports sustainable agriculture and rural development globally
Asian Development Bank (ADB)	Manila, Philippines	Invests in agricultural infrastructure and rural development across Asia
International Finance Corporation (IFC)	Washington, D.C., USA	Funding for private-sector agribusinesses and supply chains in emerging markets
International Food Policy Research Institute (IFPRI)	Washington, D.C., USA	Research on food policy, poverty alleviation, and rural development projects
International Fund for Agricultural Development (IFAD)	Rome, Italy	Loans and grants for rural poverty reduction and resilience in developing countries
Global Environment Facility (GEF)	Washington, D.C., USA	Funds projects addressing climate change, land degradation, and sustainable land management
Alliance for a Green	Nairobi,	Improves agricultural productivity and

Revolution in Africa (AGRA)	Kenya	livelihoods in Africa
Rockefeller Foundation	New York, USA	Funds projects for smallholder farmer income and climate resilience
Deutsche Gesellschaft Internationale Zusammenarbeit (GIZ)	Bonn and Eschborn, Germany	Supports global food security, rural development, and climate adaptation
Commonwealth Development Corporation (CDC Group)	London, UK	Funds agribusiness and infrastructure projects in Africa and South Asia
OPEC Fund for International Development (OFID)	Vienna, Austria	Provides funding for agricultural projects in developing countries, focusing on food security

Organization	Esta blish ed	Headquarters	Focus
Food and Agriculture Organization (FAO)	1945	Rome, Italy	Eliminate hunger, improve nutrition, and promote sustainable agriculture
International Fund for Agricultural Development (IFAD)	1977	Rome, Italy	Funding and resources for rural agriculture and poverty reduction
World Food Programme (WFP)	1961	Rome, Italy	Combat global hunger, provide food aid, support sustainable food systems
Consultative Group on International Agricultural Research (CGIAR)	1971	Montpellier, France	Research partnership developing agricultural innovations for food security
International Rice Research Institute (IRRI)	1960	Philippines	Research on rice cultivation to improve food security in rice-growing regions
International Maize and Wheat Improvement Center (CIMMYT)	1966	Mexico	Enhance productivity and sustainability of maize and wheat farming
International Crops Research Institute for the Semi-Arid Tropics (ICRISAT)	1972	Hyderabad, India	Improve crops in arid and semi-arid areas, particularly in Asia and Africa
International Center for Agricultural Research in the Dry Areas (ICARDA)	1977	Beirut, Lebanon	Promote agricultural research and sustainable farming in dry regions
Bioversity International	1974	Rome, Italy	Conservation and use of biodiversity for food and agriculture
Asian Vegetable Research and Development Center (AVRDC)	1971	Taiwan	Research on vegetable crops to improve nutrition, health, and livelihoods
International Potato Center (CIP)	1971	Lima, Peru	Research on potato, sweet potato, and other root crops for food security

Centre for International Forestry Research (CIFOR)	1993	Bogor, Indonesia	Research on sustainable forest management and conservation
World Bank Agriculture and Food	1944	Washington, D.C., USA	Funding and technical assistance for agricultural development globally
International Centre for Genetic Engineering and Biotechnology (ICGEB)	1983	Trieste, Italy; India, South Africa	Biotechnology to address agricultural, health, and environmental issues
Global Alliance for Climate-Smart Agriculture (GACSA)	2014	Hosted by FAO	Improve food security and resilience through climate-smart practices
International Institute of Tropical Agriculture (IITA)	1967	Ibadan, Nigeria	Research to improve agriculture in tropical regions, focusing on staples

Scheme	Launch Year	Coverage	Features
Pradhan Mantri Fasal Bima Yojana (PMFBY)	2016	All food crops, oilseeds, commercial/horticultural crops	Minimal premium; government subsidized; compensation based on yield loss
Restructured Weather-Based Crop Insurance Scheme (RWBCIS)	2016	Weather-based insurance for sensitive crops	Payout based on adverse weather parameters
Modified National Agricultural Insurance Scheme (MNAIS)	2010	All food crops, oilseeds, selected commercial and horticultural crops	Introduced individual farm-based assessments; government subsidized
National Agricultural Insurance Scheme (NAIS)	1999	Initially covered food crops, oilseeds, and selected commercial crops	Area approach with government subsidies; replaced by PMFBY
Coconut Palm Insurance Scheme (CPIS)	2009	Specifically covers coconut palm trees	Subsidized by central and state governments
Unified Package Insurance Scheme (UPIS)	2016	Multiple insurance products: crop, personal accident, life, asset insurance	Comprehensive coverage including various assets
Weather Insurance by State Governments		Weather-based insurance by state governments	Tailored for local weather risks and specific crops

Abbreviation	Full Form	Location	Established Year
AVRDC	Asian Vegetable Research & Development Center	Taiwan	
BIR	Biodiversity International Rome	Rome, Italy	1974
CIFOR	Centre for International Forestry Research	Bogor, Indonesia	1993

CIMMYT	International Centre for the Improvement of Maize and Wheat	Mexico	1966
CIP	International Potato Centre	Lima, Peru, South America	1971
FAO	Food and Agriculture Organization	Rome, Italy	1945
IBPGR	International Board for Plant Genetics Resources	Rome, Italy	1974
IBRD	International Bank for Reconstruction and Development (the World Bank)	Washington DC	
ICARDA	International Centre for Agricultural Research in the Dry Areas	Syria	1977
ICGEB	International Centre for Genetic Engineering and Biotechnology	Italy and New Delhi, India	1994
ICRISAT	International Crops Research Institute for the Semi-Arid Tropics	Hyderabad, Telangana, India	1972

Act/Program	Year Enacted
The Essential Commodities Act	1955
The Madhya Pradesh Sugarcane (Regulation of Supply and Purchase) ACT	1958
The Madhya Pradesh Sugarcane (Regulation of Supply and Purchase) RULES	1959
The Seed Act	1966
Sugarcane (Control) Order	1966
The Seeds Rules	1968
Insecticides Act	1968
Insecticides Rules	1971
The Seeds (Control) Order	1983
The Fertilizer (Control) Order	1985

Discipline	Father
A Value concept	Dean & friend (For P)
Agricultural chemistry	Justus von Liebig
Agro-meteorology	D.N. Walia
Agronomy	Pietro Decrescenzi
Antibiotics	Alexander Fleming
ATP Cycle	Lipmann
Bacteriology	Robert Koch
Biochemistry	Justus von Liebig
Bt-cotton in India	C.D. Mayee
Cooperative movement in India	F. Nicholson
CRI in wheat	B.L. Bhardwaj

Cropping System	Dr. S.S. Bains
Cytoplasmic inheritance	Carl Correns
DNA fingerprinting Technique	Alec Jaffrey
Drip irrigation	Simcha Blass
Economic Ecology	M.S. Swaminathan
Evergreen revolution	Swaminathan
Experimental Genetics	Thomas Hunt Morgan
Extension education	Seaman/Leagnes
Extension	J.C. Legans (in India: R.N. Singh)
Fermentation	Louis Pasteur
Field plot experiment	J.B. Boussingault
Forest Pathology	Robert Haring
Fruit and vegetable preservation	M. Nicholes Apart
Genetic Engineering	Paul Berg
Genetics	Gregor Johann Mendel
Golden revolution in India	Dr. K.C. Chadha
Golden rice	Dr. Ingo Potrykus
Green House effect	J.B. Founler
Green revolution in India	M.S. Swaminathan
Green revolution	Dr. N. E. Borlaug
Harvest index & plant Ideotype	M.C. Donald
Hybrid cotton	C.T. Patel
Hybrid Rice (India)	Ebrahimali Abubacker Siddique
Hybrid rice	Yuan Longping
Immunology	Edward Jenner
Increase yield & law	Wilcox (1929)
Indian Agriculture meteorology	L. Ramdas
Indian Ecology	R. Mishra
Indian Mycology	E.J. Butler
Indian Plant Breeding	Dr. B.P. Pal
Indian plant pathology	E.J. Butler
Indian Remote Sensing	Dr. P.R. Pishroty
Irrigation Agronomy	Dr. N.G. Dastane
Irrigation Engineering	A.M. Michele
Leaf area index	Watson (1947)
Mixed cropping	La-Flitze (1928)

Modern Genetics	T.H. Morgan
Multi cropping index	R.W. Willey
Mutation Theory	Hugo de Vries
Nematology	N.A. Cobb
Nitrogen Fixation, Soil microbiology	S.N. Winogradsky
Nutrient mobility concept	R.H. Brays
Ornamental Gardening	M.S. Randhawa
Pedology	V.V. Dokuchalev
Permanent wilting point	Richards & Smith
Photoperiodism concept	Gardener & Allard (1920)
Plant Anatomy	Grew
Plant Pathology	Anton De Bary
Plant Physiology	Stephen Hales
Plant Tissue Culture	G. Haberlandt
Polygenic inheritance	Kolreuter
Proteto (protein rich potato)	Ashish Dutta
Pure culture	Oscer Brefeld
Relay cropping	S.L. Bain
Rhizobium (Bacillus radicicola)	Beijerinck (1890)
Slow-Release Nitrogen Fertilizer	Dr. Rajendra Prasad
Soil conservation	H.H. Barnavet
Soil Science	V.V. Dokuchalev
Soil testing Technique	M.L. Troyge
Super Rice	Dr. G.H. Khush
Super wheat	S. Nagrajan
Thermoperiodism concept	Went
Tillage and Weeds	Jethro Tull
Vernalization	Lysenko
Water balance concept & PET	Thornthwaite & W. C. Penman
White Revolution	Dr. Varghese Kurien
Zoology, Biology	Aristotle

Pigment	Colour	Found In	Health Benefits
Chlorophyll	Green	Spinach, kale, broccoli, green beans	Antioxidant, detoxifying properties
Carotenoids	Yellow,	Carrots, tomatoes, sweet	Antioxidants; supports vision,

	Orange, Red	potatoes, bell peppers	immune function, skin health
Anthocyanins	Red, Blue, Purple	Blueberries, blackberries, red cabbage, eggplant	Anti-inflammatory; may protect cardiovascular and cognitive health
Betalains	Red, Purple	Beets, Swiss chard, prickly pear cactus, amaranth	Antioxidant, anti-inflammatory; supports liver health
Flavonoids	Yellow, Red, Blue	Apples, onions, tea, various herbs	Antioxidants; reduces inflammation, may protect against chronic diseases
Curcuminoids	Yellow-Orange	Turmeric	Anti-inflammatory, antioxidant; beneficial for joints and brain health
Capsanthin and Capsorubin	Red-Orange	Red bell peppers, paprika, chili peppers	Antioxidant; may reduce inflammation
Zeaxanthin	Yellow	Corn, orange and yellow peppers, egg yolk (via feed)	Supports eye health, reduces risk of macular degeneration
Xanthophylls	Yellow	Kale, spinach, corn, green leafy vegetables	Supports eye health, protects against macular degeneration
Crocin	Orange-Red	Saffron	Antioxidant; potential mood-enhancing, neuroprotective effects

Plant/Item	Characteristic	Compound/Principle
Gram leaves	Acidic taste	Malic acid/Oxalic acid
Fig	Active compound	Ficin
Brinjal	Alkaloids present	Solasodine
Broccoli	Anticancerous principle	Sulphoraphane
Cabbage	Anticancerous principle	Indole-3-carbinole
Tomato	Anticancerous principle	Lycopene
Cucumber	Bitterness	Cucurbitacin
Fenugreek	Bitterness	Trigonelline and Choline
Pepper	Bitterness	Marmelosin
Brinjal	Colour	Anthocyanin
Chilli	Colouring pigment	Capsanthin
Papain	Enzyme present	Pepsin
Pineapple	Enzyme present	Bromelain
Potato	Green colour	Solanine and Chaconine
Grape	Muscat flavour	Methyl anthranilate
Neem	Active compounds	Limbin, Nimbinin
Pepper	Odour	Oleriosin
Carrot	Colour	Carotene

Saffron	Colour	Carotenoid (crocin)
Onion	Colour	Anthocyanin
Cocoa	Principle compound	Theobromine
Coffee	Principle compound	Caffeine
Chilli	Pungency	Capsaicin alkaloid
Cole crops (Cabbage)	Pungency	Sinigrin
Garlic	Pungency	Diallyl disulfide
Mustard oil	Pungency	Glucosinolates
Onion	Pungency	Allyl propyl disulfide
Radish	Pungency	Isothiocyanate
Carrot	Colour	Anthocyanin
Tomato	Colour	Lycopene
Beetroot	Colour	B-cyanin
Turmeric	Colour	Curcumin
Cassava	Colour	Carotene
Onion	Colour	Quercetin
Papaya	Yellow pigment	Caricaxanthin
Spinach	Green colour	Chlorophyll
Turmeric	Antioxidant	Curcumin
Licorice	Sweetness	Glycyrrhizin
Ginger	Pungency	Gingerol
Green Tea	Antioxidant	Catechins
Apple	Browning upon cutting	Polyphenol oxidase
Citrus fruits	Sour taste	Citric acid
Soybean	Isoflavones (Phytoestrogen)	Genistein and Daidzein
Lavender	Aroma	Linalool
Chamomile	Calming compound	Apigenin
Strawberry	Red colour	Pelargonidin
Walnut	Antioxidant	Ellagic acid
Garlic	Antimicrobial compound	Allicin
Green Bell Pepper	Green colour	Chlorophyll
Avocado	Healthy fat	Oleic acid
Basil	Aroma	Eugenol
Black Pepper	Pungency	Piperine
Almond	Bitter taste in raw state	Amygdalin
Mango	Yellow colour	Beta-carotene

Thyme	Aroma	Thymol
Spinach	Iron content	Non-heme Iron
Coffee	Aroma and flavour	Caffeic acid
Hibiscus	Red colour	Anthocyanin
Cocoa	Mood-enhancing compound	Phenylethylamine
Rosemary	Memory-boosting compound	Carnosic acid

Pest/Disease	Affected Crops	Symptoms/Effects
Stem Rust	Wheat, Barley	Reddish-brown pustules on stems and leaves, reduced yield
Root Rot	Various crops (beans, tomatoes, cucumbers)	Root decay, stunted growth, plant death
Tomato Leaf Miner	Tomatoes, eggplants	Leaf mining, fruit damage, reduced crop quality
Peach Scab	Peaches, nectarines	Scab-like lesions on fruit, reduced marketability
Citrus Greening	Citrus fruits	Yellow mottling, fruit drop, tree death
Cabbage Maggot	Cabbage, radish, turnips	Root tunneling, wilting, stunted growth
Brown Spot Disease	Rice	Brown lesions on leaves, reduced photosynthesis
Cercospora Leaf Spot	Beet, soybean, peanuts	Dark leaf spots, premature leaf drop
Flea Beetles	Potatoes, tomatoes, leafy greens	Leaf damage, reduced photosynthesis
Verticillium Wilt	Tomatoes, potatoes	Wilting, leaf discolouration, plant death
Anthracnose	Mango, beans, peppers	Dark lesions on leaves and fruits, reduced quality
Downy Mildew	Grapes, cucumbers, spinach	Yellow spots, downy growth on leaves
Powdery Mildew	Apples, grapes, squash	White powdery spots on leaves, reduced vigor
Bean Pod Borer	Beans, cowpeas	Pod boring, reduced seed quality and yield
Botrytis Blight	Strawberries, flowers	Gray mold on flowers and leaves, decay
Black Spot	Roses, apples, strawberries	Black spots on leaves and stems, reduced aesthetic value
Apple Scab	Apples, pears	Dark spots on fruit, reduced quality
Thrips	Onions, garlic, beans	Distorted leaves, reduced yield, vector for viruses
Coffee Leaf Rust	Coffee	Orange spots on leaves, leaf drop
Pine Wilt Nematode	Pine trees	Wilted, yellowing needles, tree death

Revolution	Related To
Black Revolution	Biofuel (Jatropha) production
Blue Revolution	Fish production
Brown Revolution	Non-conventional energy sources
Golden Revolution	Fruit production (apple)
Gray Revolution	Manures and fertilizers
Green Revolution	Food grain production (wheat & rice)
Parbhani Revolution	Okra
Pink Revolution	Prawn production
Rainbow Revolution	Agriculture (1996)
Red Revolution	Meat/Tomato production
Round Revolution	Potato production
Silver Revolution	Egg production/Poultry
White Revolution	Milk production
Yellow Revolution	Oilseeds production

Botanical Name	Common Name	Plant Part Used	Chemical Found
Chlorophytum borivilianum	Safed Musli	Root	Saponins
Withania somnifera	Ashwagandha	Leaves & Root	Alkaloids
Rauvolfia serpentina	Sarpagandha	Root (Dried)	Serpentine
Plantago ovata	Isabgol	Husk of the seed	Glycoside
Acorus calamus	Sweet Flag	Rhizome (Dried)	-
Bacopa morrieri	Brahmi	Whole Plant	Hydrolytin (Alkaloid)
Papaver somniferum	Opium Poppy	Latex & Seeds	Alkaloids
Cymbopogon flexuosus	Lemon Grass	Fresh Grasses	Citral a & b
Mentha arvensis	Pudina/Mint	Herbage	Menthol
Vetiveria zizanoides	Khus/Vetiver	Root	Khusol, Vetiverone
Cymbopogon winterianus	Citronella	Fresh Herbage	Citronellol, Geraniol
Ferula foetida	Asafoetida/Hing	Gum Resin	Organic Sulphur
Ocimum sanctum	Tulsi/Basil	Leaves	Eugenol

Crop Type	Variety Name	Characteristics/Uses
Wheat	Kalyansona	High-yielding, resistant to rust

Wheat	Sonora 64	Semi-dwarf, Green Revolution variety
Wheat	HD 2967	High-yielding, rust-resistant
Wheat	PBW 343	Suitable for irrigated conditions
Rice	IR 64	Drought-resistant, high yield
Rice	Basmati 370	Aromatic, long-grain
Rice	Swarna	Flood-tolerant, high-yielding
Rice	MTU 1010	Early-maturing, high yield
Maize	Ganga 5	High-yielding hybrid
Maize	Vivek 9	Disease-resistant, suitable for hills
Maize	Dekalb 9081	Heat-tolerant hybrid
Maize	Pioneer 30V92	High productivity, drought tolerant
Barley	VLB 118	High-yield, disease-resistant
Barley	Karan 16	Rust-resistant, used for malt
Barley	RD 2668	High-yielding, used for brewing
Pulses	Pusa 992	Wilt-resistant, high-yielding
Pulses	Pusa Vishal	High-yield, rust-resistant
Pulses	Shiva	Early-maturing, virus-resistant
Pulses	Arka Bold	Drought-resistant, high yield
Cotton	BT Cotton	Genetically modified, pest-resistant
Cotton	Suraj	High-yield, suitable for rainfed areas
Cotton	H-4	High-yield hybrid
Cotton	RCH 2	Good fiber quality, pest-resistant
Sugarcane	Co 86032	High sugar content
Sugarcane	CoJ 64	Suitable for irrigated/rainfed
Sugarcane	BO 91	Tropical regions
Potato	Kufri Jyoti	Late blight-resistant
Potato	Kufri Sindhuri	Processing suitable
Potato	Atlantic	High starch, for chips
Tomato	Arka Rakshak	Wilt-resistant, high-yielding
Tomato	Roma	For canning/sauces
Tomato	Heinz 1350	For processing
Onion	Bhima Super	Storage suitable, high-yielding
Onion	Arka Kalyan	Blotch-resistant
Onion	Pusa Red	Drought-tolerant
Banana	Dwarf Cavendish	Wind-resistant, short height
Banana	Robusta	High-yielding

Banana	Nendran	For chips
Mango	Alphonso	Fragrant, premium
Mango	Dasheri	Popular, juicy
Mango	Kesar	Pulp production
Groundnut	TG 37 A	Drought-resistant, high yield
Groundnut	K 6	Disease-resistant, high oil
Groundnut	ICGS 44	High-quality oil
Mustard	Pusa Bold	High oil content
Mustard	Rohini	White rust-resistant
Mustard	Varuna	Popular, high oil content
Coffee	Cauvery	Rust-resistant hybrid
Coffee	SL28	Quality flavour
Coffee	Robusta	High caffeine content
Apple	Red Delicious	Sweet, crisp texture
Apple	Golden Delicious	Mild flavour
Apple	Granny Smith	Tart, suitable for cooking
Tea	Assam	Bold flavour
Tea	Darjeeling	Delicate aroma
Tea	Nilgiri	Fragrant, good for blending

Regulation/Act	Year
Bureau Of Indian Standards Act	1986
Livestock Importation Act	1898
AGMARK Act	1937
Essential Commodities Act	1955
The Fruit Products Order (FPO)	1955
Export (Quality Control and Inspection) Act	1963
Meat Food Product Order	1973
Standards On Weight and Measurement Act	1976
Milk And Milk Product Order	1992
Plant Quarantine (Regulation of Import into India) Order	2003
The Food Safety and Standards Act	2006

Export Standard	Focus	Region
Codex Alimentarius	International food safety, quality, and	Worldwide

	trade standards	
USDA Export Verification (EV) Program	Quality and safety verification for U.S. exports	United States
EU Export Health Standards	Food safety, quality control for agricultural exports	European Union
GlobalGAP (Good Agricultural Practices)	Food safety, sustainability, and traceability	Worldwide
ISO 22000 Food Safety Management	Food safety management systems for supply chain	Worldwide
Hazard Analysis Critical Control Point (HACCP)	Risk management for food safety in production/export	Worldwide
Phytosanitary Certification	Pest and disease-free status for plant products	Worldwide
China Good Agricultural Practices (ChinaGAP)	Food safety and quality for agricultural exports	China
Japan Agricultural Standards (JAS)	Organic and safety standards for Japanese exports	Japan
Sanitary and Phytosanitary (SPS) Measures	Ensures safety of food, animals, and plants in trade	World Trade Organization (WTO)
US Food Safety Modernization Act (FSMA)	Food safety standards for imports to the U.S.	United States
British Retail Consortium (BRC) Global Standards	Food safety and quality for exporters to the UK	United Kingdom, Worldwide
Safe Quality Food (SQF) Program	Food safety and quality assurance for global exports	Worldwide
India's APEDA Export Standards	Quality control for agricultural and processed foods	India
CanadaGAP	Good agricultural practices for exports from Canada	Canada
Organic Export Standards (various)	Organic certification for exports (USDA Organic, EU Organic, JAS)	Worldwide
Maximum Residue Limits (MRLs)	Pesticide residue limits for safe export	Worldwide
International Plant Protection Convention (IPPC)	Phytosanitary measures to control plant health risks	Worldwide
Fair Trade Certification	Ethical and sustainable practices in agricultural exports	Worldwide
Rainforest Alliance Certified	Sustainable practices for agricultural products	Worldwide

Tropism Type	Description
Exotropism	Continuation of growth in the previously established direction
Gravitropism	Growth toward gravity
Heliotropism	Response to Sunlight

Hygrotropism	Growth in response to humidity
Phototropism	Growth toward light
Thigmotropism	Growth toward solid objects

Initiative	Date of Launch
Krishi Darshan	26th Jan, 1966
Technology Mission on Oil Seeds	1986
National Horticultural Mission (NHM)	2005-06
National Food Security Mission (NFSM)	2007-08
Milk Mission	20-Apr-12
National Food Security Act	10 Sep. 2013
National Digital Literacy Mission	
National Livestock Mission	2014-15
Make in India	25th Sept 2014
Pradhan Mantri Jan Dhan Yojana	28th Aug, 2014
Swachh Bharat Mission	
DD Kisan	26th May, 2015
National Skill Development Mission	15th July, 2015
E-NAM (Electronic National Agriculture Market)	14th April, 2016
Operation Green (Production of potato, tomato & onion)	1st Feb, 2018
Pradhan Mantri Matsya Sampada Yojana	May, 2020

Initiative	Objective/Description	Year of Launch
Digital India Act 2023	Modernizes digital regulations to tackle privacy, online safety, cyberbullying, and digital rights; replaces IT Act of 2000	2023
Atmanirbhar Horticulture Clean Plant Programme	Provides high-quality, disease-free planting materials for horticulture with â,¹2,200 crore budget allocation	2023
Amrit Dharohar	Conserves wetlands to enhance biodiversity, carbon stock, and eco-tourism; supports local communities	2023
Green Credit Programme	Promotes sustainable practices by incentivizing environmental responsibility under Environment Protection Act	2023
Mahila Samman Savings Certificate	Offers a fixed savings scheme for women and girls with 7.5% interest and partial withdrawals till 2025	2023

Programme	Year of Start	Source of Funding
Grow More Food Campaign	**1942-43**	-
Community Development Programme	**1952**	Ford Foundation
National Extension Service	**2nd Oct. 1953**	
Panchayati Raj adopted	**2nd Oct. 1959**	
High Yielding Variety Programme	**1965-66**	
Drought Prone Area Programme	**1970-71**	
Training and Visit System	**1974**	World Bank
Training of Rural Youth for Self-Employment (TRYSEM)	**15th Aug., 1979**	
Integrated Rural Development Programme (IRDP)	**2nd Oct., 1980**	
Institute Village Linkage Programme (IVLP)	**1995**	
Kisan Credit Cards (KCC) Scheme	**1998**	
Agri Clinic and Agri-business Centres	**2002**	
Kisan Call Centre	**21st Jan 2004**	
Agriculture Technology Management Agency (ATMA)	**May-05**	
National Rural Employment Guarantee Programme (NREGA)	**2 Feb. 2006**	
Rashtriya Krishi Vikas Yojana (RKVY)	**Aug-07**	
Pradhan Mantri Krishi Sinchayee Yojana	**1st July, 2015**	
Soil Health Card Scheme	**17th Feb, 2015**	
Pradhan Mantri Fasal Bima Yojana (PMFBY)	**Kharif 2016**	
PM-Kisan Samman Nidhi	**1st Dec. 2018**	
One Nation, One Ration Card	**1st Jan. 2020**	

Program	Objective	Ministry	Year of Launch
PM Vishwakarma Scheme	Supports artisans and small entrepreneurs with skill development and financial aid, boosting traditional crafts	Ministry of Micro, Small and Medium Enterprises	2023
Amrit Bharat Station Scheme	Modernizes railway stations across India to enhance passenger amenities and infrastructure	Ministry of Railways	2023
PM PRANAM Scheme	Promotes reduction in chemical fertilizer usage and supports eco-friendly farming practices	Ministry of Agriculture & Farmers Welfare	2023
Agnipath Scheme	Provides short-term employment in armed forces for skill development and discipline among youth	Ministry of Defence	2022

National Technical Textiles Mission (NTTM)	Aims to make India a global leader in technical textiles through innovation and infrastructure support	Ministry of Textiles	2020

Name of Study / Plant Condition	Subject / Condition
Tsiology	Tea
Cereology	Crop cycles
Cryology	Snow, ice & frozen conditions
Xylology	Wood
Eremology	Deserts
Nephology	Clouds
Siphonapterology	Fleas
Acidophiles	Plants that grow well under acidic conditions
Chamaephytes	Plants growing in extremely cold climates
Cryophytes	Plants that grow on ice or snow
Hemicryptophytes	Plants suited to grassland conditions
Amphipytes	Plants that grow in contrasting conditions like land and water
Calcifuges	Calcium-sensitive plants
Chasmophytes	Plants with roots capable of penetrating rock fissures
Epiphyte	Plants that grow on other plants for support
Gypsophytes	Gypsum-loving plants
Heliophytes	Light-loving plants
Basophiles	Plants that prefer alkali soils
Hydrophytes	Water-loving plants
Oxylophytes	Plants tolerant to highly acidic soils
Pterophytes	Plants that grow on rocks
Phreatophytes	Plants indicating presence of sub-surface water
Phanerophytes	Plants growing in warm and moist climates
Halophytes	Plants that prefer saline conditions
Lithophytes	Plants that grow on rock surfaces
Psammophytes	Plants that prefer shady conditions

Scheme	Objective	Year of Launch
PM Vishwakarma Scheme	Supports artisans and traditional craftspeople with	2023

	skill development and financial aid	
Amrit Bharat Station Scheme	Modernizes railway stations, enhancing infrastructure and passenger amenities	2023
PM PRANAM Scheme	Promotes sustainable farming by reducing chemical fertilizer usage	2023
GOBARdhan Scheme	Establishes waste-to-wealth plants supporting a circular economy	2023
National Apprenticeship Promotion Scheme	Provides stipend support to youth through a national apprenticeship program	2023
Credit Guarantee Scheme for MSMEs	Offers collateral-free credit to MSMEs, reducing borrowing costs	2023
Pradhan Mantri Kaushal Vikas Yojana (PMKVY) 4.0	Introduces new-age skills like AI, robotics, and 3D printing for youth	2023
Mahila Samman Savings Certificate	A savings scheme for women with a 7.5% interest rate until March 2025	2023
Veer Gatha Project 3.0	Engages students in patriotism-focused creative activities honoring armed forces	2023

Plant Type	Growth Condition
Acidophiles	Plants grow well under acidic conditions
Chamaephytes	Plants growing under extremely cold climates
Cryophytes	Plants grow on ice or snow
Hemicryptophytes	Plants suitable for grassland conditions
Amphipytes	Plants grow on two contrasting conditions e.g., Land & water
Calcifuges	**Calcium**-sensitive plants
Chasmophytes	Plants with roots capable of penetrating rock fissures
Epiphyte	Plants grow on another plant for physical support
Gypsophytes	Gypsum-loving plants
Heliophytes	Light-loving plants
Basophiles	Plants prefer alkali soils
Hydrophytes	Water-loving plants
Oxylophytes	Plants tolerant to high acidic soil conditions
Petrophytes	Plants able to grow on rocks
Phreatophytes	Plants show presence of sub-surface water
Phanerophytes	Plants grow in warm and moist climates
Halophytes	Plants prefer saline conditions
Lithophytes	Plants grow on rock surfaces
Psammophytes	Plants prefer shady conditions

Plant	Edible Part	Drought Tolerance
Olives	Fruit (used for oil and culinary ingredient)	Extremely hardy in arid regions
Rosemary	Leaves (used as seasoning herb)	Thrives in dry, rocky soils
Thyme	Leaves (culinary herb)	Grows well with minimal water
Prickly Pear Cactus	Pads (nopal) and fruits (tunas)	Extremely drought-resistant, thrives in deserts
Amaranth	Leaves (greens) and seeds (grain)	Adapted to dry conditions
Tepary Beans	Beans (protein-rich)	Highly drought-resistant, grows in deserts
Moringa	Leaves, pods, and seeds	Highly resilient, grows in poor, dry soils
Sweet Potatoes	Tubers and leaves	Survives in dry conditions with mulching
Quinoa	Seeds (grain)	Adapted to dry, high-altitude environments
Figs	Fruit (fresh or dried)	Grows in hot, dry climates with low water
Purslane	Leaves and stems	Thrives in dry, poor soils
Chickpeas	Beans (protein-rich)	Well-suited to dry climates, enriches soil
Carob	Pods (used as chocolate substitute)	Thrives in arid, Mediterranean climates
Millet	Grains (cereal and porridge)	Highly resilient, thrives in arid regions
Sage	Leaves (used for seasoning)	Suited to dry, rocky soils

Plant	Nutrient Content	Drought Tolerance
Amaranth	High in protein, iron, **Magnesium**, and **Calcium**	Extremely resilient in arid climates; grows in poor soils
Moringa (Drumstick Tree)	Rich in vitamins A, C, **Calcium**, **Potassium**, and protein	Grows well in dry conditions with minimal water; improves soil fertility
Quinoa	High in protein, fiber, iron, **Magnesium**, and essential amino acids	Adapted to dry, high-altitude regions; survives in well-drained soils
Kale	Excellent source of vitamins A, C, K, **Calcium**, and **Potassium**	Can survive in low-water conditions; provides good soil cover
Chia	Rich in omega-3 fatty acids, fiber, **Calcium**, and antioxidants	Thrives in arid and semi-arid environments; deep roots prevent soil erosion
Lentils	High in protein, iron, and fiber	Resilient to low water; enriches soil **Nitrogen** through **Nitrogen** -fixing bacteria
Tepary Beans	Rich in protein, fiber, and essential minerals like **Calcium** and	Highly drought-tolerant; traditionally grown in arid regions; improves soil

	Magnesium	fertility
Sorghum	Contains protein, iron, and fiber	Deep-rooted; thrives with minimal water; used as cover crop to improve soil quality
Sweet Potatoes	High in vitamins A, C, manganese, and **Potassium**	Adaptable to low-water conditions with mulching; reduces soil erosion
Pigeon Pea	Good source of protein, iron, **Calcium**, and **Magnesium**	Tolerant to dry climates; **Nitrogen** fixer, improving soil health for future crops

Plant	Nutrient Contribution	Benefit
Legumes (e.g., Beans, Peas, Clover)	**Nitrogen** (N)	**Nitrogen** -fixing plants; enrich soil by converting atmospheric **Nitrogen**
Alfalfa	**Nitrogen** (N), **Phosphorus** (P), **Potassium** (K)	Deep roots bring up nutrients from lower soil levels; used as green manure
Buckwheat	**Phosphorus** (P), **Calcium** (Ca)	Fast-growing roots scavenge **Phosphorus**; release it upon decomposition
Comfrey	**Nitrogen** (N), **Potassium** (K), **Calcium** (Ca)	Deep taproots mine nutrients from subsoil, provide rich mulch
Mustard	Sulphur (S), **Phosphorus** (P)	Soil conditioning; suppresses soil-borne pathogens, adds organic matter
Sunflowers	**Phosphorus** (P), **Potassium** (K)	Breaks up compacted soil; adds organic matter to improve nutrient availability
Oats	**Nitrogen** (N), Organic Matter	Adds biomass and organic matter; aids water retention and microbial activity
Radishes (especially Daikon Radish)	**Nitrogen** (N), **Phosphorus** (P), Organic Matter	Breaks up compacted soils; channels for air and water, adds organic matter
Lupines	**Nitrogen** (N), **Phosphorus** (P)	**Nitrogen** -fixer; improves **Phosphorus** availability, aids soil fertility
Vetch	**Nitrogen** (N), Organic Matter	Fixes **Nitrogen** ; enriches soil with high biomass, enhances organic matter

Plant	Nutrient Requirements
Tomatoes	**Nitrogen** (N): Essential for leafy growth; moderate amounts **Phosphorus** (P): Promotes flowering and fruiting **Potassium** (K): Important for fruit size and disease resistance
Carrots	**Potassium** (K): Enhances root development and flavour **Phosphorus** (P): Supports root growth; essential for quality roots **Calcium** (Ca): Prevents root splitting and improves texture
Lettuce	**Nitrogen** (N): Crucial for leafy growth; higher levels for lush leaves **Calcium** (Ca): Prevents leaf tip burn **Magnesium** (Mg): Supports green foliage
Strawberries	**Potassium** (K): for sweetness and fruit size **Phosphorus** (P): Essential for root and fruit development **Calcium** (Ca): Prevents fruit rot and improves firmness

Blueberries	Acidic Soil: Optimal soil pH 4.5-5.5 Iron (Fe): Prevents chlorosis in acidic conditions **Magnesium** (Mg): Supports chlorophyll production
Spinach	**Nitrogen** (N): Promotes leafy growth and vibrant leaves Iron (Fe): Prevents yellowing; supports green colour **Magnesium** (Mg): Enhances chlorophyll for vibrant foliage
Potatoes	**Potassium** (K): Essential for tuber size and disease resistance **Phosphorus** (P): Supports root development and tuber formation **Calcium** (Ca): Prevents hollow heart in tubers
Cucumbers	**Nitrogen** (N): Supports vine growth and foliage development **Potassium** (K): Important for fruiting and taste **Calcium** (Ca): Prevents blossom end rot and improves quality
Broccoli	**Nitrogen** (N): Needed for leafy growth and stalk development **Calcium** (Ca): Ensures firm stalks and prevents rot Sulphur (S): Enhances flavour and nutrition
Peppers	**Potassium** (K): Improves fruit size, colour, and disease resistance **Calcium** (Ca): Prevents blossom end rot **Phosphorus** (P): Supports root and flower formation

Epithet/Crop or Nutrient	Source or Crop
[CAM Plant] Century Plant	Date palm
A true fruit	Cashewnut
Apple of paradise	Banana, Adam fig, Oldest cultivated tropical
Bio Drainage Plant	Eucalyptus
Black-eyed pea, southern pea	Cow pea
Black Plum (Shyam ber)	Jamun
Brown Gold	Died Pupa of the silk worm
Butternut squash	Pumpkin
False fruit	Apple
Food of god	Cocoa
Fountain tree	Spethodia compenulata
Glorry of East	Chrysanthemum
Love of (England) Apple	Tomato
Miracle Fruit (China)	Kiwi fruit
National fruit	Mango
Nature's Wonder	Chilli
Poor men's food	Pearl millet (Bajra)
Poor man friend	Potato
Poor men fruit	Ber
Poor men's meat, Wonder crop	Soybean

Poor men substitute	Till
Queen of milk	Saanen goat
Small holders irrigated	Oil palm
Tree of Heaven, Kalpavriksha	Coconut
Wholesome food	Musk Melon
Afla toxin	Groundnut
Antivitamin E. Factor	Field Pea
Astrogen	Tomato
Boron (B)	Tourmaline
C	Carbamate
Calcium (Ca)	Dolomite, Calcite
Clorine (CI)	Apatite
Copper (Cu)	Chalcopyrite, Olivine
Coumarin	Sweet clover
Glucocydes	White clover
HCN/Glucocydes/ Dhurin/Prussic Acid	Sorghum
Iron (Fe)	Pyrite, Magnetite
Magnicium (Mg)	Dolomite, Muscovite
Magnize (Mn)	Magnetite, Pyrolusite
Molybdenum (Mo)	Olivine
Nitrogen (N)	Organic Matter (O.M.)
Oxalic acid	Chickpea, Pearl millet, Amaranthus, Napier Grass
Phosphorous (P)	Apatite, Fe/Al Phosphate, O.M.
Polyphenolics	Sunflower
Potash (K)	Mica, Feldspar, Biotite, Orthoclase
Resins	Mango
Solanin	Potato (>20mg/100gm)
Sulpher (S)	Gypsum, Pyrite, Organic matter
Trypsin inhibitors	Peagen Pea, Soybean, Pea, Beans, Sweet potato
Zinc (Zn)	Sphalerite, Olivine, Hornblende

Nutrient	Low Range (kg/ha)	Medium Range(kg/ha)	High Range (kg/ha)
Nitrogen (N)	<280	280-560	>560
Phosphorous (P)	<10	Oct-25	>25
Potash (K)	<110	110-280	>280

Nutrient	Formula for Uptake
Nitrogen (N)	NH4+, NO3-
Phosphorous (P)	H2PO4-, HPO4--
Potassium (K)	K+
Calcium (Ca)	Ca++
Magnesium (Mg)	Mg++
Sulphur (S)	SO4--
Iron (Fe)	Fe++, Fe+++
Manganese (Mn)	Mn++, Mn+++
Boron (B)	H3BO3, H2BO3-

Category	Examples
Simple Fruit - Berry	Banana, Papaya, Grape, Sapota, Arecanut, Avocado
Simple Fruit - Modified Berry - Amphisarca	Wood Apple, Bael
Simple Fruit - Modified Berry - Balausta	Pomegranate
Simple Fruit - Modified Berry - Capsule	Aonla, Carambola, Okra, Sesame, Mustard
Simple Fruit - Drupe (Stone)	Mango, Peach, Plum, Ber, Coconut, Cherry, Cocoa, Coffee
Simple Fruit - Hesperidium	Citrus
Simple Fruit - Lomentum	Tamarind, Cole Crop
Simple Fruit - Nut	Cashewnut, Litchi, Chestnut, Walnut, Peanut, Rambutan
Simple Fruit - Peopo	Watermelon, Bottle Gourd, Cucumber
Simple Fruit - Pome	Apple, Pear, Quince, Loquat
Aggregate Fruits - Eteario of Berries	Custard Apple, Raspberry
Multiple Fruit/Composite Fruit - Syconus	Fig, Ficus bengalensis, Ficus religiosa
Multiple Fruit/Composite Fruit - Sorosis	Jackfruit, Pineapple, Mulberry, Breadfruit
Placentation	Attachment of ovules inside the ovary of flowering plants
Short-day plants	Rice, Cotton, Tobacco, Soybeans
Long-day plants	Spinach, Radish, Lettuce, Sugarbeet
Day-neutral plants	Tomato, Sunflower, Pea, Maize

Soil Testing Method	Purpose	Method

pH Testing	Measures soil acidity or alkalinity, affecting nutrient availability	pH meter or test strips in a soil-water mixture
Electrical Conductivity (EC) Test	Determines soil salinity impacting plant growth	EC meter measures electrical conductivity of a soil-water solution
Soil Texture Test (Sedimentation Test)	Identifies proportions of sand, silt, and clay for water retention and aeration	Soil mixed with water; particles settle into layers to indicate composition
Organic Matter Test (Loss on Ignition)	Determines organic matter content, essential for soil fertility	Heating soil sample to burn off organic material; weight loss indicates organic content
Nutrient Testing (Macronutrients and Micronutrients)	Measures levels of essential nutrients like N, P, K, Ca, and micronutrients	Lab analysis using chemical extraction and colourimetric/spectrophotometric methods
Cation Exchange Capacity (CEC)	Indicates soil's ability to hold and exchange nutrients, important for fertility	Lab analysis measures cations that soil can retain and supply to plants
Moisture Content Test	Determines soil's water-holding capacity	Weighing, drying, and reweighing soil sample to calculate moisture content
Soil Compaction Test	Identifies soil compaction, impacting root growth and water infiltration	Penetrometer measures resistance to penetration, indicating compaction
Microbial Activity Test	Assesses biological activity, supporting nutrient cycling and plant health	Soil respiration test measures COâ,, production as an indicator of microbial activity

S.No.	Insect (Vector)	Transmitting Disease/Pathogen
1	Aphids (Myzus persicase)	Potato leaf roll virus
2	Leafhopper	(a) Maize streak virus, (b) Rice dwarf disease virus, (c) Tungro virus of rice
3	White flies (Bemisia tabacci)	(a) Yellow mosaic of beans, (b) Vein clearing of bhindi, (c) Tomato leaf curl
4	Thrips	Tomato spotted wilt virus
5	Mites	Wheat streak mosaic virus

Disease	Causal Agent	Affected Crops	Symptoms	Impact
Powdery Mildew	Various Erysiphales fungi	Vegetables, cereals, grapes, ornamentals	White, powdery growth on leaves and stems	Reduces photosynthesis, weakens plants
Downy Mildew	Various Peronospora	Grapes, lettuce, spinach, cucurbits,	Yellow spots on leaves with downy	Kills seedlings, reduces crop

	ceae fungi	onions	growth underneath	quality
Late Blight	Phytophthora infestans	Potatoes, tomatoes	Dark, water-soaked spots on leaves and stems	Severe yield losses, caused Irish Potato Famine
Early Blight	Alternaria solani	Tomatoes, potatoes	Dark ring spots on leaves, premature leaf drop	Reduces photosynthesis, fruit quality
Anthracnose	Various Colletotrichum species	Beans, cucumbers, tomatoes, peppers, fruit trees	Sunken, dark lesions on fruits and leaves	Reduces marketable yield, can defoliate plants
Fusarium Wilt	Fusarium oxysporum	Tomatoes, cucumbers, bananas, cotton	Yellowing leaves, brown vascular tissue in stems	Plant wilting and death, persists in soil
Verticillium Wilt	Verticillium species	Tomatoes, potatoes, strawberries, ornamentals	Yellowing leaves, brown vascular tissue in stems	Reduces plant vigor, difficult to control
Rust Diseases	Various Pucciniales fungi	Wheat, barley, coffee, beans, ornamentals	Reddish pustules on leaves and stems	Significant yield loss in grains, coffee
Black Spot	Ascochyta and Alternaria species	Peas, beans, potatoes, tomatoes	Dark spots on leaves and stems with yellow halos	Reduces leaf area, lowers photosynthesis
Gray Mold	Botrytis cinerea	Strawberries, grapes, tomatoes, lettuce, ornamentals	Gray fuzzy mold on fruits and leaves	Reduces yield, spreads in humid conditions
Sclerotinia Stem Rot (White Mold)	Sclerotinia sclerotiorum	Beans, soybeans, sunflowers, carrots	White cottony growth on stems, black sclerotia	Stem rot and plant death, affects yield
Rice Blast	Magnaporthe oryzae	Rice	Diamond-shaped lesions on leaves	Severe yield losses in rice regions

Feature Name	Examples
Antenna Type	
Setaceous	Cockroaches, leaf hopper
Feliform	Grasshopper
Moniliform	Termites
Serrated	Pulse beetle
Pectinate	Sawfly
Bipectinate	Silkworm moth
Plumes	Male mosquito

Whorled	Mango mealy bug
Clavate	Butterfly
Geniculate	Bees, ants, weevils
Aristate	Housefly
Mouth Part	
Maxilla	Cutting food
Mandible	Crushing food
Labium	Lower lip
Labrum	Upper lip
Hypopharynx	Works like a tongue
Mouthpart Type	
Piercing and sucking	Mosquito, aphids, bugs, leafhopper
Sponging	Housefly
Siphoning	Butterfly, moth
Rasping and lapping	Honey bee

Type of Metamorphosis	Insect Order	Examples
Complete/Complex/Indire ct	Lepidoptera	Butterfly, moths, loopers, borers, bollworms, silkworms
Complete/Complex/Indire ct	Coleoptera	Beetles, weevils (most damaging order)
Complete/Complex/Indire ct	Diptera	Mosquitoes, houseflies, midges, shoot flies, flies
Complete/Complex/Indire ct	Hymenopter a	Sawflies, bees, ants, wasps (mostly predators)

Particulars	Specification
Development of primary agriculture stages	(1) Hunter-gatherer (2) Animal husbandry (3) Early Agricultural (4) Modern Agricultural Development
Dwarf varieties origin	Dr. Norman Borlaug (Mexico)
Dwarf varieties first tested in India	Lerma Rosa-64-A, Sonora 64, S-227
Early agricultural tools	Made from bone
Truck Gardening origin	Derived from French 'torquer', meaning 'to share' or 'swap' (to barter or exchange)

Advancement	Description
Precision	Uses GPS, IoT, and data analytics for efficient crop management, optimizing

Agriculture	inputs like water, fertilizers, and pesticides.
CRISPR Gene Editing	Allows precise gene editing in plants to improve yield, disease resistance, and drought tolerance.
Vertical Farming	Indoor, multi-layer farming systems that reduce land usage, use LED lighting, and enable year-round crop production.
Drones for Agriculture	Used for aerial imaging, crop health monitoring, and spraying pesticides, enabling real-time field analysis.
Artificial Intelligence (AI)	Analyzes large datasets for crop health, yield prediction, and efficient farming practices.
Blockchain in Food Supply Chain	Enhances traceability and transparency, tracking produce from farm to table to ensure food safety and quality.
Biopesticides	Environmentally friendly pesticides derived from natural materials to control pests with minimal ecological impact.
Automated Machinery	Autonomous tractors, planters, and harvesters improve productivity and reduce labor costs.
Soil Health Monitoring Sensors	Sensors provide real-time data on soil moisture, nutrient levels, and temperature, enabling precise water and nutrient management.
Smart Irrigation Systems	Automatically adjust water usage based on soil moisture and weather data, conserving water and optimizing growth.
Drought-Resistant Crop Varieties	Genetically enhanced varieties withstand drought conditions, safeguarding food security in arid regions.
Synthetic Biology for Crops	Engineering crops to produce high-value compounds (like vitamins) or biofuels, adding new functionalities to plants.
Climate-Resilient Crops	Development of crop varieties that can withstand extreme weather conditions, such as floods, heat, and cold.
Plant-Based Proteins	Advancements in crop breeding and processing to improve taste and nutrition of plant-based protein alternatives.
Digital Farming Platforms	Platforms like FarmLogs and Climate FieldView offer data-driven insights for farm management decisions.
Mobile Apps for Farmers	Apps provide access to market prices, weather forecasts, and farming tips, especially benefiting smallholder farmers.
Nano-fertilizers	Slow-release fertilizers that enhance nutrient efficiency and reduce environmental impact.
Agroforestry Practices	Integrates trees and shrubs into agricultural landscapes to improve biodiversity, soil health, and carbon sequestration.
Biodegradable Mulch Films	Plastic alternatives that decompose naturally, reducing plastic waste in agricultural fields.
Carbon Farming	Practices that capture and store carbon in soil, helping to mitigate climate change and offering carbon credits.

Category	Area (Million Ha)	Production (Million Tonnes)	Top Producing State(s)	Notes
Total Horticulture	28.63	352.23	Andhra Pradesh, Maharashtra, Uttar Pradesh	Decline of 0.91% in total production compared to 2022-23 estimates

Fruit Producti on	-	112.63	Andhra Pradesh, Maharashtra, Gujarat	Increases seen in mango, banana, and guava production
Vegetabl e Producti on	-	204.96	West Bengal, Uttar Pradesh, Madhya Pradesh	Decrease due to reduced production of potato, onion, and brinjal; tomato production increased
Onion	-	24.2 (Lakh Tonnes)	Maharashtra, Karnataka, Madhya Pradesh	Production decrease of about 60 Lakh Tonnes year-over-year
Potato	-	56.7 (Lakh Tonnes)	Uttar Pradesh, West Bengal, Bihar	Notable decrease in production in Bihar and West Bengal
Tomato	-	21.2 (Lakh Tonnes)	Andhra Pradesh, Madhya Pradesh, Karnataka	Production increased by 4.37% over the previous year

Crop Type	Kharif Production (LMT)	Rabi Production (LMT)	Total Production (LMT)	Top Producing States
Foodgrains	1541.87	1551.61	3093.48	Uttar Pradesh, Punjab, Madhya Pradesh
Rice	1114.58	123.57	1238.15	West Bengal, Uttar Pradesh, Punjab
Wheat	-	1120.19	1120.19	Punjab, Madhya Pradesh, Haryana
Maize	227.2	97.5	324.7	Karnataka, Madhya Pradesh, Maharashtra
Shree Anna (Millets)	128.91	24.88	153.79	Rajasthan, Karnataka, Maharashtra
Tur (Arhar)	33.39	-	33.39	Maharashtra, Karnataka, Madhya Pradesh
Gram	-	121.61	121.61	Madhya Pradesh, Maharashtra, Rajasthan
Oilseeds	228.42	137.56	365.98	Rajasthan, Maharashtra, Madhya Pradesh
Soybean	125.62	-	125.62	Madhya Pradesh, Maharashtra, Rajasthan
Rapeseed & Mustard	-	126.96	126.96	Rajasthan, Haryana, Uttar Pradesh
Sugarcane	-	-	4464.3	Uttar Pradesh, Maharashtra, Karnataka
Cotton	323.11 Lakh Bales	-	323.11 Lakh Bales	Gujarat, Maharashtra, Telangana
Jute	92.17 Lakh Bales	-	92.17 Lakh Bales	West Bengal, Bihar, Assam

Ra nk	State	Primary Crops	Contributions
1	Uttar Pradesh	Sugarcane, Wheat, Rice, Potato	Largest producer of sugarcane, major contributor to wheat and rice production, with robust potato yield
2	West Bengal	Rice, Jute, Vegetables	Highest rice producer, dominating jute production, with strong vegetable output
3	Madhya Pradesh	Wheat, Soybean, Pulses	Leads in wheat and soybean production, significant in pulses production
4	Karnatak a	Coffee, Maize, Sugarcane, Sunflower	Leading coffee producer, also known for maize, sunflower, and a growing horticulture sector
5	Maharas htra	Cotton, Soybean, Onion, Sugarcane	Top cotton producer, substantial contributor to soybean, onion, and sugarcane production
6	Punjab	Wheat, Rice, Milk	contributor to India's food grain stock, especially wheat and rice, with significant dairy output
7	Andhra Pradesh	Rice, Tobacco, Fruits	Known for rice, prominent in tobacco and diverse fruit production (mango, banana)
8	Gujarat	Groundnut, Cotton, Castor, Fruits	Major producer of groundnut and castor seed, strong in cotton and horticultural output
9	Haryana	Wheat, Rice, Milk	High productivity in wheat and rice, strong dairy industry
10	Tamil Nadu	Rice, Coconut, Spices	Major rice and coconut producer, recognized for spices and floriculture

Crop	Top High-Yielding Regions (States)	Notes
Banana	Tamil Nadu, Maharashtra, Gujarat	Tamil Nadu consistently ranks highest, with Maharashtra and Gujarat also major producers.
Mango	Uttar Pradesh, Andhra Pradesh, Karnataka	Known for varieties like Alphonso, Dasheri, and Kesar.
Grapes	Maharashtra, Karnataka, Tamil Nadu	Maharashtra is the leading producer, especially for table and wine grapes.
Papaya	Andhra Pradesh, Gujarat, Madhya Pradesh	Andhra Pradesh leads due to Favourable climate and efficient cultivation practices.
Potato	Uttar Pradesh, West Bengal, Bihar	High productivity regions, but production can be impacted by weather variations.
Onion	Maharashtra, Karnataka, Madhya Pradesh	Maharashtra contributes significantly to India's onion supply, especially in export.
Tomato	Andhra Pradesh, Madhya Pradesh, Karnataka	Andhra Pradesh has shown increased yield recently due to improved varieties and practices.
Chilli	Andhra Pradesh, Maharashtra, Karnataka	Andhra Pradesh is known for high-yield spicy chilli varieties.
Turmer ic	Tamil Nadu, Maharashtra, Odisha	Primarily used in culinary and medicinal applications, both domestically and for export.
Pomegr anate	Maharashtra, Karnataka, Gujarat	Maharashtra is a major producer with a focus on export quality.

Apple	Himachal Pradesh, Jammu & Kashmir, Uttarakhand	Major regions due to suitable climate in Himalayan states.
Guava	Uttar Pradesh, Maharashtra, Bihar	Known for varieties like Allahabad Safeda, these states have high-quality yields.
Litchi	Bihar, West Bengal, Jharkhand	Bihar is known for the Shahi litchi variety and accounts for a large portion of India's production.
Pineapple	West Bengal, Assam, Tripura	West Bengal and the northeastern states are producers due to Favourable climate conditions.
Orange	Maharashtra, Madhya Pradesh, Assam	Nagpur in Maharashtra is especially famous for high-quality oranges.
Watermelon	Uttar Pradesh, Karnataka, Maharashtra	These regions yield high-quality watermelons, with varieties adapted to local climates.
Coconut	Kerala, Tamil Nadu, Karnataka	Kerala leads in coconut production, essential for oil, culinary, and industrial uses.
Cashew Nut	Maharashtra, Kerala, Karnataka	These coastal regions offer ideal climates for cashew production.
Lemon	Andhra Pradesh, Maharashtra, Gujarat	Grown widely for high juice content and export, especially Andhra Pradesh's varieties.
Custard Apple	Maharashtra, Gujarat, Madhya Pradesh	Known for sweetness and high yield, Maharashtra is a top producer.
Green Peas	Uttar Pradesh, Madhya Pradesh, Punjab	High yield in cooler seasons; Punjab practices include both fresh and processing varieties.

State	Fruits Produced	Notes
Andhra Pradesh	Bananas, Mangoes	Favourable climate for diverse fruit production
Maharashtra	Mangoes (Alphonso), Grapes, Pomegranates	Leading producer with notable varieties like Alphonso mangoes
Uttar Pradesh	Mangoes, Guavas	High production in mangoes and guavas
Karnataka	Bananas, Grapes, Papayas	Supports diversified fruit cultivation
Tamil Nadu	Bananas, Mangoes	High productivity in bananas and mangoes
Gujarat	Pomegranates, Mangoes	Innovative cultivation techniques in semi-arid areas
West Bengal	Litchis, Mangoes	Rich soil and monsoon support multiple fruits, including litchis

Fruit	Growth in Export Value (%)	Export Notes	Markets
Banana	63	Highest export value, strong demand in Middle East and Europe	Middle East, Europe, Southeast Asia
Mango (Kesar, Dasheri)	120	Kesar and Dasheri varieties showing major growth	Middle East, Europe, Southeast Asia

Grapes		Popular in European and Middle Eastern markets	Europe, Middle East
Pomegranate		Significant export presence, especially in West Asia	West Asia, Europe
Orange		Steady export demand from various international markets	Europe, Middle East

State	National Contribution (%)	Vegetables Produced	Notes
Uttar Pradesh	14.80%	Peas, Okra, Cauliflower, Spinach	Top state for vegetable production with a diverse output
West Bengal	14%	Brinjal, Cabbage, Cauliflower	Favourable climate for high yields in brinjal and cabbage
Madhya Pradesh		Tomato, Brinjal, Staple Vegetables	High productivity in staple vegetables
Maharashtra		Onions, Tomatoes, Cabbage	Major contributor to domestic and export markets
Andhra Pradesh		Tomatoes, Brinjal, Leafy Vegetables	Known for high yields in tomatoes and leafy vegetables

Crop	Top Producing States	Notes
Banana	Tamil Nadu, Maharashtra, Gujarat	Leads in both productivity and area cultivated
Mango	Uttar Pradesh, Andhra Pradesh, Karnataka	Top producers with significant national contributions
Grapes	Maharashtra, Karnataka, Tamil Nadu	Largest producer, especially in Maharashtra
Papaya	Andhra Pradesh, Gujarat, Madhya Pradesh	High productivity regions
Potato	Uttar Pradesh, West Bengal, Bihar	Productivity impacted by climate variations
Onion	Maharashtra, Karnataka, Madhya Pradesh	Major producers with fluctuating productivity
Tomato	Andhra Pradesh, Madhya Pradesh, Karnataka	Production increases, particularly in Andhra Pradesh
Chilli	Andhra Pradesh, Maharashtra, Karnataka	Major contributors to national chilli supply
Turmeric	Tamil Nadu, Maharashtra, Odisha	Prominent production, high export demand

Category	Crop	Top Producing States	Notes
Fruits	Banana	Tamil Nadu, Maharashtra, Gujarat	Tamil Nadu consistently a top producer
Fruits	Mango	Uttar Pradesh, Andhra Pradesh, Karnataka	Significant portion of India exports
Fruits	Grapes	Maharashtra, Karnataka,	Maharashtra leads, especially for

		Tamil Nadu	table grapes
Fruits	Papaya	Andhra Pradesh, Gujarat, Madhya Pradesh	High productivity led by Andhra Pradesh
Vegetables	Potato	Uttar Pradesh, West Bengal, Bihar	Slight productivity dip due to climate
Vegetables	Onion	Maharashtra, Karnataka, Madhya Pradesh	Productivity decrease noted in Maharashtra
Vegetables	Tomat o	Andhra Pradesh, Madhya Pradesh, Karnataka	Increased production in Andhra Pradesh
Spices and Other Crops	Chilli	Andhra Pradesh, Maharashtra, Karnataka	Main suppliers of India's chilli
Spices and Other Crops	Turme ric	Tamil Nadu, Maharashtra, Odisha	High domestic and international demand

Scientist	Contribution
Gregor Mendel	Father of Genetics, foundational work on inheritance principles with pea plants, essential for hybrid development.
Norman Borlaug	Father of the Green Revolution, developed high-yield, disease-resistant wheat varieties, significantly boosting food security globally.
M.S. Swaminathan	Led India's Green Revolution, introduced high-yielding wheat and rice varieties, enhancing food security in India.
Barbara McClintock	Discovered jumping genes (transposons) in corn, advancing genetic mutation research and crop improvement.
Henry Wallace	Founder of Hi-Bred Corn Company, pioneering hybrid corn production, boosting corn yields in the U.S.
William Bateson	Coined the term genetics and promoted Mendelian genetics, foundational to plant breeding.
Paul Berg	Pioneer in genetic engineering, contributing to the development of genetically modified crops for pest resistance.
Luther Burbank	Developed over 800 plant varieties, including the Russet Burbank potato, instrumental in horticultural hybridization.
Yuan Longping	Father of Hybrid Rice, created high-yield hybrid rice varieties, improving rice productivity, particularly in Asia.
Nikolai Vavilov	Identified centers of origin for crops, promoted plant genetic diversity preservation, foundational for crop improvement.
E.M. East & G.H. Shull	Developed the concept of hybrid vigor (heterosis) in corn, crucial for creating high-yielding hybrid varieties.
Ingo Potrykus	Co-developed Golden Rice, a genetically modified rice enriched with Vitamin A to address malnutrition.
Charles Darwin	Theories on natural selection and variation informed crop domestication and selective breeding.
Cyril Darlington	Research on plant cytogenetics and chromosomal structure, aiding genetic variation studies essential for crop improvement.
Hugo de Vries	Introduced mutation theory, foundational to understanding genetic diversity in plant breeding.
Dr. G.H. Khush	Developed over 300 rice varieties at IRRI, greatly impacting global rice

	production.
C.T. Patel	Pioneer in hybrid cotton breeding in India, improving cotton yields.
Ebrahimali Siddique	Key contributor to hybrid rice research in India, adapting it for Indian agricultural needs.
William Beal	Early corn breeder who experimented with selective breeding, contributing to hybrid corn development.
George Washington Carver	Promoted crop rotation and soil health, introduced alternative crops to improve soil fertility in the U.S.
Hans Jenny	Developed CLORPT model for understanding soil formation, advancing soil science.
Fritz Haber & Carl Bosch	Invented Haber-Bosch process for synthesizing ammonia, revolutionizing nitrogen fertilizer production, greatly increasing crop yields.
Justus von Liebig	Father of Agricultural Chemistry, researched plant nutrition, crucial to understanding soil fertility.
C.T. de Wit	Contributed to plant physiology and resource-use efficiency studies in agriculture.
Alexander von Humboldt	Early work on ecosystems, climate, and plant distribution, informing later agricultural ecology research.
Lysenko Trofim	Soviet agronomist known for controversial theories influencing agricultural policy in the USSR.
Elvin C. Stakman	Plant pathologist whose work on cereal rust diseases laid the groundwork for plant disease research and resistant crop development.
Ephraim Wales Bull	Developed the Concord grape, a disease-resistant variety adapted to American climates.
Sir Rowland Biffen	Pioneered wheat breeding for disease resistance, contributing to rust-resistant wheat varieties.
Donald Forsha Jones	Created the first practical method for producing hybrid corn, transforming the corn industry.
Cyril G. Hopkins	Soil fertility research advocate, promoted balanced fertilization and sustainable soil management.
E.J. Russell	Soil scientist at Rothamsted Experimental Station, focused on soil chemistry and fertility research.
Hugh Hammond Bennett	Father of Soil Conservation, instrumental in U.S. soil conservation policy development.
William Albrecht	Researched soil health's role in crop and animal productivity, emphasizing mineral balance in soil.
R.A. Fisher	Pioneered statistical methods in agriculture, essential for experimental design and data analysis in agronomy.
Albert Howard	Father of Organic Farming, promoted sustainable farming and soil health, author of An Agricultural Testament.
Cecil Salmon	Introduced Norin 10 wheat from Japan, key to semi-dwarf wheat varieties for the Green Revolution.
Walter C. Lowdermilk	Studied land degradation and erosion, contributing to U.S. conservation policies.
Pedro Sanchez	Improved tropical soil management practices, awarded World Food Prize for

	contributions to food security.
Gurdev Singh Khush	Developed high-yielding rice varieties at IRRI, enhancing food security globally.
Thomas Hunt Morgan	Nobel laureate geneticist whose work on chromosomal inheritance influenced plant breeding research.
John Bennet Lawes	Established the first agricultural research station at Rothamsted, developed early artificial fertilizers.

Policy Milestone	Year & Region	Description
Homestead Act	1862, USA	Encouraged Western migration in the U.S. by providing settlers with 160 acres of public land, significantly expanding agricultural land.
Agricultural Adjustment Act (AAA)	1933, USA	New Deal policy to stabilize crop prices by paying farmers to reduce production, marking a shift toward government support in agriculture.
Food and Agriculture Organization (FAO) Establishment	1945, Global	FAO founded to lead global efforts to defeat hunger, improve nutrition, and promote agricultural productivity and sustainability.
Soil Conservation Act	1935, USA	Introduced soil conservation measures in response to the Dust Bowl, promoting sustainable land use practices to prevent soil erosion.
Common Agricultural Policy (CAP)	1962, Europea n Union	EU policy providing subsidies, price supports, and rural development programs to ensure food security and stable agricultural markets.
The Green Revolution	1960s–1970s, Global	Agricultural transformation with high-yield crop varieties, fertilizers, and irrigation to increase food production, especially in Asia and Latin America.
Minimum Support Price (MSP) Policy	1965, India	Indian policy to protect farmers from price fluctuations by ensuring a minimum price for essential crops.
National Environmental Policy Act (NEPA)	1969, USA	Required environmental impact assessments for federal projects, including agricultural developments, marking a focus on environmental sustainability.
Farm Credit Act	1971, USA	Strengthened availability of affordable loans for American farmers, ensuring access to capital and promoting farm stability.
Pradhan Mantri Fasal Bima Yojana (PMFBY)	2016, India	Crop insurance scheme in India providing financial support for crop failure due to natural disasters, pests, or diseases.
Food Security Act	1985, USA	Established the Conservation Reserve Program, paying farmers to remove environmentally sensitive land to improve soil and water quality.
Farm Bills (USA)	Revised every 5 years,	Recurring bill in the U.S. governing agricultural and food policy, including subsidies, crop insurance, and nutrition programs.

	USA	
Agricultural Biodiversity Policy	1996, International	Promoted by the Convention on Biological Diversity, focusing on conserving genetic diversity in crops and livestock.
National Food Security Act	2013, India	Indian act providing subsidized food grains to two-thirds of India's population, aiming to ensure food security as a right for all.
Sustainable Development Goals (SDGs)	2015, United Nations	Goal 2, Zero Hunger, of the UN's SDGs targets ending hunger, achieving food security, and promoting sustainable agriculture by 2030.
African Union's Comprehensive Africa Agriculture Development Programme (CAADP)	2003, Africa	African Union program to boost agricultural productivity through investment in infrastructure, technology, and policy reforms.
European Green Deal	2020, European Union	Targets sustainable agriculture practices, aiming to reduce greenhouse gases, protect biodiversity, and promote organic farming in the EU.
Paramparagat Krishi Vikas Yojana	2015, India	Indian scheme promoting organic farming through financial assistance and training for farmers to adopt organic practices.
Global Alliance for Climate-Smart Agriculture (GACSA)	2014, FAO	FAO-led initiative to enhance food security and climate resilience through sustainable agricultural practices worldwide.
One District One Product (ODOP)	2018, India	Indian strategy promoting agricultural diversification, focusing on unique agricultural products in each district.
National Action Plan on Climate Change (NAPCC)	2008, India	Includes the National Mission for Sustainable Agriculture, focusing on adapting agriculture to climate change through resource management.
Kisan Credit Card (KCC) Scheme	1998, India	Indian scheme providing affordable credit to farmers for crop production, improving access to financial support.
Biological Diversity Act	2002, India	Promotes conservation of biological resources, including agro-biodiversity, through sustainable use and equitable sharing of benefits in India.
National Bamboo Mission	2006, India	Focuses on commercial cultivation of bamboo in India to improve farmer incomes and sustainable livelihoods.
National Agricultural Research System (NARS)	Various Countries	Global agricultural research support system with institutions, universities, and extension systems supporting R&D.

Area of Contribution	Description
Agricultural Research and Innovation	Leads India's agricultural research efforts, covering crop science, horticulture, animal science, fisheries, natural resource management, and agricultural engineering. Develops new crop varieties, improved practices, pest control

	methods, and farm equipment innovations.
Education and Training	Oversees and accredits state agricultural universities and deemed universities to standardize education. Provides scholarships and fellowships, and organizes training programs for faculty, researchers, and students.
Crop Improvement and Breeding	Focuses on developing high-yielding, disease-resistant, and climate-resilient varieties of major crops, achieving self-sufficiency in food grains with significant developments during the Green Revolution.
Animal Husbandry and Fisheries Development	Conducts research in animal genetics, breeding, nutrition, and health, improving livestock productivity and sustainability. Supports aquaculture and fisheries growth, contributing to nutritional security and rural livelihoods.
Soil and Water Management	Focuses on soil health and water management practices for sustainable agriculture, with initiatives like the Soil Health Card Scheme. Researches irrigation, water-saving technologies, and soil conservation for resource management.
Climate Resilience and Sustainability	Leads climate-smart agriculture research, developing resilient crop varieties and practices. Supports the National Mission for Sustainable Agriculture with practices like conservation agriculture, agroforestry, and integrated farming systems.
Technology Transfer and Extension Services	Through Krishi Vigyan Kendras (KVKs), ICAR delivers agricultural technologies and knowledge at the district level, conducting training sessions, demonstrations, and workshops to support the farming community.
Food Security and Nutrition	Supports national food security through research on staple crops and biofortification, increasing nutritional crop quality. Works on combating malnutrition by enhancing crop varieties with essential nutrients like zinc and iron.
Policy Support and Data Collection	Provides scientific data and recommendations to policymakers, influencing agricultural policies such as MSP and crop insurance. Collaborates with government agencies and international organizations for global agricultural standards.
International Collaborations	Collaborates with international agricultural research organizations like FAO and CGIAR, enhancing research capabilities and sharing knowledge on food security, climate change, and sustainable agriculture.

Policy Milestone	Date	Description
Union Budget 2024-25: Increased Agricultural Allocation	July 2024	Increased allocation to ₹1.52 lakh crore for agriculture and allied sectors, emphasizing digital infrastructure for agriculture and supporting natural farming practices.
Agricultural Infrastructure Fund (AIF) Expansion	August 2024	Expansion of AIF scheme to support agricultural infrastructure, focusing on storage facilities, cold chains, and processing units to reduce post-harvest losses and improve market connectivity.

Export Policy Adjustments for Agricultural Commodities	September - October 2024	Adjustments in export policies including lifting the ban on non-basmati white rice exports with a floor price of $490 per metric ton and removing export tax on parboiled rice. MSP for wheat increased by 6.6% to encourage expansion of wheat cultivation.
Emphasis on Sustainable and Climate-Resilient Practices	Recent	Promotes sustainable agriculture and climate resilience through NMSA, focusing on soil conservation, organic farming, and practices to enhance productivity and mitigate climate change impacts.

Reform	Year	Description
Land Reform Acts	1950s – 1970s	Aimed to abolish the Zamindari system, enforce land ceilings, and redistribute land to landless farmers, reducing land inequality and increasing ownership among small farmers.
Green Revolution	1960s – 1970s	Introduction of high-yielding varieties (HYVs) of crops, particularly wheat and rice, along with fertilizers, irrigation, and pesticides, leading to a significant increase in food grain production.
National Agriculture Policy	2000	Policy aiming for a 4% annual growth in agriculture, focusing on sustainable practices, conservation, and employment in rural areas.
Kisan Credit Card (KCC) Scheme	1998	Introduced to provide farmers with easy access to credit, enabling them to purchase inputs and meet farming expenses, improving financial inclusion.
National Food Security Mission (NFSM)	2007	Aimed at increasing rice, wheat, and pulse production through productivity and area expansion, targeting self-sufficiency and reducing import dependence.
Pradhan Mantri Fasal Bima Yojana (PMFBY)	2016	Crop insurance scheme designed to protect farmers against crop loss due to natural disasters, pests, and diseases, providing financial stability and encouraging sustainable farming.
Pradhan Mantri Krishi Sinchai Yojana (PMKSY)	2015	Scheme to enhance irrigation coverage and improve water-use efficiency, promoting techniques like drip and sprinkler systems to support 'per drop more crop'.
Soil Health Card Scheme	2015	Provides soil health cards with soil test results and nutrient recommendations, promoting balanced fertilizer use and improving soil fertility.
e-NAM (National Agriculture Market)	2016	An online trading platform connecting mandis across India to create a unified market, improving transparency and price discovery for farmers.
Agriculture Infrastructure Fund (AIF)	2020	Government initiative for developing agricultural infrastructure like cold storage, warehouses, and processing units, aimed at reducing post-harvest losses and improving market linkages.
Model Agricultural Land Leasing Act	2016	Act allowing farmers to lease land without ownership loss, facilitating efficient land use and supporting tenant farmers.
Amendments to Essential Commodities Act	2020	Amendments to deregulate production, storage, and distribution of certain food items to encourage private investment and reduce government's market role.

Farm Laws [Later Repealed]	2020	Farmers' Produce Trade and Commerce Act, Price Assurance and Farm Services Act, and the Essential Commodities Amendment Act aimed at market reforms, later repealed due to protests.
National Mission for Sustainable Agriculture (NMSA)	2014	Mission under the National Action Plan on Climate Change promoting sustainable practices, soil conservation, and organic farming to enhance climate resilience.
Minimum Support Price (MSP) Policy	Ongoing	Policy setting price floors for essential crops to provide a safety net against market fluctuations, offering income security for farmers.
Operation Greens	2018	Scheme to stabilize the supply of tomato, onion, and potato, ensuring affordability, and focusing on infrastructure for storage, processing, and transportation.

Initiative	Description
Digital India Act 2023	Modernizes digital regulations to address privacy, online safety, cyberbullying, and digital rights, replacing the outdated IT Act of 2000 with a more accountable and secure framework.
Atmanirbhar Horticulture Clean Plant Programme	Aims to provide disease-free, high-quality planting materials for horticulture with a budget of ₹2,200 crore to enhance productivity and sustainability.
Amrit Dharohar	Three-year program focusing on wetland conservation to improve biodiversity, carbon sequestration, and eco-tourism, supporting local communities.
Green Credit Programme	Encourages sustainable practices by offering incentives for environmental responsibility, promoting actions to reduce carbon footprints and waste under the Environment (Protection) Act.
Mahila Samman Savings Certificate	A savings scheme for women and girls offering fixed deposits with a 7.5% interest rate and partial withdrawals, available until 2025.

Short Form	Full Form
NSSO	National Sample Survey Office (1950)
PDS	Public Distribution System (1947, with significant reforms in 1997)
PFA	Prevention of Food Adulteration Act (1954)
PMFBY	Pradhan Mantri Fasal Bima Yojana (2016)
PMKSY	Pradhan Mantri Krishi Sinchai Yojana (2015)
PPVFRA	Protection of Plant Varieties and Farmers Rights Authority (2001)
RCF	Rashtriya Chemicals & Fertilizers (1978)
RCGM	Review Committee on Genetic Manipulation (1989)
RKVY	Rashtriya Krishi Vikas Yojana (2007)
RKVY-RAFTAAR	Rashtriya Krishi Vikas Yojana - Remunerative Approaches for Agriculture and Allied Sector Rejuvenation (2017)
SAU	State Agricultural University (First - GBPUAT, 1960)

SHG	Self-Help Group (1972)
SHM	Soil Health Management (Part of NMSA, 2014)
SRI	System of Rice Intensification (1983, India adoption from the 2000s)
SWOT	Strengths, Weaknesses, Opportunities, Threats (Concept from 1960s)
TRIFED	Tribal Cooperative Marketing Development Federation of India (1987)
WTO	World Trade Organization (1995)
BIS	Bureau of Indian Standards (1986)
CACP	Commission for Agricultural Costs and Prices (1965)
CAZRI	Central Arid Zone Research Institute (1959)
CGIAR	Consultative Group on International Agricultural Research (1971)
CIMMYT	International Maize and Wheat Improvement Center (1966)
CRIDA	Central Research Institute for Dryland Agriculture (1985)
CSIR	Council of Scientific and Industrial Research (1942)
CSO	Central Statistical Office (1951, now part of the Ministry of Statistics and Programme Implementation)
CSS	Centrally Sponsored Scheme (Varies by specific schemes)
DAHD	Department of Animal Husbandry and Dairying (1919)
DD Kisan	Doordarshan Kisan (2015, a TV channel dedicated to agriculture)
DGFT	Directorate General of Foreign Trade (1991)
DRDO	Defence Research and Development Organisation (1958, includes agricultural research applications)
DRIP	Drip Irrigation Program (Widespread adoption in India from the 1970s)
FAO	Food and Agriculture Organization (1945)
FARM	Farmers' Agricultural Resource Management (Varies, specific programs)
FICCI	Federation of Indian Chambers of Commerce & Industry (1927)
FPO	Farmer Producer Organization (2002)
FRP	Fair and Remunerative Price (Sugarcane - 2009)
GDP	Gross Domestic Product (Concept from 1934)
GIS	Geographic Information System (Concept from the 1960s, Agricultural application varies)
GM	Genetically Modified (First GM crop - 1994, widespread agricultural use from 1990s)
HYV	High-Yielding Variety (Green Revolution era, 1960s in India)
ICMR	Indian Council of Medical Research (1911, relevant for food and agriculture in health context)
ICRISAT	International Crops Research Institute for the Semi-Arid Tropics (1972)
ICT	Information and Communication Technology (Adopted in various agricultural applications since the 1990s)
IFFCO	Indian Farmers Fertilizer Cooperative Limited (1967)

IFPRI	International Food Policy Research Institute (1975)
IFS	Integrated Farming System (Adopted since the 1970s)
IRRI	International Rice Research Institute (1960)
ISRO	Indian Space Research Organization (1969, agricultural applications varied)
KCC	Kisan Credit Card (1998)
KVIC	Khadi and Village Industries Commission (1956)
KVK	Krishi Vigyan Kendra (1974)
LPG	Liberalization, Privatization, and Globalization (Economic policy shift in India - 1991)
MIDH	Mission for Integrated Development of Horticulture (2014)
MIT	Micro Irrigation Technology (Widespread adoption since the 1970s)
MNCFC	Mahalanobis National Crop Forecast Centre (2012)
MSP	Minimum Support Price (1965)
NAIP	National Agricultural Innovation Project (2006)
NBAIM	National Bureau of Agriculturally Important Microorganisms (2001)
NBSS	National Bureau of Soil Survey (1976)
NCS	National Centre for Sustainable Agriculture (Varies, based on specific programs)
NDRI	National Dairy Research Institute (1923)
NFSM	National Food Security Mission (2007)
NGC	National Green Corps (2001)
NGO	Non-Governmental Organization (Concept from 1945, after the establishment of the UN)
NGS	Next Generation Sequencing (First introduced in 2005)
NHB	National Horticulture Board (1984)
NHM	National Horticulture Mission (2005)
NICRA	National Innovations on Climate Resilient Agriculture (2011)
NMOOP	National Mission on Oilseeds and Oil Palm (2014)
NMSA	National Mission for Sustainable Agriculture (2014)
NPV	Net Present Value (Economic concept, broadly adopted in agriculture since the mid-20th century)
NRCPB	National Research Centre on Plant Biotechnology (1985)
NREGA	National Rural Employment Guarantee Act (2005, now MGNREGA)
NRLM	National Rural Livelihood Mission (2011)
NSC	National Seed Corporation (1963)
NSFM	National Food Security Mission (2007)
NSS	National Service Scheme (1969)
ICAR	Indian Council of Agricultural Research

IBPS-AFO	Institute of Banking Personnel Selection - Agricultural Field Officer
NABARD	National Bank for Agriculture and Rural Development
FSSAI	Food Safety and Standards Authority of India
AIEEA	All India Entrance Examination for Admission (conducted by ICAR)
JRF/SRF	Junior Research Fellowship / Senior Research Fellowship (conducted by ICAR)
IARI	Indian Agricultural Research Institute (entrance exams for postgraduate courses)
UPCATET	Uttar Pradesh Combined Agriculture and Technology Entrance Test
BHU PET	Banaras Hindu University Postgraduate Entrance Test (for agriculture courses)
MP PAT	Madhya Pradesh Pre-Agriculture Test
TS EAMCET-AGRI	Telangana State Engineering, Agriculture and Medical Common Entrance Test (for agriculture)
AP EAMCET-AGRI	Andhra Pradesh Engineering, Agriculture and Medical Common Entrance Test (for agriculture)
AGRICET	Agriculture Common Entrance Test (conducted by Acharya N.G. Ranga Agricultural University for diploma holders)
Rajasthan JET	Rajasthan Joint Entrance Test for Agriculture
MCAER PG CET	Maharashtra Council of Agricultural Education and Research Postgraduate Common Entrance Test
CG PAT	Chhattisgarh Pre-Agriculture Test
KEAM-AGRI	Kerala Engineering Architecture Medical Entrance Exam (for agriculture courses)
GBPUAT	Govind Ballabh Pant University of Agriculture and Technology Entrance Exam
ICAR AIEEA PG	ICAR All India Entrance Examination for Admission for Postgraduate courses
AAU VET	Assam Agricultural University Veterinary Entrance Test
PAU CET	Punjab Agricultural University Common Entrance Test
OUAT	Orissa University of Agriculture and Technology Entrance Exam
BCECE AGRI	Bihar Combined Entrance Competitive Examination for Agriculture
JET Agriculture	Joint Entrance Test for Agriculture (various states)
CPAT	Combined Pre-Agriculture Test (various states)
ICAR NET	ICAR National Eligibility Test
ASRB ARS	Agricultural Scientists Recruitment Board Agricultural Research Service
SKUAST	Sher-e-Kashmir University of Agricultural Sciences and Technology Entrance Exam
RAJUVAS RPVT	Rajasthan University of Veterinary and Animal Sciences Rajasthan Pre-Veterinary Test

BHU UET-AGRI	Banaras Hindu University Undergraduate Entrance Test for Agriculture
JCECE AGRI	Jharkhand Combined Entrance Competitive Examination for Agriculture
AGRI POLYCET	Agriculture Polytechnic Common Entrance Test (various states)
HORTICET	Horticulture Common Entrance Test (conducted by Dr. YSR Horticultural University)
TNAU UG/PG	Tamil Nadu Agricultural University Undergraduate/Postgraduate Entrance Exam
UPCATET	Uttar Pradesh Combined Agriculture and Technology Entrance Test
ICAR AICE-JRF/SRF	ICAR All India Competitive Examination for Junior Research Fellowship/Senior Research Fellowship
LUVAS VLDA	Lala Lajpat Rai University of Veterinary and Animal Sciences Veterinary and Livestock Development Assistant Entrance Exam
CAEPHT	Central Agricultural University Pre-Entrance Test (for agricultural engineering and technology)
PJTSAU	Professor Jayashankar Telangana State Agricultural University Entrance Exam
BAU	Bihar Agricultural University Entrance Exam
UPSC	Union Public Service Commission
CGPSC	Chhattisgarh Public Service Commission
MPPSC	Madhya Pradesh Public Service Commission
ACABC	Agri-Clinics and Agri-Business Centers Scheme (2002)
AFL	Agriculture Field Laboratory (Varies by institution, no single establishment date)
AI	Artificial Insemination (Concept from the early 1900s, widespread use from 1930s)
AIEEA	All India Entrance Examination for Admission (Conducted by ICAR since 1998)
APEDA	Agricultural and Processed Food Products Export Development Authority (1985)
APMC	Agricultural Produce Market Committee (APMC Act - 1963)
ASCI	Agriculture Skill Council of India (2013)
ATMA	Agricultural Technology Management Agency (2005)
BCS	Bio-Control Agents (Concept adopted in the 1970s)

Term	**Definition (Important terms)**
Abiotic Factors	Non-living environmental factors such as soil, water, and climate that influence crop growth and agricultural productivity.
Agribusiness	Commercial agriculture enterprises involved in the production, processing, and distribution of agricultural products.
Agri-tourism	A form of commercial enterprise that links agricultural production with tourism to attract visitors to a farm for education and entertainment.
Agrochemicals	Chemical products used in agriculture, including pesticides, herbicides, fungicides, and fertilizers, to manage pests and enhance crop growth.

Agro-Climatic Zones	Regions classified based on climate and agricultural practices, influencing crop suitability and farming techniques.
Agroecology	The study of ecological processes applied to agricultural production systems, focusing on sustainable farming practices.
Agroecosystem	An ecological system managed and modified by humans for agricultural production, including crops, livestock, soil, and water.
Agroforestry Systems	Farming systems that combine trees, crops, and/or livestock on the same land, enhancing biodiversity and productivity.
Agroforestry	Integrating trees and shrubs into agricultural landscapes to enhance biodiversity, improve soil health, and provide additional income sources.
Allelochemicals	Chemicals produced by plants that influence the growth, survival, and reproduction of other plants, often involved in allelopathy.
Allelopathy	The chemical inhibition of one plant by another due to the release of toxic substances, affecting crop growth and yield.
Alluvial Soils	Fertile soils composed of silt, sand, clay, and organic matter, found in river plains and deltas.
Anhydrous Ammonia	A nitrogen fertilizer applied as a gas directly into the soil.
Annual Crops	Crops that complete their life cycle within one year, from germination to seed production.
Anthracnose	A group of fungal diseases affecting plants, causing dark lesions on leaves, stems, flowers, or fruits.
Anthropogenic	Environmental changes or processes that are caused by human activities, such as deforestation, pollution, and climate change.
Aquaculture	The cultivation of aquatic organisms such as fish, crustaceans, and seaweed in controlled environments for commercial purposes.
Aquaponics	A system combining conventional aquaculture with hydroponics in a symbiotic environment.
Aquifer	An underground layer of water-bearing rock or sediment that can store and transmit groundwater, crucial for irrigation.
Arable Land	Land capable of being plowed and used to grow crops.
Biochar	A form of charcoal produced from organic materials through pyrolysis, used as a soil amendment to improve fertility.
Biocontrol	The use of natural predators, parasites, or pathogens to manage agricultural pests and reduce reliance on chemical pesticides.
Biodiversity	The variety of plant and animal life in a particular habitat, essential for ecosystem health and resilience in agricultural systems.
Biodynamic Agriculture	A farming method emphasizing holistic development and interrelationships of soil, plants, and animals.
Biodynamic Farming	A farming method treating farms as unified organisms, emphasizing integration of crops and livestock and recycling nutrients.
Biofertilizers	Natural fertilizers containing living microorganisms that enhance soil fertility.
Biofuel	A fuel derived directly from living matter, such as ethanol or biodiesel.
Biogas	A mixture of gases produced by the breakdown of organic matter without oxygen, used as a renewable energy source.
Biopesticides	Pesticides derived from natural materials used to control pests and diseases

	in an environmentally friendly manner.
Buffer Strip	Strips of vegetation planted between fields and water bodies to trap pollutants and prevent soil erosion.
Buffer Zone	An area of land designated to separate and protect different land uses.
Carbon Farming	Agricultural practices aimed at reducing greenhouse gas emissions and increasing carbon sequestration in soils and vegetation.
Carbon Footprint	The total amount of greenhouse gases emitted by human activities, including agricultural practices.
Carbon Sequestration	The process of capturing and storing atmospheric carbon dioxide in soil, plants, and other carbon sinks.
Catch Crop	A fast-growing crop planted between successive plantings of main crops to improve soil fertility.
Certified Organic	Products grown and processed according to specific standards avoiding synthetic chemicals and GMOs.
Chlorosis	The yellowing of leaves due to insufficient chlorophyll.
Climate Mitigation	Strategies and practices aimed at reducing sources of greenhouse gases to combat climate change.
Climate-Smart Agriculture	An integrated approach to managing landscapes that addresses food security and climate change.
Climatic Zones	Regions of the world classified by climate affecting types of crops grown.
Cold Chain	A temperature-controlled supply chain maintaining quality and safety of perishable products from farm to consumer.
Commodity Crop	Crops traded on commodity markets.
Compaction	The compression of soil particles leading to reduced pore space and poor water infiltration.
Companion Planting	Growing different plants together for mutual benefits.
Composting	Recycling organic waste into humus-rich soil amendment through aerobic decomposition.
Conservation Agriculture	Soil management practices minimizing soil disturbance to maintain soil health.
Cover Crop	A crop grown to cover the soil, to improve soil health, reduce erosion, and manage weeds.
Crop Diversification	Growing a variety of crops on the same farm to reduce risk, improve soil health, and increase biodiversity.
Crop Insurance	Financial protection for farmers against crop loss due to natural calamities, pests, and diseases.
Crop Residue	Remains of crops left in the field after harvest, used for soil conservation.
Crop Rotation	The practice of growing different types of crops in succession on the same land to maintain soil fertility and control pests and diseases.
Crop Yield	The total quantity of crop produced on a given area of land, typically measured in bushels, pounds, or tons per acre/hectare.
Cultural Practices	Agricultural practices such as crop rotation, planting dates, and pest management to optimize production and minimize environmental impact.
Deciduous	Trees and shrubs that shed their leaves annually, often used in agroforestry and permaculture for seasonal benefits.

Defoliation	The loss of leaves from a plant due to natural processes, pests, diseases, or environmental conditions.
Deforestation	The clearing of forests for agricultural or other purposes, leading to loss of biodiversity and disruption of ecosystems.
Desertification	The process by which fertile land becomes desert due to drought, deforestation, or inappropriate agricultural practices.
Drip Irrigation	A micro-irrigation system where water is delivered directly to the root zone of plants through a network of tubes and emitters.
Ecological Intensification	Enhancing agricultural productivity through the optimal use of ecosystem services, rather than relying on external inputs.
Ecosystem Approach	A strategy for managing land, water, and living resources equitably promoting conservation and sustainable use.
Ecosystem Services	The benefits that humans receive from ecosystems, such as pollination, water purification, climate regulation, and soil fertility.
Endemic	A species or condition regularly found and restricted to a particular geographic area.
Erosion Control	Practices designed to prevent soil erosion, such as planting cover crops, building terraces, and creating windbreaks.
Evapotranspiration	The combined process of water evaporation from the soil and transpiration from plants, influencing water management in agriculture.
Fallow Land	Agricultural land that is left unplanted for one or more growing seasons to restore soil fertility and reduce pest and disease cycles.
Farm Mechanization	The use of machinery and technology in farming to increase efficiency and reduce labor.
Farmers' Produce Trade and Commerce (Promotion and Facilitation) Act	A 2020 act that allows farmers to sell their produce outside the designated Agricultural Produce Market Committee (APMC) markets.
Farming Systems Research (FSR)	An interdisciplinary approach to improve agricultural production systems considering the socio-economic context of the farmers.
Farm-to-Table	A movement that promotes serving local food acquired directly from the producer.
Field Capacity	The amount of soil moisture held after excess water has drained and the downward movement has decreased.
Food Miles	The distance food travels from production to consumption, impacting its environmental footprint.
Food Security	The state of having reliable access to sufficient, safe, and nutritious food for a healthy life.
Food Sovereignty	The right of people to define their food systems, prioritizing local production and sustainable farming practices.
Genetic Diversity	The variety of genes within a species, important for crop resilience and adaptation to environmental conditions.
Genetically Modified Organisms (GMOs)	Organisms whose genetic material has been altered using genetic engineering techniques to introduce desirable traits.
Grafting	A horticultural technique where tissues from one plant are inserted into

	those of another.
Green Manure	Crops grown to be ploughed back into the soil to improve fertility and organic matter content.
Green Revolution	A period of agricultural transformation in the 1960s-1970s introducing high-yielding varieties of seeds, fertilizers, and advanced irrigation.
Greenhouse Effect	The trapping of heat in Earth's atmosphere by greenhouse gases, leading to global warming.
Greenhouse Gases (GHGs)	Gases in the atmosphere, such as CO2 and CH4, that trap heat and contribute to global warming.
Hardpan	A dense soil layer that is impermeable to water and roots, hindering plant growth.
Hedgerow	A row of shrubs or trees planted along field edges to act as a windbreak and reduce soil erosion.
Herbicide Resistance	The ability of a plant to survive and reproduce despite herbicide application.
High-Yielding Varieties (HYVs)	Crop varieties developed to produce higher yields under optimal conditions.
Hydraulic Fracturing (Fracking)	A method of extracting underground resources, such as oil or gas, which can impact water availability for agriculture.
Hydroponics	A method of growing plants without soil, using nutrient-rich water solutions.
Integrated Crop Management (ICM)	A farming system that combines the best agricultural practices for economic and ecological balance.
Integrated Farming Systems (IFS)	Combining different agricultural enterprises to optimize resource use and enhance sustainability.
Integrated Nutrient Management (INM)	The combined use of fertilizers, manures, and biofertilizers to enhance soil fertility.
Integrated Pest Management (IPM)	Managing pests sustainably by combining biological, cultural, and physical tools in ways that minimize risks.
Integrated Water Management (IWM)	A holistic approach to managing water resources that considers the entire water cycle.
Intercropping	Growing two or more crops together in proximity to optimize resource use.
Irrigation Efficiency	The effectiveness of irrigation methods in delivering water to crops, crucial for conserving water.
Kisan Credit Card (KCC)	A government scheme providing farmers timely access to credit for their agricultural needs.
Land Tenure	The rights and arrangements by which land is owned, used, and transferred, affecting investment and productivity.
Legume	Plants that have symbiotic nitrogen-fixing bacteria enriching soil fertility.
Livelihood	The process by which households diversify activities to improve income and

Diversification	reduce vulnerability.
Livestock Integration	The practice of integrating animal husbandry with crop production to enhance farm productivity.
Marginal Land	Land that is less suitable for conventional agriculture due to poor soil fertility or water availability.
Microbial Inoculants	Beneficial microorganisms applied to seeds or soil to enhance growth, nutrient uptake, and disease resistance.
Microclimate	The climate of a small, specific place within a larger area, influenced by vegetation and water bodies.
Micro-Irrigation	Efficient irrigation systems like drip and sprinkler irrigation that deliver water directly to the plant root zone.
Minimum Support Price (MSP)	A government-fixed price at which it buys crops from farmers, ensuring a minimum profit for their harvest.
Monoculture	Growing a single crop species over a large area, which can lead to increased vulnerability to pests and diseases.
Mulch	A layer of material, such as straw or leaves, spread over the soil surface to conserve moisture and suppress weeds.
Mycorrhiza	A symbiotic association between fungi and plant roots that enhances nutrient and water uptake.
Nematodes	Microscopic, worm-like organisms in soil that can be beneficial or harmful to plants.
Nitrate Leaching	The process by which nitrogen in the form of nitrate moves through the soil and into groundwater, potentially causing pollution.
Nitrogen Fixation	The process by which certain plants, especially legumes, convert atmospheric nitrogen into forms usable by plants.
No-Till Farming	An agricultural practice where the soil is not ploughed, reducing soil erosion and improving soil health.
Nutrient Cycling	The movement and exchange of organic and inorganic matter back into the production of living matter.
Organic Certification	A certification process ensuring producers adhere to organic farming standards.
Organic Farming	Agricultural practices that rely on natural processes and inputs, avoiding synthetic chemicals.
Permaculture Principles	Guidelines for designing sustainable agricultural systems that mimic natural ecosystems.
Permaculture	A system of agricultural design principles that simulate natural ecosystems for sustainability.
Pest Management	Managing pests to minimize damage to crops using chemical, biological, cultural, and physical methods.
Photosynthesis	The process by which green plants use sunlight to synthesize nutrients from $CO2$ and water.
Phytoremediation	Using plants to clean up contaminated soil and water, absorbing pollutants through roots.
Phytosanitary	Relating to the health of plants, particularly the prevention and control of pests and diseases.
Polyculture	Growing multiple crop species in the same space to promote biodiversity and reduce pest risks.

Poultry Farming	Raising domesticated birds such as chickens and ducks for their meat or eggs.
Precision Agriculture	Farming management based on observing, measuring, and responding to variability in crops using technology.
Precision Farming	A modern farming practice using technology such as GPS and remote sensing to manage field variability.
Rainwater Harvesting	The collection and storage of rainwater for agricultural use, reducing dependence on groundwater.
Regenerative Agriculture	Farming practices that restore soil health, increase biodiversity, and enhance ecosystem resilience.
Remote Sensing	The use of satellite or aerial imagery to collect information about Earth's surface for agriculture.
Resilience	The capacity of agricultural systems to withstand and recover from adverse conditions.
Rhizosphere	The region of soil directly influenced by root secretions and associated soil microorganisms.
Riparian Buffer	Vegetated areas next to water bodies that help protect water from adjacent land uses.
Rotational Grazing	Moving livestock between pastures to allow forage plants to recover and maintain ecosystems.
Salinization	The accumulation of salts in soil, reducing fertility and crop yields.
Silage	Fermented, high-moisture fodder stored for livestock feeding when fresh forage is unavailable.
Silviculture	The practice of controlling the establishment, growth, and quality of forests.
Silvopasture	Agroforestry that combines trees, forage plants, and livestock in an integrated system.
Smart Farming	The use of information technology, robotics, and data analysis to optimize agricultural processes.
Soil Amendment	Substances added to soil to improve its physical or chemical properties, like compost or gypsum.
Soil Conservation	Techniques to prevent soil erosion and degradation to maintain soil health and productivity.
Soil Erosion	The removal of the topsoil layer by natural forces, leading to reduced soil fertility.
Soil Health Card Scheme	A government initiative providing farmers with information on soil nutrient status and improvement recommendations.
Soil Organic Matter (SOM)	The organic component of soil crucial for soil health and fertility.
Soil pH	A measure of the acidity or alkalinity of soil, affecting nutrient availability and microbial activity.
Soil Profile	A vertical section of soil revealing its layers, differing in physical, chemical, and biological properties.
Stubble Mulching	Leaving crop residues on the soil surface after harvest to protect against erosion.
Subsidy	Financial assistance provided by the government to reduce the cost of agricultural inputs.
Subsistence	Small-scale farming focused on producing enough food to meet the needs of

Farming	the farmer's family.
Sustainable Agriculture	Farming practices meeting current food needs without compromising future generations.
Sustainable Intensification	Increasing productivity on existing farmland while minimizing environmental impact.
Sustainable Livelihoods	Strategies providing communities with means to generate income without degrading the environment.
Terrace Farming	Creating stepped levels on hilly terrain to reduce erosion and enhance water retention.
Transgenic Crops	Crops genetically engineered to express genes from other species, providing traits like pest resistance.
Transpiration	The process by which plants release water vapor through their leaves.
Trellising	Support structures for climbing plants to improve air circulation and ease of harvest.
Urban Agriculture	The practice of cultivating, processing, and distributing food in or around urban areas.
Value Chain	The full range of activities required to bring a product from production to delivery to consumers.
Varietal Resistance	The inherent ability of certain crop varieties to resist pests, diseases, or environmental stresses.
Varietal Trials	Tests conducted to evaluate the performance of different crop varieties under specific conditions.
Vermiculture	The cultivation of earthworms for use in composting, producing nutrient-rich vermicompost.
Vertical Farming	Growing crops in vertically stacked layers using controlled-environment agriculture technology.
Vertical Integration	The combination of two or more stages of production, under a single management.
Water Harvesting	The collection and storage of rainwater or runoff for agricultural use, enhancing water availability.
Water Use Efficiency (WUE)	The ratio of crop yield to the amount of water used, emphasizing efficient water management.
Watershed Development	The integrated development of a watershed area to improve water availability and agricultural productivity.
Watershed Management	Managing the natural resources within a watershed area to balance environmental, social, and economic needs.
Watershed	An area of land where all the water that falls in it drains into a common outlet, like a river or lake.
Weed Management	The practice of controlling unwanted plants that compete with crops for nutrients, water, and light.
Wildlife Corridor	Areas of habitat that connect wildlife populations separated by human activities or structures.
Xeriscaping	Landscaping techniques that reduce or eliminate the need for irrigation by using drought-resistant plants.
Yield Gap	The difference between the actual crop yield achieved by farmers and the potential yield under optimal conditions.
Yield Potential	The maximum possible yield a crop can achieve under optimal conditions,

	influenced by genetic and environmental factors.
Zero Tillage	A conservation agriculture practice where crops are planted directly into the residue of previous crops.
Zero-Budget Natural Farming (ZBNF)	A farming practice promoting natural crop growth without synthetic fertilizers and pesticides.
Zoonotic Diseases	Diseases that can be transmitted from animals to humans, often associated with livestock farming.
Zoonotic Pathogens	Disease-causing organisms that can be transmitted from animals to humans, often found in livestock settings.

Important Varieties mostly preferable by farmers in India

Horticulture

Fruits

1. **Mango**
    - **Alphonso**: Known for its sweetness, richness, and flavor; popular in Maharashtra and Gujarat.
    - **Banganapalli**: Popular in Andhra Pradesh; known for its sweet flavor and firm flesh.
    - **Dasheri**: Originates from Uttar Pradesh; known for its sweet taste and aroma.
    - **Langra**: Popular in Uttar Pradesh and Bihar; known for its distinctive taste.
2. **Banana**
    - **Robusta**: Widely grown in Tamil Nadu and Maharashtra; known for its high yield and disease resistance.
    - **Grand Naine**: Popular across India; known for its good yield and quality.
3. **Apple**
    - **Red Delicious**: Popular in Himachal Pradesh and Jammu & Kashmir; known for its sweetness and crispness.
    - **Golden Delicious**: Grown in Himachal Pradesh; known for its sweet taste and firm texture.
4. **Guava**
    - **Allahabad Safeda**: Known for its white flesh and high vitamin C content; popular in Uttar Pradesh.
    - **Lucknow 49**: Also known as Sardar; popular in Uttar Pradesh and Maharashtra.
5. **Citrus**
    - **Nagpur Orange**: Known for its sweet and tangy flavor; popular in Maharashtra.
    - **Kinnow**: A Mandarin variety popular in Punjab and Rajasthan.
6. **Grapes**

- **Thompson Seedless**: Popular in Maharashtra; known for its sweetness and use in raisin production.
- **Anab-e-Shahi**: Known for its large size and good flavor; grown in Andhra Pradesh.

7. **Papaya**
   - **Red Lady**: Known for its high yield, sweet taste, and disease resistance; popular in Southern India.
   - **Pusa Dwarf**: Popular in Northern India; known for its dwarf stature and high fruit production.
8. **Pomegranate**
   - **Bhagwa**: Known for its large, sweet fruits and disease resistance; popular in Maharashtra.
   - **Ganesh**: Known for its sweet taste and good yield; popular in Maharashtra and Gujarat.
9. **Sapota (Chikoo)**
   - **Kalipatti**: Known for its sweetness and high yield; popular in Gujarat and Maharashtra.
   - **Pala**: Known for its high yield and good quality; popular in Karnataka.
10. **Pineapple**
    - **Kew**: Known for its large size and sweet flavor; popular in Assam and West Bengal.
    - **Queen**: Smaller and more aromatic; popular in Meghalaya and Manipur.
11. **Lychee**
    - **Shahi**: Known for its high yield and sweet flavor; popular in Bihar.
    - **China**: Known for its good fruit size and quality; popular in Bihar and West Bengal.
12. **Jackfruit**
    - **Varikka**: Known for its firm and sweet bulbs; popular in Kerala.
    - **Panruti**: Known for its high yield and quality; popular in Tamil Nadu.
13. **Custard Apple (Sitaphal)**
    - **Balanagar**: Known for its large fruit size and sweet taste; popular in Andhra Pradesh and Maharashtra.
    - **Arka Sahan**: Hybrid variety is known for its good yield and quality; popular in Karnataka.

14. **Strawberry**
    - **Chandler**: Known for its sweet taste and good yield; popular in Himachal Pradesh and Maharashtra.
    - **Sweet Charlie**: Known for its early fruiting and disease resistance; popular in Mahabaleshwar, Maharashtra.
15. **Litchi**
    - **Shahi**: Known for its sweet taste and high yield; popular in Bihar.
    - **Bombai**: Known for its large size and juicy flesh; popular in West Bengal.
16. **Passion Fruit**
    - **Kaveri**: Hybrid variety is known for its high yield and quality; popular in Kerala and Karnataka.
    - **Purple**: Known for its sweet flavor and high yield; popular in North-Eastern states.

Vegetables

1. **Tomato**
    - **Pusa Ruby**: Known for its high yield and disease resistance; popular in Northern India.
    - **Arka Vikas**: Developed by IIHR Bangalore; known for its high yield and good quality.
2. **Brinjal (Eggplant)**
    - **Pusa Purple Long**: Known for its long, purple fruits and high yield; popular in Northern India.
    - **Arka Nidhi**: Known for its resistance to bacterial wilt; grown in Karnataka.
3. **Onion**
    - **Pusa Red**: Known for its high yield and good storage quality; popular in Northern India.
    - **N-53**: Known for its bulb size and shelf life; popular in Maharashtra.
4. **Cabbage**
    - **Golden Acre**: Known for its compact head and resistance to black rot; popular in Northern India.
    - **Pusa Mukta**: Known for its disease resistance and high yield.
5. **Cauliflower**

- **Pusa Snowball**: Known for its compact curds and high yield; popular in Northern India.
- **Snowball 16**: Known for its good curd quality and resistance to diseases.

6. **Potato**
   - **Kufri Jyoti**: Known for its high yield and resistance to late blight; popular in Northern India.
   - **Kufri Pukhraj**: Known for its early maturity and high yield; popular in Uttar Pradesh and Punjab.
7. **Okra (Lady's Finger)**
   - **Pusa Sawani**: Known for its high yield and disease resistance; popular in Northern India.
   - **Arka Anamika**: Known for its high yield and good quality; popular in Karnataka.
8. **Carrot**
   - **Pusa Kesar**: Known for its high yield and good color; popular in Northern India.
   - **Nantes**: Known for its sweet flavor and tEnder texture; popular in Karnataka and Maharashtra.
9. **Peas**
   - **Arkel**: Known for its early maturity and sweet taste; popular in Northern India.
   - **Pusa Pragati**: Known for its high yield and disease resistance; popular in Punjab.
10. **Bitter Gourd**
    - **Pusa Vishesh**: Known for its high yield and good quality; popular in Northern India.
    - **Preethi**: Known for its high yield and disease resistance; popular in Kerala.
11. **Capsicum (Bell Pepper)**
    - **Indra**: Known for its thick flesh and high yield; popular in Karnataka and Himachal Pradesh.
    - **California Wonder**: Known for its sweet taste and disease resistance; popular in Tamil Nadu.
12. **Cucumber**
    - **Poinsett**: Known for its high yield and resistance to downy mildew; popular in Tamil Nadu and Karnataka.
    - **Pusa Sanyog**: Known for its good quality and yield; popular in Northern India.

13. **Bottle Gourd**
    - **Pusa Naveen**: Known for its smooth skin and high yield; popular in Northern India.
    - **Arka Bahar**: Known for its uniform size and good quality; popular in Karnataka.
14. **Spinach**
    - **Pusa Harit**: Known for its high yield and good quality leaves; popular in Northern India.
    - **All Green**: Known for its fast growth and disease resistance; popular in Maharashtra.

Flowers

1. **Marigold**
    - **Pusa Narangi Gainda**: Known for its bright orange flowers and high yield; popular in Northern India.
    - **Pusa Basanti Gainda**: Known for its yellow flowers and disease resistance; popular in Northern India.
2. **Rose**
    - **Taj Mahal**: Known for its deep red color and long stems; popular in Maharashtra.
    - **First Red**: Known for its large flowers and good vase life; popular in Tamil Nadu.

Spices

1. **Turmeric**
    - **Salem**: Known for its high curcumin content; popular in Tamil Nadu.
    - **Rajapuri**: Known for its aroma and color; grown in Maharashtra.
2. **Chilli**
    - **Guntur Sannam**: Known for its spiciness; popular in Andhra Pradesh.
    - **Byadagi**: Known for its color and mild pungency; grown in Karnataka.
3. **Black Pepper**
    - **Panniyur 1**: Known for its high yield and disease resistance; popular in Kerala.

- **Karimunda**: Known for its quality and high yield; popular in Kerala.

4. **Cardamom**
    - **Njallani**: Known for its high yield and large capsules; popular in Kerala.
    - **Green Gold**: Known for its quality and high yield; popular in Kerala.
5. **Coriander**
    - **CO 4**: Known for its high yield and aromatic leaves; popular in Tamil Nadu.
    - **Pant Haritma**: Known for its high yield and disease resistance; popular in Northern India.
6. **Fenugreek**
    - **Pusa Early Bunching**: Known for its early maturity and high yield; popular in Northern India.
    - **Kasuri**: Known for its strong aroma and good quality; popular in Rajasthan and Punjab.
7. **Turmeric**
    - **Erode**: Known for its high curcumin content and bright color; popular in Tamil Nadu.
    - **Duggirala**: Known for its high yield and quality; popular in Andhra Pradesh.

Important Varieties in Agriculture

Cereals

1. **Rice**
    - **IR64**: Known for its high yield and disease resistance; popular in Andhra Pradesh and Tamil Nadu.
    - **Sona Masuri**: Known for its aroma and quality; popular in Karnataka and Andhra Pradesh.
    - **Basmati**: Known for its aroma and long grains; popular in Punjab and Haryana.
2. **Wheat**
    - **HD 2967**: Known for its high yield and disease resistance; popular in Punjab and Haryana.
    - **PBW 343**: Known for its high yield and adaptability; popular in Punjab.
3. **Maize**

- Ganga 5: Known for its high yield and adaptability; popular in Bihar and Uttar Pradesh.
- **Dekalb**: Hybrid varieties known for high yield; popular in Karnataka and Maharashtra.

4. **Sorghum**
   - **CSH 14**: Known for its high yield and drought tolerance; popular in Maharashtra and Karnataka.
   - **Maldandi**: Known for its good quality grain and fodder; popular in Maharashtra.
5. **Barley**
   - **RD 2668**: Known for its high yield and disease resistance; popular in Rajasthan and Haryana.
6. **Finger Millet (Ragi)**
   - **Indaf 9**: Known for its high yield and drought tolerance; popular in Karnataka.
   - **GPU 28**: Known for its high yield and disease resistance; popular in Tamil Nadu.
7. **Pearl Millet (Bajra)**
   - **HHB 67**: Known for its high yield and drought tolerance; popular in Rajasthan and Gujarat.
   - **ICTP 8203**: Known for its high yield and resistance to downy mildew; popular in Maharashtra.
8. **Foxtail Millet (Kangni)**
   - **SIA 3156**: Known for its high yield and adaptability; popular in Karnataka and Andhra Pradesh.
   - **CO 7**: Known for its high yield and short duration; popular in Tamil Nadu.
   - **K 551**: Known for its high yield and quality; popular in Uttar Pradesh

Pulses

1. **Pigeon Pea (Arhar)**
   - **Pusa 992**: Known for its high yield and disease resistance; popular in Uttar Pradesh and Maharashtra.
   - **ICPL 88039**: Known for its early maturity and high yield; popular in Karnataka.
2. **Chickpea (Gram)**

- **Pusa 256**: Known for its high yield and disease resistance; popular in Madhya Pradesh and Rajasthan.
- **JG 11**: Known for its early maturity and high yield; popular in Andhra Pradesh.

3. **Green Gram (Moong)**
    - **Pusa Vishal**: Known for its high yield and short duration; popular in Northern India.
    - **CO 6**: Known for its high yield and disease resistance; popular in Tamil Nadu.
4. **Black Gram (Urad)**
    - **T 9**: Known for its high yield and early maturity; popular in Uttar Pradesh and Madhya Pradesh.
    - **PDU 1**: Known for its disease resistance and high yield; popular in Tamil Nadu.

Oilseeds

1. **Groundnut**
    - **TMV 2**: Known for its high yield and disease resistance; popular in Tamil Nadu and Karnataka.
    - **GG 20**: Known for its high yield and good quality; popular in Gujarat.
2. **Mustard**
    - **Pusa Bold**: Known for its high yield and disease resistance; popular in Haryana and Rajasthan.
    - **Varuna**: Known for its adaptability and high yield; popular in Uttar Pradesh.
3. **Sunflower**
    - **Morden**: Known for its high yield and oil content; popular in Karnataka and Andhra Pradesh.
    - **KBSH 1**: Hybrid variety is known for its high yield; popular in Karnataka.
4. **Soybean**
    - **JS 335**: Known for its high yield and wide adaptability; popular in Madhya Pradesh and Maharashtra.
    - **Pusa 9712**: Known for its high yield and disease resistance; popular in Northern India.
5. **Sesame**

- TNV 7: Known for its high yield and good oil content; popular in Tamil Nadu.
   - **GT 10**: Known for its high yield and disease resistance; popular in Gujarat.
6. **Castor**
   - **GCH 4**: Known for its high yield and resistance to wilt; popular in Gujarat.
   - **Jyothi**: Known for its high yield and adaptability; popular in Andhra Pradesh
7. **Red Gram (Tur)**
   - **BSMR 736**: Known for its high yield and disease resistance; popular in Maharashtra.
   - **Maruti**: Known for its short duration and high yield; popular in Karnataka.
8. **Lentil**
   - **Pusa Masoor 5**: Known for its high yield and disease resistance; popular in Northern India.
   - **Pant L 406**: Known for its high yield and good quality; popular in Uttar Pradesh.
9. **Linseed (Flax)**
   - **Shubhra**: Known for its high yield and oil content; popular in Uttar Pradesh.
   - **Parvati**: Known for its high yield and disease resistance; popular in Madhya Pradesh.
10. **Safflower**
   - **A1**: Known for its high yield and drought tolerance; popular in Maharashtra.
   - **Bhima**: Known for its high yield and oil content; popular in Karnataka.

Fibre Crops

1. **Cotton**
   - **Bt Cotton**: Known for its high yield and resistance to bollworms; popular in Maharashtra, Gujarat, and Andhra Pradesh.
   - **Suraj**: Known for its high yield and quality; popular in Gujarat and Maharashtra.

- **LRA 5166**: Known for its high yield and resistance to bollworms; popular in Tamil Nadu.
- **H 777**: Known for its high yield and quality; popular in Gujarat and Maharashtra.

2. **Jute**
    - **JRO 524**: Known for its high yield and quality; popular in West Bengal and Assam.
    - **JRO 8432**: Known for its high yield and disease resistance; popular in Bihar and Odisha.
    - **JRO 8432**: Known for its high yield and disease resistance; popular in Bihar and Odisha.
    - **JRC 7447**: Known for its high yield and good quality; popular in West Bengal and Assam.

Agricultural Statistics

- **Foodgrains production** in 2021-22 reached **285.71 million tonnes** as per the 4th advance estimates.
- **Kharif foodgrains production** for 2021-22 was **141.03 million tonnes.**
- **Rabi foodgrains production** for 2021-22 reached **144.68 million tonnes.**
- **Horticulture production** for 2021-22 reached **342.33 million tonnes** as per the 3rd advance estimates.
- **Milk production** for 2020-21 stood at **209.96 million tonnes.**
- **Meat production** for 2020-21 was recorded at **87.98 lakh tonnes.**
- **Livestock population** as per the 20th census in 2019 was **536.76 million.**
- **Fish production** in 2020-21 was **162.48 lakh tonnes.**
- **Rice procurement** for the Kharif marketing season 2022-23 was **478.27 lakh tonnes.**
- **Wheat procurement** for Rabi marketing season 2022-23 reached **187.92 lakh tonnes.**
- **Nutri/coarse grains procurement** for 2022-23 was **263 thousand tonnes.**
- **Cotton procurement** in 2021-22 was **15 lakh bales.**
- **GVA from agriculture and allied sector** for 2022-23 at constant 2011-12 prices was **Rs. 22,21,092 crore.**
- The **growth rate of GVA** in the agriculture sector for 2022-23 is **3.3%.**
- The **share of agriculture in total GVA** for 2022-23 is **21.1%.**
- **Agricultural exports** in 2021-22 valued at **Rs. 3,75,662 crore.**
- **Agricultural imports** for 2021-22 were worth **Rs. 2,31,850 crore.**
- **Total cultivators** as per Census 2011 was **118.8 million.**
- **Total agricultural laborers** per the 2011 Census stood at **144.3 million.**
- **Agricultural workers** accounted for **54.6%** of the total workforce as per the 2011 Census.
- **Operational holdings** in 2015-16 numbered **146.45 lakh.**
- **Marginal holdings** (less than 1 hectare) accounted for **68.45%** of total operational holdings in 2015-16.
- **Small holdings** (1-2 hectares) represented **17.62%** of total operational holdings.
- **Irrigated area** under paddy cultivation in Madhya Pradesh is a

significant portion of the state's agricultural land.

- **Crop calendar** for Madhya Pradesh indicates paddy sowing occurs in **June-July** and harvesting in **October-November**.
- **Crop calendar for Uttar Pradesh** highlights paddy sowing in **June-July** and wheat sowing in **November-December**.
- **Crop calendar for Chhattisgarh** focuses on paddy cultivation in **June-July** and harvesting by **October-November**.
- **State-wise consumption of fertilizers** indicates Uttar Pradesh is among the highest consumers of fertilizers in India.
- **Monsoon rainfall performance** from 1989 to 2022 highlights variability affecting crop productivity.
- **Minimum support price (MSP)** for key crops has been critical in ensuring farmers' profitability.
- **Total area under horticultural crops** increased, showing sustained growth in **Madhya Pradesh**.
- **Soybean cultivation** is a significant contributor to Madhya Pradesh's agricultural economy.
- **Madhya Pradesh** leads in **pulse production**, particularly in crops like gram and lentils.
- **Wheat productivity** in **Uttar Pradesh** remains high, making it a leading wheat-producing state.
- **Rice production** in **Chhattisgarh** is a vital component of the state's agricultural output.
- **Groundnut production** is increasing in **Gujarat and Madhya Pradesh**, contributing significantly to India's oilseed production.
- **India's share in world agriculture** is significant, especially in the production of wheat, rice, and pulses.
- **Fertilizer usage per hectare** varies significantly across states, with the highest consumption in states like **Punjab and Haryana**.
- **Electricity consumption for agricultural purposes** continues to rise, reflecting the growing mechanization in farming.
- **Sugarcane production** in India, led by **Uttar Pradesh and Maharashtra**, has seen a steady increase.
- **Lentil production** has seen a notable rise, especially in **Madhya Pradesh and Uttar Pradesh**.
- **Gram production** is predominantly focused in **Madhya Pradesh, Maharashtra, and Uttar Pradesh**.
- **Cotton purchases** by Cotton Corporation of India saw substantial volumes from **Madhya Pradesh and Gujarat**.

- **All-India index numbers of yield** for principal crops reflect gradual improvements in crop productivity.
- **Minimum support prices (MSP)** for oilseeds and pulses have provided a buffer for farmers, particularly in **Madhya Pradesh and Rajasthan**.
- **Rainfall distribution data** for India from 1992 to 2022 underscores its role in agricultural yield variability.
- **Net irrigated area** in India for 2019-20 was **75.46 million hectares**.
- **Gross irrigated area** in 2019-20 was **112.23 million hectares**.
- **Average size of operational holdings** has been declining, reflecting increased fragmentation.
- **Area under organic farming** in major states like **Madhya Pradesh** continues to expand.
- **Tomato production** in India saw the highest yields in states like **Madhya Pradesh and Karnataka**.
- **Fish production** data indicates **West Bengal and Andhra Pradesh** are leading contributors.
- **Export of agricultural commodities** from India has shown a steady rise, with **rice and wheat** being major contributors.
- **Livestock sector growth** is driven by states like **Uttar Pradesh and Rajasthan**.
- **Institutional credit flow** to agriculture has increased, with major disbursements in **Madhya Pradesh and Uttar Pradesh**.
- **Indebtedness among agricultural households** is significant, with **Madhya Pradesh** being a key focus.
- **Coconut production** shows significant growth, especially in **Kerala and Tamil Nadu**.
- **Horticultural crops area** in **Madhya Pradesh** continues to increase, contributing to national fruit and vegetable production.
- **Agricultural trade indices** for 2021-22 highlight growth in both exports and imports.
- **Irrigation potential** created under the Accelerated Irrigation Benefit Programme (AIBP) was substantial for states like **Madhya Pradesh**.
- **Foodgrains production** reached **285.71 million tonnes** in 2021-22.
- **Horticulture production** in 2021-22 was **342.33 million tonnes**.
- **Gross cropped area** for 2019-20 was **211.36 million hectares**.
- **Milk production** in 2020-21 was **209.96 million tonnes**.
- **Percentage of net area sown** in 2019-20 was **45.64%**.
- **Meat production** in 2020-21 stood at **87.98 lakh tonnes**.
- **Percentage share of agricultural exports** in national exports was

11.94% for 2021-22.

- **Livestock population** reached **536.76 million** in 2019.
- **Gross value added (GVA) from agriculture** was **Rs. 22,21,092 crore** in 2022-23.
- **GVA growth rate in agriculture** was **3.3%** in 2022-23.
- **Share of agriculture in total GVA** for 2022-23 was **21.1%**.
- **Percentage share of agricultural imports** to national imports was **5.07%** in 2021-22.
- **Total number of cultivators** as per the 2011 Census was **118.8 million.**
- **Total number of agricultural laborers** as per the 2011 Census was **144.3 million.**
- **Net irrigated area** in 2019-20 was **75.46 million hectares.**
- **Gross irrigated area** in 2019-20 was **112.23 million hectares.**

Agronomy

Kharif crop

Cereals

Rice

- **Transplanting** method is commonly used in rice cultivation for better plant stand.
- **Irrigation at critical stages** like tillering and flowering improves rice yield significantly.
- Rice is sensitive to **water stagnation** and requires well-drained fields.
- **Weed management** early in the crop cycle (2-3 weeks) is crucial for productivity.
- **Hybrid varieties** offer higher yields but require higher inputs and care. Best biofertiilzer for rice is **azolla**.
- **Bronzing disease** of rice is associated with high concentrations of ferrous.
- Brown rice **de-hulled** rice.
- Effect of puddling on soil bulk density it increases the bulk density.
- Father of golden rice ***Ingo Potrykus.***
- Golden yellow rice is rich in **vitamin A.**
- Harvest index of rice is **40%.**
- Highest nitrogen loss in rice field **denitrification**.
- Hulling% of rice **65%.**
- Hydrothermal treatment of rice grain before milling parboiling.
- The idea of super rice **G.S khush**.
- Killer disease of rice **tungru virus.**
- Length of extra-long rice **7mm** or more
- Micronutrient essential for rice **silicon.**
- The most critical stage of irrigation **booting stage**.
- Nitrogen use efficiency of rice is **30-40%.**
- The optimum plant population **per hill per m^2 is 50 hills per m^2.**

- Origin of **Southeast Asia.**
- Parboiling rice conserves vitamin **B12.**
- Plastic rice is made by mixing potato, sweet Potatoes, and resin and shaped into grain.
- Seed rate of **depog** method 1.5-3 kg/m2.
- SRI was first developed by ***Fr. Henri de Laulanie*** under drought conditions in **Madagascar** in 1983.
- The bioherbicide used in rice cultivation is **collego.**
- The gas emitted from rice fields is **methane**.
- The value of albedo for rice is **12%.**
- A variety suitable for waterlogged conditions is **jalmanga**.
- White-eye of rice is due to **iron deficiency.**
- A widely used nitrogenous fertilizer in rice is **ammonium sulfate.**
- Yield increasing by adopting SRI is **50-90%.**

Maize

- **Kharif maize** is sown with the onset of monsoon rains in India.
- Maize responds well to **NPK fertilizers**, especially nitrogen for vegetative growth.
- **Intercropping maize with pulses** like pigeon pea enhances soil fertility and productivity.
- **Water management** during flowering and grain filling stages is critical for yield.
- **Fall armyworm** is a major pest affecting Kharif maize, requiring integrated pest management.
- America produces 40% of the total world production of Maize.
- Carbohydrate percent in maize > **70%** highest in cereal crops.
- **Cross technique** among the **inbred line**.
- **Double cross technique** for hybrid seed production by **D.F. Jones** in **1920.**
- Due to more consumption of ***maize*** people suffer from **pellagra disease** because maize is deficient in **Vit-B** and **Tryptophane**.
- The first all-India Coordinated Maize Improvement Project was started in **1957** in **New Delhi**.
- The gene responsible for quality protein maize is **Opaque-2**.
- The idea of Hybrid maize was first conceived by ***E.M. East*** and ***G.H. Shull*** in 1910 by a single.
- In maize yellow color due to the presence of **cryptoxanthin**.
- Insect of maize — maize borer ***(Chilo partellus).***

- The leading state of **rabi** maize is **Bihar**.
- **Lysine** and **Tryptophane** Amino Acids rich in **Quality Protein Maize**.
- Maize is deficient in tryptophane and **lysine amino acids.**
- Maize crops are cultivated in all 3 seasons ie. ***Kharif, Rabi, Jayad***, but more production is obtained from Rabi Season(15-25% more).
- Maize is a **C_4 plant**.
- Maize is a **non-tiller plant**.
- Maize is a cross-pollinated crop it is known as **protandry.**
- Maize is a **frost** susceptible crop.
- Maize is a **monoecious plant** / on which male and female parts are present on the same plant but differently.
- Maize is also known as the **queen** of cereals.
- Maize is the backbone of **America**.
- Maize is an indicator plant for **zinc (Zn)** deficiency.
- Maize is susceptible to **sensitive water logging**.
- The male part of maize is known as Tessel and the female part is known as Silk.
- The maturation of the male part is first and the female part is later in maize, this stage is known as **protandry**.
- Production of **maize** is the **highest** among **all cereal crops**.
- Protein % in **maize > 10%.**
- The protein in maize is called **zein -10%.**
- The red and purple colour of maize leaves due to a deficiency of **phosphorus.**
- Removal of male flowers in maize is known as ***De- tasselling.***
- Sowing of maize in East the **east-west** direction for more receiving of sunlight.
- Suitable temperature for maize cultivation > **32°C**.
- **Teosinte** is the closest wild relative of modern maize.
- Useful Herbicide in maize **simazine** and **Atrazine.**
- White bud disease in maize is due to a deficiency of **Zn**.

Sorghum

- Sorghum can be grown in **rainfed conditions**, making it ideal for arid and semi-arid regions.
- **Ratooning** in sorghum allows multiple harvests from a single planting.
- Sorghum is highly **drought-tolerant**, often grown in low rainfall areas.
- **Fodder sorghum** is commonly used in dual-purpose systems for both grain and forage.
- **Hoeing and weeding** are essential practices at the early stages to boost

growth.

- **Africa** is the leading country of sorghum production.
- CSH-**9** is a Drought and salinity-tolerant variety of sorghum.
- For fodder purposes, sorghum is harvested at the **knee stage**.
- Green fodder of sorghum is **toxic** for animals because it has **HCN (Hydrogen Cyanide).**
- HCN is also called **Prusic** acid or **Dhurin**, a **synthesis** of HCN in **roots**.
- HCN is increased with drought conditions and decreased with rains.
- Inflorescence is **Panicle**.
- **Maharashtra** is the leading state in India in sorghum production.
- The optimum plant population is 185000 plants/ha.
- Protein % in sorghum **10-12%.**
- Regularly higher dose of sorghum in food causes **"Pellagra disease"** Due to a deficiency in Vit-B.
- Sorghum is a C_4 plant.
- Sorghum is also an **Exhaustive crop**.
- Sorghum is known as "**camel crop"** because it can stand against
- Sorghum is often a **cross-pollinated crop.**
- **Striga** is a partial root parasite of sorghum.
- The HCN toxic limit is **200 ppm.**
- When sorghum is used for fodder purposes for animals harvesting is done after the **flowering stage**.

Pearl Millet

- **Pearl millet (Bajra)** is the most **drought-tolerant** cereal grown in Kharif season.
- **Intercropping pearl millet** with legumes like cowpea improves soil health.
- **Grain and fodder yields** of pearl millet are high under proper irrigation and nutrient management.
- **Early sowing** helps escape terminal drought and ensures better yields.
- **Vernacular names** include Bajra, Bajri, Sajje, Cambu across various Indian states.
- Among the cereals, the water requirement for pearl millet is lowest (250 mm) but sensitive to **waterlogging**.
- Bajra is a **cross-pollinated** crop.
- Bajra is a stable food for Poor men.
- The first Hybrid of **Bajra > HB-1** in **1965** from Ludhiana (male sterile Tift 23A)
- Highly **drought-tolerant** crop among cereals.

- The maturation of female flowers is first known as **protogyny.**
- India is the leading producing country of **Bajra** production in the world.
- The leading state of Bajra production in India is **Rajasthan** in both area & production.
- Mineral percent in Bajra is **2.7%** higher than other cereal crops.
- Optimum Plant population 175000-200000 plant/ha.
- Sensitive to waterlogging and acidic soil.

Finger Millet

- **Finger millet (Ragi)** is highly tolerant to **alkalinity** and thrives in pH > 11 soils.
- **Rainfed conditions** are suitable for finger millet, with minimal water requirement.
- The crop has **short duration varieties**, making it a good option for contingency planning.
- **Nutrient management** with organic and inorganic fertilizers improves productivity.
- **Threshing and storage** are important to prevent grain damage due to moisture.

Pulses

Pigeon Pea

- **Pigeon pea (Arhar)** is a highly **nutritious pulse**, rich in protein (21%).
- It is drought-tolerant and grown as **sole, mixed, or intercrop** with cereals.
- **Sowing time** is critical; delayed sowing affects flowering and pod filling.
- **Waterlogging** during flowering hampers pod development and reduces yields.
- **Harvesting in stages** is common due to its indeterminate growth pattern.
- Pigeon pea is mainly grown in **tropical** and **subtropical climate**
- Pigeon pea is sensitive to salinity **(>8 pH).**
- The protein percentage in urd been is **25-26%.**
- South Indian dishes like ***Dosa***, ***Itley***, and ***Wada*** are prepared by **urd bean.**
- break the seed coat by Thermal energy.
- Urd bean is also known as meet crop.

Chick Pea crop

- Blood purification factor is present in **gram.**
- Chickpea has **tape rooted system**.
- Chickpea is also known as the king of **pulse crops.**
- Chickpeas is a **self-pollinated** and **long-day plant.**
- flowering and **pod development** is a Critical stage for Irrigation.
- Germinated seed of gram is used to **scare disease.**
- Gram cultivation required a loose and well-aerated rough **seed bed.**
- Gram is an important source of **Fe, Ca, niacin.**
- Gram seed is sown **8-10 cm deep** in the soil to escape from wilt disease.
- Its leaves are recommended for Intestired disorder patients due to the presence of **maleic** and **oxalic acid.**
- Late planting of chickpeas is done to protect the seedling from **wilt** disease.
- The most important pest of gram is the **pod borer**.
- **Nipping** is done in Gram for the development of lateral branches
- Sheep and goats are grazing in the **gram field for Nipping.**
- The chemical is used for **Nipping TIBA (75ppm).**
- The sour taste is found in chickpeas because of the presence of maleic acid (90-96%) and **oxalic acid (4-10%).**

Mung Bean and Urd Bean

- **Mung bean (Green Gram)** is a **short-duration** pulse ideal for Kharif.
- It is commonly **intercropped** with cereals like sorghum and maize.
- **Weed management** in the early stages is critical for mung bean yield.
- **Pod harvesting** is done in stages, as pods mature at different times.
- Mung bean is a source of **plant-based protein** (24-26%).
- **Urd bean (Black Gram)** is grown as a **catch crop** after rice.
- It is highly **protein-rich**, making it a staple in vegetarian diets.
- **Intercropping with oilseeds** like groundnut or sesame improves yield and soil fertility.
- **Tolerates high temperatures**, suitable for tropical regions.
- **Sequential cropping** with cereals like rice and wheat is common in rainfed areas.
- Green gram and Black gram are catch crops grown in the **summer season** and tolerance to **Sunstroke (Loo)**.
- Green gram also known as golden gram is an **important short-duration crop.**
- The harvest index is **19%** lowest among pulses.
- In India, the Highest production of ***Arhar*** is UP.
- The highest productivity of pigeon peas in **Bihar (115 kg/ha).**

- It can tolerate moisture stress to a greater extent because of its **deep/tap-rooted system**.
- It is a cross-pollinated crop. An average cross-pollination 1st 20%.
- It required light-textured, well-drained soil.
- It requires a soil pH range of **5-8.**
- Moong and urd come in pulses crop after gram and pigeon pea.
- Moong is **the third Rank** after gram and pigeon pea among pulse crops.
- Moong or green gram is grown for **multiple purposes** like pulse green manure **catch crop** and **cover crop.**
- Moong bean is the **hardiest** crop among all the pulses.

Oilseeds

Groundnut

- **Groundnut** is widely grown in **light sandy soils** that facilitate easy pod development.
- **Rainfed groundnut** relies on monsoon rains for pod formation and kernel filling.
- **Weed control** is critical for groundnut due to slow initial growth.
- **Pod maturity** varies, making staged harvesting important.
- **Calcium application** enhances pod development and kernel quality.

Soybean

- **Soybean** is a high **protein and oil** crop (40% protein, 20% oil).
- **Soybean cultivation** has expanded in **Madhya Pradesh**, the leading producer.
- **Water management** during flowering and pod filling ensures better yields.
- **Nitrogen fixation** in soybean reduces the need for synthetic nitrogen fertilizers.
- **Intercropping soybean** with sorghum or maize enhances soil nitrogen.
- **20% oil** is present in soybean protein.
- **Andhra Pradesh** is first in the productivity of soybeans.
- Due to the presence of the enzyme **lip oxidase**, soybean is not used as '***Dal***' which produces **off flavour**.
- First nodules are visible 10" days after sowing.
- It is called **Gold of America.s**
- It is called the wonder crop and meat of the poor.

- **Lysine** is highly present in soybean protein.
- **Madhya Pradesh** is first in both area & production in India and second in Maharashtra.
- MP is known as a Soya state.
- The National Soybean Research Institute is in **Indore (MP).**
- The protein content in soybean is **40-42%.**
- Soybean area in MP 5.12 mh and productivity **5.8 mh (54%)**
- Soybean in most **oilseed crops** in the world (50%).
- Soybean is a long-day plant and C_3 type.
- World first rank crop as a source of vegetable oil.
-

Sesame

- **Sesame** is a **drought-tolerant** crop suitable for arid Kharif conditions.
- **Early sowing** improves yields, as sesame is sensitive to heavy rains at flowering.
- **Hand weeding** is necessary in sesame due to its slow initial growth.
- **Nutrient application** of phosphorus increases seed oil content.
- **Sequential cropping** of sesame after cereals or pulses is common in rainfed systems.

Castor

- **Castor** is grown for **oil-rich seeds**, with diverse industrial uses.
- **Deep ploughing** and **early sowing** help in better crop establishment.
- **Irrigation at flowering** increases seed yield significantly.
- **Resistant to drought**, castor is grown in semi-arid regions.
- **Intercropping with legumes** helps maintain soil fertility and improves overall yield.

Fibre Crops

Cotton

- **Cotton** thrives in **black soil** regions under rainfed conditions.
- Requires **adequate irrigation** at critical stages of flowering and boll formation.
- **Pest management** (bollworm) is critical for improving cotton yields.
- Cotton is a **long-duration** crop, typically harvested 6-7 months after planting.
- **Intercropping with legumes** helps in maintaining soil fertility.
- **'Kandy'** is an international unit of unit **Kandy = 99kg.**
- **15-25% oil** is found in cotton seed.
- **'epidermal cell'** is an Outgrowth Cotton fiber.
- Cotton fiber is called lint in the present **99% cellulose.**

- Cotton seed is called ***Binolla***, Toxic agent **gossypol** is present in this.
- Crinkle leaf of cotton due to **'Mn' Toxicity.**
- Fiber length and fiber fineness are 'genetic traits.'
- Fiber thickness is measured by **Nippiness.**
- First hybrid cotton **H-4** (G-67* A. nector less) 1970.
- The first interspecific hybrid variety of cotton is ***Varalaxmi*** **(*G. hirsutum*** (F) * ***G. Barbadence*** (M).
- Little leaf in cotton due to **'Zn'** deficiency
- The coloured cotton is discovered by **'K.C. Mandloi (Khandawa).**
- The fiber maturity is measured by an **'Areometer'**.
- The fiber quality is seen by fiber **length.**
- The hybrid cotton is discovered by C.T. Patel (GJ).
- The weight of one bale of cotton is **168+3kg.**

Jute

- **Jute** grows best in **well-drained alluvial soils** with high water retention capacity.
- Requires **high humidity** and ample water supply during the growing period.
- **Retting** is a unique process used for **fiber extraction** in jute.
- **Manual weeding** is necessary for jute during the early stages of crop growth.
- **Golden fiber** revolution is related to **jute.**
- The ideal stage for Harvesting is the small pod stage or Initiation of pod formation ***Viz*** **-135-140 DAS.**
- In India, west Bengal has first position both in **area** and **production**.
- India's **first Rank** in both area and production of Jute in the world.
- It most important fiber crop in India
- Jute fiber is also called '**Bast**.
- Jute fiber is known as golden fiber.
- Jute fiber is obtained from the secondary Phloem of the stem.
- Jute is a cash crop in India.
- *Ligno* cellulose is present in Jute fiber.
- Mesta grows on soils where jute cannot grow.
- Jute provides **high biomass** and is known for its **biodegradable fibres**.

Forage Crops

Sorghum (Forage)

- **Sorghum** is suitable for both **rainfed and irrigated** conditions for forage.

- It can be harvested **at 50% flowering** to maximize green fodder yield.
- **Intercropping with legumes** improves soil health and productivity.
- **Water management** during flowering and grain formation is crucial.
- Sorghum is highly **drought-tolerant** and widely used as a **dual-purpose crop** (grain and fodder).

Cowpea (Forage)

- **Cowpea** is a **fast-growing legume**, excellent for intercropping with cereals.
- It can fix **atmospheric nitrogen**, improving soil fertility.
- **Green fodder** is ready for harvest **50-55 days** after sowing.
- **Short-duration crop**, ideal for forage purposes in Kharif.
- Tolerates **drought conditions**, making it suitable for dryland areas.

Cluster Bean (Forage)

- **Cluster bean** (Guar) is highly **drought-resistant**, making it ideal for arid zones.
- It improves soil fertility through **nitrogen fixation**.
- Provides **green fodder** and **dry pods** for animal feed.
- Responds well to **organic manure** for better growth.
- **Weed control** is essential during the early stages of crop growth.

Maize (Forage)

- **Maize** is harvested at the **milky stage** for high-quality green fodder.
- It can be **intercropped with legumes** for better land utilization.
- **Water management** during silking and grain-filling stages ensures high fodder yield.
- Requires **fertilization** at critical stages for optimal growth.
- **Varieties like Ganga 5** and **African Tall** are popular for fodder production.

Guinea Grass

- **Guinea grass** is a perennial forage crop that grows well in **well-drained soils.**
- First cut is taken **75 days after sowing**, subsequent cuts every **45 days**.
- Responds well to **NPK fertilization** after each cut for continuous growth.
- It provides **high green fodder yields**, making it ideal for intensive livestock systems.
- **Intercropping with legumes** like hedge lucerne enhances fodder nutrition.

Napier Grass

- **Napier grass** (Elephant Grass) is known for its **high biomass yield**, especially in irrigated areas.
- Harvesting starts **75-80 days after planting**, with cuts at regular **45-day intervals.**
- Requires **heavy fertilization** (especially nitrogen) for optimal growth.
- **Intercropping with legumes** improves both **yield and soil health**.
- Widely used in **dairy farming** for its **high nutritional value** as fodder.

Wheat (Triticum sp.)

- **World's leading cereal** in area cultivated.
- Suitable for **bread, cakes, and bakery products**.
- **Varieties** include common, durum, and emmer wheat.
- **Optimal growth temperature**: 20-22°C for vegetative growth.
- **Critical irrigation stages**: CRI, flowering, and grain filling.
- Biofertilizer used in **wheat > Azotobacter.**
- Dwarf varieties of wheat were developed **by Dr. Norman Borlaug in 1963.**
- The export quality of wheat is reduced due to **"karnal bunt".**
- First dwarf wheat seen in Japan.
- First Triticale is developed by **Rimpu** scientists in **Swindon.**
- Gene found in wheat **> Rht— 1, Rht-2,** and **Norin -10** for dwarfness.
- The gene responsible for dwarfness in wheat is **Norin-10 (N-10).**
- Germination % - **85%**
- Gluten Protein present in wheat > **11-12%.**
- The ***Goojo*** method is used to produce hybrid seed production in wheat.
- The harvesting stage of wheat is **55%.**
- Inflorescence of wheat is **called spike/Ear.**
- Man-made cereal is **Triticale** (Wheat rye — Developed by Rimpu)
- The meaning of cereals is **Goddess of Grain**.
- Moisture percent at the time of Harvesting > **25-30%.**
- Moisture percent at the time of storage is **10-12%.**
- Mustard is a very common crop that is usually intercropped in **wheat**.
- The name of the Absolute weed in wheat is ***Bathua***.
- Noble prize was awarded to ***Norman Borlaug*** in 1970 for peace.
- Problematic weed in wheat crop> **Hirankhuri.**
- The ratio of wheat and mustard rows is **9:1.**
- Regional Wheat Research Institute of MP. In panwarkheda ,Hoshangabad.
- The seed of wheat is called **caryopsis**.

- Temperature at the time of germination in **wheat 20-25°C**.
- The test weight of wheat is 40-42 gm while the test weight of ***Phalaris minor*** is 2gm.
- Test weight of wheat seed 40 gm. And ***Phalaris minor*** is 2 gm.
- The central zig-zag axis in **wheat grain** 1st is called "Rachis".
- The word "Cereal" is derived from the Roman word "Ceres"
- Varieties ***Larma rojo, Sonara -63,*** and ***Mayo-64*** are released in Mexico (CIMMYT)
- The variety of triticale is **DT -46.**
- Wheat and Rice are responsible for a **green revolution** in the world.
- Wheat is a Rabi season crop and sowing is done first fortnight of **November.**
- Wheat is responsible for the success of the **green revolution** in India.
- Wheat is the **second largest** cereal crop In India.
- Wheat is the largest **staple food crop** of the world then Rice
- Wheat ranks first in the world among cereals both **concerning** area and **production.**

Barley (Hordeum vulgare)

- **Hardy crop**, tolerates **drought, salinity**, and alkalinity.
- Used for **malt, beer, whisky**, and animal feed.
- High in **protein** and has medicinal properties.
- Performs well in **cool climates**, sensitive to frost.
- **Irrigation** is crucial during tillering and grain filling stages.

Chickpea (Cicer arietinum)

- **Largest pulse crop** in India and globally significant.
- **Two types**: Desi (small-seeded) and Kabuli (large-seeded).
- **Nitrogen-fixing** legume, important for soil health.
- Thrives in **dry areas** with moderate rainfall.
- **Nipping** practice enhances branching and yield.

Lentil (Lens culinaris)

- **Rich source of protein**, iron, and vitamins.
- Thrives in **cool, dry climates**, tolerant to frost.
- **Microsperma and macrosperma** varieties exist.
- Grows on **alluvial and black cotton soils.**
- Requires **minimal irrigation** during flowering and grain filling.

Peas (Pisum sativum)

- **Third most important** Rabi legume after chickpea and lentil.
- Suitable for **cool climates** and can tolerate drought.

- Requires **well-drained soils**, sensitive to salinity.
- Used in **snacks, soups, and dried pulse products**.
- **Rhizobium inoculation** enhances nodulation and yields.

Rajma (Phaseolus vulgaris)

- Cultivated for **both fresh pods (vegetables)** and dried seeds.
- **High protein content**, good for vegetarian diets.
- Grows well in **hilly regions** during Kharif and small Rabi areas.
- Requires **well-drained soil**, sensitive to salinity.
- **Seed rate** varies by seed size, 120-140 kg/ha for large seeds.

Mustard (Brassica sp.)

- **Second most important** oilseed after groundnut.
- Contains **erucic acid and glucosinolates**, not regular cooking oil.
- **Canola** varieties low in erucic acid are favored.
- Used for **vegetable oil**, soap, lubricants, and animal feed.
- Grows in **Rabi season**, prefers well-drained soils.
- Due to the presence of toxic **glucosinolates** in its cake, it is an unsuitable source of protein for both humans and cattle.
- The Harvest Index of Mustard is 25%.
- **NRCHB -506**- It is the first hybrid of mustard in India developed by the Directorate of Rate Seed and Mustard Research, Bharatpur.
- Pungency is due to Isothiocyanate, an enzymic hydrolysis product of glucosinolates (In all crucifers).
- **Pusa Jai Kisan** (Bio -902) first variety of Brassica Juncea (Mustard) developed in the world by **Prof. V.L. Chopra**.
- The help of biotechnology through somatic hybridization in India.

Sunflower (Helianthus annuus)

- **Robust oilseed crop**, 40-50% oil content.
- High in **vitamins A, D, and E**, and good keeping quality.
- **Hulls** are used in **animal feed** or as fuel.
- Performs well under **moist conditions** but sensitive to drought.
- **Decortication** produces high-fiber byproducts for roughage.
- '**Chaffiness**' means non-filling of seed.
- **Birds** (particularly parrots) rats & squirrels cause damage to sunflowers when it is raised in Isolated and stray pockets.
- **Helios** means **'Sun'** and Anthus means '**Flower**.'
- High temperature above 38°C during post-anthesis periods reduces seed field and oil content.
- The highest **FUFA** quantity is present in sunflower oil.

- Insecticidal spray during the flowering period is harmful because it affects the visit of honeybees.
- It has a high seed multiplication ratio (>180).
- It's growing in all three seasons.
- Karnataka is first in India, both area and production and U.P. is first in productivity of sunflower.
- Russia is first in both area and production of sunflower.
- Seeds should be dried well to the moisture content at 9-10% before storage.
- Spraying of borax (0.2% ie 2 g/lit) directly to the capitulum at the ray floret opening. stage increases seed filling yield and oil content.
- Sunflower is a day-neutral plant of the Compositae family
- Sunflower comes in four main oilseed crops in the world.
- Sunflower oil is best for heart disease patients because presents high level of unsaturated fatty acids and vita-E is more.

Safflower (Carthamus tinctorius)

- Cultivated for **oil production**, oil content 35-45%.
- Traditionally known for **dye production**.
- **Thistle-like herb**, grown in marginal soils.
- **Oil cake** used in **animal feed** and as manure.
- Contains **bitter flavour compounds** that can be reduced in processing.
- 2-3 irrigations are required for safflower cultivation.
- In India, Maharashtra is first in both area and production.
- In the world, India is first in both area and production.
- Percentage of unsaturated fatty acid -78%.
- Safflower can grow in dried areas.
- Safflower contains 32-36% oil (used for food) and 41% linolic acid and is also used for making paint, and varnish.
- The Safflower crop is known as fencing crop/Border crop.
- Safflower oil is best for heart patients.
- The colour is obtained from its flower.
- Topping 40-50 DAS to increase later branching.

Linseed (Linum usitatissimum)

1. Primarily used for **industrial oil**, rich in linolenic acid.
2. **Flax fibres** are strong, used in **linen production**.
3. Oil is used in **paints, varnishes, and inks**.
4. **Oilcake** is good for **milch animals** and as manure.
5. Grows in **cooler climates**, suitable for **rainfed** conditions.
6. **'Seedball' word** is used for linseed seeds

7. **Canada** is first in both the area and production of linseed.
8. **Flex** is used for making sports material
9. The flower color of linseed is Bue.
10. Highest cultivation of linseed in **M.P.**
11. It is called oilseed cum **fiber**,
12. Linseed is a less water-requireable crop.
13. Linseed is grown for both oilseed and fiber purposes.
14. Linseed is grown in the ***Rabi*** season.
15. The fiber of linseed is called ***Flex.***

Sugarcane (Saccharum officinarum)

- **Main source of sugar**, also used for **alcohol and ethanol**.
- Grows well in **tropical and subtropical** regions.
- **High water requirement**, crucial for **irrigation management**.
- **By-products** used in animal feed and **biofuel production**.
- Requires **fertile, well-drained soils** for optimal growth.
- **Burning of canes** is done to Improve sucrose and **Juice quality**.
- **The critical stage** of Irrigation in sugarcane is the Formative stage.
- Earthing in sugarcane should be done in June-July.
- For **brix reading**, juice should be taken from the **middle portion of the stalk**.
- A higher dose of **Nitrogen** decreases sucrose content.
- **Highest sugar** consumption in India in our world.
- Highest sugar industry in **Maharashtra**.
- Lodging concept Is given by scientist **HF. Clement**, it is the foliar diagnosis comparing the nutrient status of comparable leaves of high and low-field crop plants generally used in sugarcane in Hawaii **(1935).**
- Most popular planting method in **north** India.
- Saline soils are **unsuitable** for sugarcane.
- The state has the highest productivity of sugarcane in **Tamil Nadu**.
- **Tying** and **Earthing** are done in sugarcane to prevent the crop lodging.
- Under high temperatures, sucrose gets covered in glucose and the quantity of the produce becomes **poor**.

Sugar beet (Beta vulgaris)

- Grown in **cooler climates** for **sugar production**.
- High in **sugar content**, up to 18% by weight.
- Tolerates **frost**, grows well in **temperate zones**.
- Requires well-drained soils with **adequate nutrients**.
- Used in **biofuel production** and animal feed.

Tobacco

- The best tobacco for Cigarettes is **Flue Cured Virginia** (FCV).
- Central Tobacco Research Institute, situated at ***Rajahmundry, A.P.*** **(1947).**
- **Flue curing is** mainly used for cigarettes.
- In India, the first hybrid variety of tobacco is **GTH-1**.
- The maximum exportable tobacco type is **FCV**.
- Mild acidic (**pH 5-6**) are the best soils for Tobacco.
- The most widely distributed disease of **Tobacco Mosaic viral**.
- ***Nicotiana rustica a plant*** smaller than tobacco, with Nicotine content is 3.5-8.0%, Mostly grown in **heavysoils**.
- ***Nicotiana tabacum***, Plant height 150-250cm, Large and narrow leaf, Nicotine content is 0.5-5.5%,Grown in light soils.
- Non-Virginia type crops **cover maximum** area and production.
- **Potash** is essential for smoking tobacco.
- **Priming** is a Process in which mature leaves are removed; Leaf priming harvesting **(5-6)** is done mainly for Cigarette & wrapper tobacco.
- Removal of **lateral suckers' auxiliary buds** is called **De- Suckering**.
- **Remove flower heads** to improve the **size** and **quality** of leaves known as **topping**.
- Seed rate for the nursery of tobacco is **20-30 gm per 100m**.
- Seed rate of tobacco **2-3 Kg/ha**.
- **Stalk cut harvesting** is done mainly for Bidi, Hookah, Cigar, and Cheroot.
- There are two species of Indian tobacco, ***Nicotiana tabacum*** & ***Nicotiana rustica.***
- Tobacco best for Bidi & hookah is **non-Virginia type.**
- Tobacco **Caterpillar** is the most important pest in the **nursery**.
- Tobacco, Botanical name ***Nicotiana spp***.

Mentha (Mint)

- **Widely grown** for its **essential oil** content.
- Common types include **Japanese mint** and **Peppermint**.
- Used in **cosmetics, culinary**, and **medicinal** purposes.
- Requires **cool, moist climate** for optimal growth.

- **Intercropping** with other crops helps control weeds.

Lemongrass (Cymbopogon spp.)

- Primarily grown for **citral**, used in **Vitamin A** production.
- Requires **warm, humid climates** with **well-drained** soils.
- **High water requirement** and susceptible to **water-logging**.
- Oil yield increases after the **second year** of planting.
- **Distillation method** affects the **quality** and **yield** of oil.

Citronella (Cymbopogon winterianus)

- A **perennial aromatic herb** cultivated for its **essential oil**.
- Thrives in **tropical and subtropical** regions with **high rainfall**.
- Propagated **vegetatively** through **slips**.
- Oil is primarily used in **insect repellents** and **fragrances**.
- Requires **four harvests** per year for optimal oil production.

Berseem (Trifolium alexandrinum)

- **Annual leguminous fodder** crop grown in **irrigated** areas.
- Tolerates **water-logged conditions**, making it ideal for **low-altitude** regions.
- **Nitrogen-fixing** crop, improves soil fertility.
- Requires **5-6 cuttings** per year for maximum **green fodder** production.
- Grows best in **cool, dry climates** with **clay loam soils**.

Lucerne (Medicago sativa)

- Known as the **queen of fodder crops**, a **perennial legume**.
- Provides **high-protein** green fodder with **multiple cuttings** per year.
- Prefers **well-drained loamy soils**, sensitive to **acidic soils**.
- Requires **adequate irrigation** and **phosphorous-rich soils** for growth.
- Popular for its ability to **rejuvenate soil** and **fix nitrogen**.

Oats (Avena sativa)

- **Dual-purpose crop**, used for **fodder** and **grain production**.
- Thrives in **cool climates** and grows well under **irrigated** or **rainfed** conditions.
- **Nutrient-rich fodder**, containing up to **14.6% protein**.
- Provides **3-4 cuttings** in a season under **ideal conditions**.
- Grows well in **all soil types** except waterlogged soils.

Horticulture

General Horticulture

- All fruits in general are acidic.
- Aonla has a higher amount of Vit. C.
- The aroma of over overripe fruit of banana is due to Isopentanol.
- **Asparagus** is a perennial crop.
- Avocado fruit is also known as butter fruit.
- Bael is the richest source of **Vit-B2 (riboflavin).**
- Baradari is an important feature of the **Mughal Garden**.
- Best planting material for pineapple Slip.
- Best suited crop as intercrop in Banana Papaya.
- Blackheart of potato due to **Oxygen deficiency**.
- Blacktip in mango is caused by to harmful effect of brick kiln fumes which contain carbon monoxide (CO), SO, and acetylene.
- Blanching in vegetables is done to inactivate enzyme activities.
- **Blanching** is an important process for Cauliflower.
- **Blindness** (absence of curd or head in Cole crops) is a disorder of Cole crops **due to frost.**
- ***Bolero*** is the variety of Marigold.
- Botanically pineapple is a syncarpous (multiple) fruit known as sorosis and 1 it has originated in Brazil.
- Botanically, Chinese guava is ***Psidium friedrichsthalia***.
- Bronzing in guava is caused by a deficiency of Zn.
- Buttoning (The formation of small curds in cauliflower) is due to a **deficiency of nitrogen.**
- Calcium carbide is used for artificial ripening in bananas.
- **California** Paper shell is a variety of almonds.
- The causal organism of Fig rust is ***Ceratolium fici.***
- The chief pollinating agent in onion is a **Honey bee.**
- **Cider** is prepared by **Apple** & **pear**.
- Citranges have originated as a result of a cross between Trifoliate orange & sweet orange.
- Citrus grandis (Pummelo), Citrus latifolia (Tahiti lime), and Citrus medica (Citron) are the three mono-embryonic species of Citrus.
- Coconut fat rich source of **Lauric acid.**
- Coconut is propagated by **Seeds**.

- Coffee leaf rust is caused by the ***Hemelia vestratrix.***
- The concentration of sugar used for preservation is **60-70 %.**
- Contender is a popular variety of French bean tolerant to powdery mildew and mosaic.
- Crescent is well known for its flower arrangement.
- Cricket Ball, CO 1 (Cricket ball x Oval), CO 2, DHS 1, DHS 2, PKM 2, PKM 3, Kallipati, Calcutta.
- The cross protection technique is effective in checking the tristeza virus in acid lime (C. aurantifolia).
- Deciduous types of ber ***Z. jujuba.***
- Developed small curds in young plants with less developed leaves are known as buttoning.
- The development of an embryo without fertilization is known as **Apomixis**.
- The development of fruits without fertilization is called **Parthenocarpy**.
- Dioecious fruit plants **Papaya, dale palm, grape.**
- Double century is the variety of **coconut**.
- A dwarf mutant cultivar of papaya Pusa Nanha (Dioecious) was developed at the IARI Regional Station, Pusa Bihar.
- An early variety of ***ber*** is Gola.
- Edible banana fruit is seedless because of **Embryo abortions**.
- The edible part of cauliflower is **curd.**
- Edible parts of **asparagus** are **Underground young shoots** (known as spears).
- ***Feni*** (drink) is prepared from cashew apple & Coconut.
- The finest fruit of the world is **Mongo steen**.
- Flower pedicels of velvety curds elongate and such condition is known as fuzziness.
- The forking of carrots is due to **Compact soil.**
- Foster, Thompson, and burgundy pigmented grapefruit (Citrus paradisi) are periclinal chimeras by somatic mutations in white grapes.
- Fruit crop suitable for the cold desert of cold arid zone Apricot.
- Fruit of Bael is botanically known as a hard-shelled berry containing marmelosin an active ingredient (in all parts) and this fruit is the richest source of Riboflavin.
- The fruit of okra is a **Capsule**.
- Fruit of rose known as **Hips**.
- Fruit with maximum iron content Karonda.

- GA_3 is the most used growth regulator for berry elongation and quality improvement in grapes.
- Garlic is propagated by **bulbils.**
- Gladiolus is an indicator plant for fluoride pollution even at very low concentrations. (1 ppb). 1,50,000 corms can be accommodated in one ha area.
- Granulated fruits of Citrus are characterized by a decrease in total solubility.
- Grapes are generally dried in the **sun.**
- Guava and Jamun both belong to the family Myrtaceae.
- Guava bears mostly on Current season growth.
- The harvesting stage for long-distance transport of muskmelon is the **Half-slip stage.**
- ***Helopeltis antonii*** (tea mosquito bug) causes shoot blight or inflorescence blight and can be controlled by a spray of carbaryl (0.05%), quinalphos (0.05%), or phosphomidon (0.03%).
- High-density planting in pineapple accommodates plants of about 60,000 / ha.
- The highest oil-producing tree plant is Oil Palm.
- The Horticulture Society of India was established in 1942.
- Inarching in mango in India was suggested by S.K. Mukherjee.
- Incompatibility and polyploidy are two serious problems in **ber** improvement.
- India ranked first in vegetable production in the year 2004-05, whereas in the year 2007-08, China ranked first.
- India's share in the fruit production in the World is **10%.**
- Inflorescence of cabbage known as **Cat ken.**
- Inflorescence of cauliflower is known as **Cyme.**
- Jackfruit is commonly propagated through seeds, air layering, grafting, and budding.
- Jade Cross, Hills Ideal, and Rubine are improved varieties of Brussels sprouts ***(Brassica oleracea var gemmifera)*** and 500 g of seed is enough to raise seedlings for one ha.
- Jam is prepared by boiling the fruit pulp with enough sugar (minimum 68 %) to a reasonably thick consistency, whereas jelly is prepared by fruit juices/ or clear water extract from the fruit.
- **Kent** is the mutant variety of Coffee.
- Kesar (saffron) belongs to the family of **Iridiceae.**
- King of arid fruit Ber.

- King of temperate fruits Apple.
- Kinnow is a hybrid between ***Citrus nobilis*** & ***Citrus deliciosa***.
- Kinnow Mandarin is a hybrid between the king (***Citrus nobilis***) and leaf (***Citrus deliciosa***) developed at Citrus Experiment Station, California by **HB Frost** in 1935.
- Kniffin system of training in grape was developed by **William Kniffin (USA).**
- Largest importer of cut flowers in the world **Germany.**
- The largest producer of citrus in the world USA.
- Lime is a good source of **Vitamin C.**
- Litchi is propagated through air layering, is native to southern China, and belongs to the family Sapindaceae. (Bihar is the leading producer of Litchi).
- Little leaf of brinjal is transmitted by leaf hopper (***Amrasca biguttula***).
- M9 is a dwarf rootstock of apple that evolved as a chance seedling, whereas M27 is an ultra dwarf rootstock developed as a result of a cross between M13 x M9.
- Mango is mostly propagated through **Veneer grafting**.
- The mango variety suitable for high-density planting is ***Amrapali.***
- Monoecious species of papaya Carica monoica.
- The most salt-tolerant fruit crop is the **Date palm**.
- The most suitable fruit for avoiding scurvy is **Aonla.**
- Multi-storeyed cropping is popular in **Coconut plantations**.
- Oil Palm plantation crop is also known as smallholder irrigated crops.
- Oleoresin is an important product of **Chilli seeds**.
- Only citrus fruit that contains malic acid sweet lime.
- The origin place of the Date palm is **Iraq**.
- The outer layer of papaya seed which hinders germination is called Sarcotesta.
- ***Pajaro*** is a variety of Strawberry.
- Peach leaf curl is caused by the fungus ***Taphrina deformes***.
- The planting season for deciduous plants is **Jan- Feb**.
- Plants grow without terminal buds and fail to form any curd in cauliflower is called blindness.
- Pollination in fig carried by fig wasp (***Blastophaga pens***).
- Pollination in oil palm is carried by **Weevil**.
- **Polyembryony** is present in fruit crops Mango, Citrus, and Jamun.
- Pomology is derived from the **Greek word**.
- Predominant organic acid present in grape **Tartaric acid**.

- Pungency and red color in chili are due to capsaicin and capsaithin pigments, respectively.
- Pusa Bedana is a seedless hybrid having aborted embryos and false seeds, whereas Sugar Baby is an introduction from the USA.
- Pusa Majesty and Pusa Delicious varieties of papaya are Gynodioecious.
- **Pusa ruby** is a variety of tomatoes.
- Pusa snowball is a variety of **Cauliflower**.
- Queen of beverage crop Tea.
- The Quincunx system accommodates (Times) more plants than the square system.
- Rangpur lime is the most preferred rootstock for sweet orange and mandarin in Central and South India.
- The richest source of vitamin **'C'** is **Barbados** cherry.
- Round are improved varieties of Sapota (Climacteric fruit).
- Rubber is native to Brazil.
- **Saffron** is obtained from **Style** and **Stigma**.
- Sago (***Sabudana***) is prepared from the roots of **Cassava/Topiaca**.
- Sanjose scale is the most serious pest of **Apple**.
- The seed of carrot is known as **Schizocarp**.
- Seedlessness in grapes is due to Stenospermocarpy.
- The sex form of watermelon is Monoecious Seed rate of hybrid tomato is **100-150 g/ha**.
- The sex ratio in cucurbits is modified by **silver nitrate.**
- Skiffing is practiced in tea and it is the lightest form of pruning, whereas collar pruning is the severe most pruning used for rejuvenation of tea gardens.
- Sodium benzoate is used to preserve colored juices/pulps along with citric acid (only in non-acid fruits), whereas KMS is used to preserve most of the pulps/juices.
- Spacing recommended for ***Pusa Nanha*** variety of papaya **1.25 x 1.25 m^2.**
- Spray of NAA @ 200 ppm in Oct-Nov followed by de-blossoming (Feb-March) to control the malformation.
- ***Swaran roopa*** is the early variety of Litchi.
- Tea is commonly propagated by **Softwood cutting**.
- The common chemical preservative for colorless fruits is **KMS.**
- The dwarf variety of mango ***Amrapali***.
- The exclusion of micro-organisms is known as **asepsis**.
- The fruit of the pineapple is known as **Sorosis.**

- The hard fruits of citrus are due to **Boron** deficiency
- The main insect responsible for pollination in mango Common house fly.
- The nutrient that improves the quality of fruit is K.
- The term stenospermocarpy was coined in 1936 by Stout.
- The bromine in cacao is extracted from Bark.
- Thompson seedless, Pusa seedless, Delight, Perlette, and Beauty Seedless belong to Stenospermocarpy, whereas Black Corianth shows vegetative Parthenocarpy.
- To enhance the vase life of gladiolus spikes, pulsing with 20% sucrose and 200 ppm hydroxyl quinoline citrate for 24 hrs is excellent. Cut spikes can be stored successfully for 2 weeks at 1-2°C.
- Turnip is grown for roots and propagated through seeds. (d) Cauliflower is grown for curd (economic part), whereas, the economic part of cabbage is head.
- **Umran** is the Iate ripening cultivar of ***ber.***
- Under metaxenia, pollens have a direct effect on somatic tissues of fruit resulting in early or late ripening, and changes in colour and size of fruit and seed.
- The vector for transmission of the tristeza virus in citrus is Toxoptera citricida.
- Watermelon fruit is the richest source of Iron amongst cucurbits and it contains about 92 % water, 7 % carbohydrates, 0.2 % protein, and 0.3 minerals.
- whereas the highest Vit. C containing fruit is Barbados cherry.
- **The Cacao** beverage crop is referred to as the food of God.
- Whiptail of cauliflower due to **Mo deficiency**.

Mango

- Widely grown in **India** for 400 years, called "**King of Fruits**"
- **Alphonso** popular but prone to **spongy tissue disorder**
- **Totapuri** essential for **processing** due to high quality
- **High-density planting** boosts yield
- Varieties like **Mallika** and **Arka Puneet** have superior qualities
- ***Alphanso*** Variety is suitable for processing in mango.
- **Amrapali** (Dwarf Variety) is a cross of ***Dasheri x Neelam (DNA)***.
- ***Amrapali*** is a dwarf mango variety.
- ***Arka anmol*** is a cross of ***Alphanso x Janardan pasand (AJA)***.
- **Arka aruna** is a cross of ***Banganpali x Alphanso (ABA)***.

- Botanical name ***Mangifera Indica***, Origin **Indo-Burma**.
- ***The cagging*** technique of breeding was first used by **Dr. N. Singh**.
- **Clustering/*Jhumka*** in mango occurs due to **Low temperature, improper pollination,** and **fertilization.**
- Control of Blacktip by **Borax spray**.
- De-blossoming is done for the Control of **malformation**.
- Fruit-type mango is a **drup.**
- Good mango varieties have a 20% TSS.
- India ranked first in mango production (>50% share of the world).
- The inflorescence of mango is **Panicle**.
- Internal fruit necrosis is due to **Boron** deficiency.
- Langra and Dashari are **Alternate-bearing** varieties.
- Leaf scorching occurs due to **Potassium** deficiency.
- Mango is a type of Climacteric and tropical fruit.
- Mango is the richest source of **Vitamin A**.
- Mango malformation is caused by **cold temperatures**.
- Mango pollination by **houseflies**.
- mango powdery mildew (***Odium manifested***) is the **primary disease.**
- Mango propagation occurs using the **Veneer grafting** method.
- **Neelam** and **Totapuri** are **Regular-bearing** varieties.
- Off season variety is ***Niranjan*** & ***Madhulica***.
- Primary Mango Pests (***Amritodues atkinsoni***).
- Quarantine important pest of mango is the **Stone weevil.**
- Ratna is a cross of ***Neelam x Alphanso*** **(RNA)**.
- The recently developed method of Epicotyl stone grafting (MH).
- Seedless mango is known as ***Sindhu***.
- ***Sindhu*** is a cross of ***Ratna x Alphanso (RAS).***
- Spongy tissue is due to **Convection heat** (Highly susceptible Alphonso).
- ***Sugandha*** Hybrid variety of regular bearing and free from malformation.
- The sweetest mango verity is ***chausa***.
- **U.P.** first in mango production.

Papaya

- Yields **papain**, used in **medicine** and **industry**
- Dioecious, hermaphrodite, and gynodioecious **types** exist
- **Tamil Nadu** ideal for cultivation, low disease incidence

- Needs **controlled pollination** for purity
- Prefers **well-drained soil**, intolerant to frost
- Banana is propagated by **Suckers/ Corms**.
- **Bunchy top** disease of Banana transmitted by **aphids.**
- **Bunchy top** is the most serious disease of Banana.
- Cut rhizomes used for propagation are known as **Peepers.**
- The diploid banana variety is **Lady Finger**.
- The ideal temperature range to grow bananas is **20-40 °C.**
- In the world, the largest producer of India. In India, **Tamilnadu.**
- Infectious chlorosis in bananas is caused by **viruses**.
- Most of the cultivated edible banana is **Triploid in nature**.
- ***Narendra*** is the best variety for making chips.
- Ripe banana has a sugar content of **26% to 27%.**
- Scientific name is ***Musa acuminate***, native of ***Southeast Asia***.
- Seedless of banana is due to **Vegetative parthenocarpy**.
- A serious fungal disease of Bananas is **Sigatoka leaf spot.**
- **Spadix** is an Inflorescence of the banana.
- Temperature and humidity for banana storage are **13°C** and **85-90%**.
- The stem above the ground in a banana is known as **Pseudostem**.
- Vector of bunchy top virus spread by Aphids.
- The weight of sword suckers generally used **500-750 gm.**
- ***Carica papaya*** Tropical America.
- **CO-5** variety is suitable for papain production.
- **Damping off** Is a most serious/ disease of papaya seedlings.
- Enzyme, **Pepsin** is present in the dried latex of papaya.
- Milk is obtained from the unripe fruit of papaya known as **Papain**.
- Papaya is commercially propagated by **Seed**.
- Papaya is most susceptible to ***Waterlogging***.
- Papaya leaf curl virus is transmitted by **Whiteflies**.
- **Papin** is extracted from **Unmatured fruit**.
- Percent of male plants required in dioecious varieties is **10%.**
- Seed rate of papaya **200-300 gm/ha**.
- The yellow pigment in Papaya is due to ***Caricaxanthin***.

Pineapple

- Thrives in **mild tropical climates** on well-drained **hill slopes**
- Primary varieties: **Kew, Mauritius, Queen**

- **Uniform flowering** induced by **NAA** and **Ethephon**
- **High-density planting** increases yield
- Major pest: **mealy bugs**, controlled by **insecticides**

Banana

- Originates from **Southeast Asia**, one of the oldest fruits
- Derived from **M. acuminata** and **M. balbisiana** hybrids
- **Sword suckers** preferred for propagation
- **Micropropagation** through tissue culture
- **High-density planting** with irrigation improves yield

Avocado

- Types **A** and **B** needed for **pollination**
- Sensitive to **poor drainage** and saline soils
- **Ripens post-harvest** within 6-12 days
- Nutrient deficiency affects **fruit size** and growth
- **Cross-pollination** essential due to dichogamy

Sapota

- Known as **chiku**, thrives in **coastal India**
- Best in **deep alluvium** or **sandy loam** soil
- Grafted on **Manilkhara hexandra** for high returns
- Tolerates **salts** in soil and irrigation
- **8x4 m high-density** planting boosts yield

Guava

- **"Poor man's apple"**, rich in **vitamin C** and **calcium**
- Grows in **subtropical/tropical climates**, drought-resistant
- Propagated by **air layering, grafting**
- **Micronutrient spray** improves yield
- **Pruning** removes suckers, stimulates fruiting
- ***Arka mirdula*** is Soft soft-seeded dwarf variety of Guava.
- **Bronzing** in Guava occurs due to **Zn** deficiency.
- Guava is susceptible to **Acidic soils.**
- Guava, red-fleshed variety of **Hafsi.**
- **Hybrid 45** is a cross of the **Allahabad safeda x Sardar** (Lucknow -49).
- In India, **Uttar Pradesh** with higher production.
- ***Psidium guajava.*** Family **Myrtaceae**, 2n = 22, Origin West Indies to Peru.
- The Seedless Guava variety is ***Behat coconut***.
- The most common and cheapest method of Guava propagation was **Stooling/Air layering.**

Jackfruit

- Large fruit grown in **humid climates** up to 1200 m altitude
- Firm and soft **flesh varieties** exist
- **Hybrids** like **Singapore Jack** bear fruit early
- Seeds **edible**, used in cooking
- Grows best in **loamy soils**, slight acidity

Tamarind

- **Drought-tolerant**, acidic fruit high in **tartaric acid**
- Grows in varied soils, **prefers loamy**
- **Seed propagation** common; grafting improves quality
- Used in **medicine, food preservation, seasoning**
- **Long-lived**, low maintenance

Carambola (Starfruit)

- **Star-shaped**, high juice content
- Grows in warm, humid climates with **deep clay loam soils**
- Varieties like **Golden Star** are **crisp, juicy**
- Requires **heavy irrigation**
- Propagated by **grafting, air-layering**

Mangosteen

- Slow-growing tree with **sweet flesh**
- Thrives in **warm, humid climates, organic soils**
- Seed-propagated, **grafting** preferred for quicker fruiting
- Takes **8-10 years** to bear fruit, high market demand
- Known for **medicinal, antioxidant** properties

Passion Fruit

- **Vine** grown for juicy fruit high in **vitamins A, C**
- Prefers **well-drained** sandy loam, pH 5.5-6.5
- Needs **trellis support**, grown in hilly areas
- Varieties like **Purple Passion** for juice
- Major pests: **fruit flies, aphids**

Rambutan

- Tropical "**hairy litchi**" with sweet flavour
- Warm, humid climates with **rich soils**
- Annual rainfall **2000-2800 mm** needed
- Used **fresh, canned, syrup** products
- Popular varieties: **Rohug-Rian, Seematjan**

Longan

- Related to **lychee**, sweet flavour

- Best in warm climates, **high humidity**
- Moisture essential during **flowering, fruiting**
- Varieties: **Kohala, Biew Kiew**
- Propagated by **air-layering**

Durian

- Known as "**King of Fruits**" for strong odor
- Needs **high humidity, well-drained soils**
- Fruits in **7-10 years**, popular varieties: **Golden Pillow**
- **Odor** from **sulfur compounds**
- **Pruned** for air circulation, quality

Citrus

- Grows in subtropical climates, **500-1500 m elevation**
- **Nagpur Santra** top mandarin variety in India
- **Fruit cracking** managed with **light irrigation**
- **Granulation** prevented by nutrient balance
- High-density planting improves **yield, quality**

Grapes

- Needs **warm, dry summers**, cool winters
- **Biannual pruning** in Tamil Nadu
- Resistant rootstocks: **Vitis riparia**
- **Seedless grapes** like Anab-e-Shahi for fresh use
- **GA3 spray** increases berry size
- The best variety for Raisin is **Kismis Bely**.
- **The Bower Training system** of grapes is mostly used in **India**.
- Calyx end rot occurs due to **Ca** deficiency.
- Due to improper pollination and fertilization in grapes, caused **Berry/ Blossom** drop.
- Grape is a Deciduous crop.
- Grape is propagated by **Hardwood cuttings**.
- Hen & chicken disease occurs due to **Bo** deficiency.
- **Magnesium** is universally deficient in **grapes**.
- The major disease of grapes Downey Mildew (***Plasmophora viticola***).
- **Milky latex** created by **unripe sapota** fruits is known as **Chuckle** (It forms the base for makingChicklets and chewing gum).
- **NAA (50 ppm)** is used to reduce post-harvest fruit drop in grapes.
- Pink berry formation occurs due to **High temperatures**.
- The planting time of the rooted cutting of the grapes is **Jan - Feb**.
- The planting time of unrooted cuttings of the grapes is ***October***.

- Powdery mildew of grapes is caused by ***Erysiphe viti.***
- Scientific name ***Vitis vinifera*** (15-25% sucrose in present).
- ***Tartaric acid*** is present in grapefruits.
- **Thompson seedless** is the most cultivated famous variety of grapes.

Pomegranate

- Thrives in **cool winter, hot summer**
- Soft-seeded types like **Ganesh** in demand
- **Fruit cracking** managed by soil moisture
- **Rooted cuttings** common for propagation
- Multi-stem **training** prevents pest issues

Litchi

- Suited for **subtropical regions** with dry winters
- **Muzaffarpur** variety prized for sweetness
- Propagated by **air-layering, cuttings**
- Major pests: **leaf rollers, bark feeders**
- **Mulching, irrigation** key in dry climates

Apple

- Requires **temperate climate** with cold winters
- Dwarf rootstocks like **M9** improve yield
- **Pruning** essential for productive growth
- **Apple scab** controlled with fungicides
- **Controlled atmosphere** storage extends life
- Scientific name ***Malus domestica***, Origin **Asia Minor**.
- Apple is propagated by **Shield budding** and **grafting**.
- **Himachal Pradesh** is the Apple Bowl of India.
- Redness in Apple is due to **Anthocyanin**.
- The country is leading in Apple production in **China.**
- The aroma of ripe apple is also due to **Isopentanol**.

Loquat

- Best in **subtropical, temperate climates**
- Primarily propagated by **seeds, grafting**
- **Pruning** improves air flow, fruit quality
- High in **pectin**, good for jams
- **Fruit flies** managed with traps, insecticides

Pear

- Thrives in **temperate climates** with cold winters
- Two types: **European, Asian** pears
- **Fire blight** resistant varieties like **Moonglow**

- **T-budding, grafting** on quince rootstocks
- Tatura trellis **boosts orchard yield**

Peach

- Needs **warm climate**, sandy loam soil
- Resistant rootstocks like **Nemaguard**
- High in **sugars, carotenoids**
- **Sunscald, split pit** common disorders
- T-budding propagation for **varietal purity**

Plum

- Suited for cold winters, warm summers
- Japanese plums **frost-sensitive**
- Used in **jams, dried prunes**
- **Myrobalan rootstocks** improve resistance
- **Pruning, thinning** enhance fruit quality

Apricot

- Prefers **temperate climate**, alkaline soil
- Rootstocks like **P. armeniaca** resist nematodes
- **Early frost** affects fruit set
- High in **vitamins A, C**, suitable for drying
- T-budding, **grafting** common propagation

Cherries

- Suited to **temperate regions**, prone to **frost**
- Main types: **sweet** and **sour cherry**
- **Netting** prevents bird pests
- Harvested carefully as **overripe fruit** deteriorates
- Budding, grafting on **Mahaleb, Mazzard** rootstocks

Berries

- Strawberries prefer **cool climate**, well-drained soil
- Varieties determine **cropping pattern**
- **Runners** used for propagation
- **Mulching, drip irrigation** improve yield
- Pests: **aphids, spider mites**

Persimmon

- Best in **subtropical, temperate regions**
- Types: **astringent, non-astringent**
- Minimal pruning needed; **thinning** for quality
- Grafted on **D. lotus, D. virginiana** rootstocks
- Issues: **sunscald, cracking**

Kiwifruit

- Requires **subtropical to temperate climate**
- High trellis systems like **T-bar**
- Male-female vine **ratio 1:8** for pollination
- **Wind-sensitive**, windbreaks necessary
- Susceptible to **root rot**

Walnut

- Temperate climate with cold winters
- **Black walnut rootstock** resists disease
- **Grafted propagation** for quality
- Irrigation critical in **nut development**
- **Long-lived**, high-yield

Almond

- Thrives in **warm climate**, well-drained soil
- **Frost-sensitive** during bloom
- High in **oil**, used in snacks, confectionery
- **Pruning** improves tree health
- T-budding onto peach or almond rootstocks

Pecan Nut

- Needs **warm climate**, alluvial soil
- **Grafted pecans** improve quality
- Heavy **irrigation** required during growth
- **Pecan nut weevil** managed by IPM
- High in **oils, protein**

Hazelnut

- Prefers **temperate climates**
- **Pollination** needs compatible varieties
- Propagated by **layering, grafting**
- **Suckers** removed regularly
- Eastern filbert **blight** managed by fungicides

Chestnut

- Grows in **temperate climates**
- **Grafted** for varietal integrity
- Bears nuts in **5-7 years**
- **Hand-harvested** when ripe
- **Consumed roasted, boiled**

Other fruit crops

- Acid content is a very important consideration for the preparation of Jelly.
- Anola is commercially propagated by **T-budding/ patch.**
- **Ber** is a King of arid fruit and a poor man Apple.
- Ber is commercially propagated by the **Ring & T- T-budding**.
- Central Research Institute for Banana is situated in ***Tiruchirappalli (TN).***
- Century plant is known as the **Date palm**.
- Cider is prepared by **Apple & Pear**.
- Citrus is commercially propagated by **Seeds/ Air layering**.
- Citrus, Fruit type of Hesperidum.
- Coconut is propagated by **Seeds.**
- Concentration of salt preservation **10-25%.**
- Country first in area and production of **pomegranate India**.
- The country is leading in Litchi and Peaches production in **China**.
- ***Cricket ball*** and ***Murrabba*** are a famous variety of **Sapota**.
- **Daru** is a Wild type of pomegranate.
- Date palm is commercially propagated by **Offshoot/ suckers**.
- Date palm is rich in **Iron**.
- The development of an embryo without fertilization is called **Apomixis.**
- The development of fruits without fertilization is called **Parthenocarpy**.
- The element of **Boron** is improving the quality of fruits.
- Family of cashew **Anacardiaceae.**
- Fruits can be processed at a temperature of **100°C.**
- Guava is commercially propagated by **Stooling / Air layering**.
- The hardness of citrus fruit is due to **Boron** deficiency.
- A highly salt-tolerant fruit tree is the **Date palm**.
- *Kinnow* is a cross between **King sweet x Willow Leaf mendarins**.
- Laddu is a variety of **Mandarin (Citrus fruit**).
- Leathery rind skin found in **Citrus.**
- Little leaf and Dieback of citrus due to **Cu** deficiency.
- Little leaf of Litchi Due to **zinc** deficiency.
- **Maharashtra** first in pomegranate production.

- ***Makhana is*** also known as **Fox nuts**.
- **Mesocarp** Is the Edible part of Papaya & Mango, Ber - **Pericarp**, Litchi - **Fleshy aril**, Apple & strawberry- **Thalamus**, Coconut- **Endosperm**, Pineapple - bracts, Pomegranate - **Juicy seed coat**, Citrus- **juicy placenta hair**.
- The National Horticulture Board is situated in ***Gurugram (Haryana)***.
- Origin of Date palm, **Iraq.**
- Polyembryony is present in fruits like **Mango, Citrus, and Jamun**.
- Pomegranate is commercially propagated by **Cutting/ Air layering**.
- **Queen** of fruits **Litchi**.
- Rayan as the rootstock is a commercial method of **Sapota**.
- The red colour of pomegranate is due to **Anthocyanin**.
- Research Centre for Date palm is situated at **Bikaner.**
- ***Sapota*** is commercially propagated by **Inarching**.
- Seed less variety of **acid lime (Kagzi Lime)**.
- Vitamin **C** is lost during processing.
- Yellow leaf of citrus due to **Mo** Deficiency.

warm-season vegetables

Tomato

- **Tomato** originated in **Peru**, and its name derives from the **Aztec word** "Tomato."
- Rich in **Vitamin C (27 mg)** and **Vitamin A (900 IU)**, making it a prime protective food.
- **Lycopene** provides the **red color**, while **carotene** gives a **yellow hue** in fruits.
- Optimal growth in warm climates, but **sensitive to frost**.
- Used in **sauces, soups, and salads**, and is a good **appetizer**.
- A period of drought followed by sudden heavy irrigation during fruiting may cause **Cracking of Fruits,**
- BER (Blossom end rot) disease is due to **Ca** deficiency.
- Botanical name ***Solanum lycopersicum*** (old name is ***Lycopersicon esculentium***), Pimpinellifolium (small fruited), or currant tomato wild species, Origin in Peru.
- The chemical used for sauce preservation is **Sodium benzoate**.

- The Edible Parts of Tomato is **Pericap** and Placenta, it is also called fruits **Protective Food.**
- Fruit borer (***Helicoverpo spp.***) is a major pest of tomato.
- Fruit cracking occurs due to a deficiency of **Boron** deficiency.
- The fruit type of tomato is **Berry.**
- Plant type of tomato **Day neutral** and self-pollinated plant.
- **Puffiness** occurs due to **Poor pollination, temperature fluctuation,** and **heavy rains.**
- Seed rate of tomato 400-500 gm/ha, Hybrid **100-150 gm/ha.**
- Sunscald occurs due to the exposure of fruits in high temperatures> **40°C.**
- Susceptible for Frost, Red colour is due to **Lycopene.**
- **Tomato Leaf curl virus** is a most serious virus disease.
- Tomato leaf curl virus is transmitted by **Whiteflies.**

Brinjal (Eggplant)

- **Brinjal** (Eggplant) is a **warm-season crop** and thrives in **well-drained soils.**
- Susceptible to **bacterial wilt** and **little leaf disease**; **hybrids** are developed for resistance.
- A large number of **F1 hybrids** are used to improve **yield** and **disease tolerance.**
- Known for **long purple fruits,** like varieties such as **Pusa Hybrid 6.**
- Requires **moderate irrigation** and thrives in **temperatures between 20°C-30°C.**

Chilli

- **Chillies** are grown for their **pungency** and used both **green and dried.**
- Require **well-drained sandy loam soils** and prefer **warm climates.**
- **Whitefly** is the major vector for **yellow vein mosaic virus** (YVMV).
- Important in **spices** and **medicinal** applications due to **capsaicin content.**
- Best grown in areas with **moderate rainfall** and plenty of **sunlight.**

Muskmelon

- **Muskmelon** is a **summer crop,** best grown in **sandy loam soil** with good drainage.
- **Pollination** is by **honey bees,** with optimal flowering at **25°C-30°C.**
- The edible part is mostly **pericarp,** offering **high water content.**
- Commonly used for **dessert purposes** due to its **sweet flavour.**
- Fruits are **rich in vitamins,** including **Vitamin C.**

Watermelon

- **Watermelon** requires **well-drained, sandy soil** for best growth.
- Grows well in **warm climates**, with an ideal temperature range of **25°C-30°C.**
- Pollination is usually done by **bees**, and the fruits have a **high-water content.**
- **Rich in Lycopene**, beneficial for **heart health.**
- Grown mostly for **refreshing summer fruit**, high in **water** and **sugar content.**

Cucumber

- **Cucumber** is grown widely as a **warm-season crop** requiring **well-drained sandy loam soils.**
- Gynomonoecious and gynoecious forms are important for **F1 hybrid production.**
- **Pollination** occurs early morning, and **cross-pollination** is common.
- **Cucurbitacins**, which are bitter compounds, are present in some parts of the plant.
- **Sex modification** with plant growth regulators can improve the yield by increasing female flowers.

Bitter Gourd

- **Bitter gourd** thrives best in **warm climates** with **well-drained fertile soils.**
- It requires frequent **irrigation** during the fruiting stage for better yields.
- The plant is highly sensitive to **high temperatures** beyond 35°C, affecting fruit setting.
- **Bitter gourd juice** is valued for its **medicinal properties**, especially for treating **diabetes.**
- Seeds should be **scarified** or soaked for better germination.

Pumpkin

- **Pumpkin** is a vigorous **warm-season vine crop** that prefers **well-drained loamy soils.**
- **High yields** of 30-35 t/ha are achieved with proper spacing and soil management.
- **Cross-pollination** by bees plays a crucial role in the successful setting of fruits.
- **Fruits** should be harvested at **immature stages** to ensure better market quality.
- **Pruning** and **training on bowers** are recommended to maximize sunlight exposure and yield.

Okra

- **Okra** is a **warm-season crop** that thrives well in **tropical and subtropical climates.**
- **Yellow vein mosaic virus (YVMV)** is a major disease controlled through **resistant varieties.**
- Flowers are **cross-pollinated**, and optimal pollen fertility is achieved in the morning.
- **Axillary buds** must be removed to promote growth and flowering at the proper height.
- Okra tolerates **chromosome polymorphism**, which allows the development of high-yielding hybrids.

Cowpea

- **Cowpea** grows well in **warm conditions**, between 21-35°C, in **fertile loose soils.**
- Widely used for **fodder**, **green manure**, and **intercropping** in sustainable agriculture.
- **Rhizobium inoculation** is essential to enhance **nitrogen fixation** in new cultivation areas.
- **Aphids** and **Cercospora leaf spot** are common pests and diseases.
- Cowpea produces **edible pods** with high protein content, used as a vegetable or pulse.

Sweet Potato

- **Sweet potato** is propagated mainly through **terminal stem cuttings** due to high heterozygosity.
- It is grown for its **sweet root tubers**, which are rich in **starch (16%)** and **sugar (4%).**
- Requires **well-drained, fertile sandy loam soils** with a pH below **5.2** for optimal growth.
- The tubers are used in making **starch**, **syrup**, and **alcohol** and consumed boiled or baked.
- **Scarification** of seeds is required for promoting **germination**, as seeds have hard coats.

Cluster Beans (Guar)

- **Cluster beans** are known for being a **drought-tolerant crop** grown in **well-drained sandy loam soils.**
- The seeds are used for **guar gum**, widely utilized in the **textile and cosmetic industries.**
- Cultivated as both **vegetable and fodder**, it offers **high protein content** in its fruits.

- **Irrigation** is critical during flowering and fruiting stages to ensure **high yields**.
- **Pests** such as **Fusarium wilt** and **bacterial blight** are common, requiring management practices.

Amaranth

- **Amaranth** is a **short-duration crop** that responds well to **frequent irrigation**, especially for **leaf production**.
- It can be cultivated in **both tropical and subtropical regions** and is known for its **iron and calcium content**.
- The crop is sensitive to **premature flowering (bolting)**, which affects quality and yield.
- **Multi-cut varieties** can be harvested every **25-35 days**, making it ideal for leafy green production.
- Requires **light hoeing** to prevent soil crusting and promote **aeration**.

Basella (Malabar Spinach)

- **Basella** thrives in **warm, humid conditions** and is a **perennial climbing plant** cultivated for its edible leaves.
- The plant prefers **well-drained, fertile loam soils** rich in organic matter.
- **Basella alba** and **Basella rubra** are the two common types, known for their **succulent leaves**.
- Harvesting can be done in **multiple cuts**, and leaves are marketed as **spinach alternatives**.
- The plant has high content of **vitamin A** and **calcium**, making it nutritionally important.

Moringa

- **Moringa** (drumstick tree) is a **drought-resistant perennial** grown for its nutrient-rich leaves, flowers, and pods.
- The tree requires **well-drained sandy loam soil** and thrives best in **tropical climates**.
- **Moringa leaves** are rich in **vitamins A and C**, **calcium**, and are used in various **medicinal and nutritional applications**.
- Pods are harvested when **immature** and used in curries and soups, with multiple **harvests per year**.
- The plant tolerates a wide range of **soil pH levels**, making it versatile in **diverse agro-climatic conditions**.

Tapioca (Cassava)

- **Tapioca** is cultivated for its **starch-rich tubers**, often used for making **chips, sago, and vermicelli**.

- The crop is highly adaptable to **poor soils** and can be grown in **rainfed conditions**, especially in **Kerala**.
- **Cassava** requires a **well-drained soil** and thrives in **slightly acidic to neutral pH** conditions.
- **Tubers** are harvested after **8-12 months** and are a critical ingredient in **cattle feed** and **industrial products**.
- It produces **latex** and contains **cyanogenic glucosides**, which need to be removed through processing.

Carrot

- **Carrot** prefers **deep, loose, well-drained soils** for optimal root growth and quality.
- Rich in **beta-carotene**, which converts to **Vitamin A** in the body.
- **Temperature** around **16°C-18°C** is ideal for root development.
- Common varieties include **Nantes** and **Kuroda**, suited for different seasons.
- Carrot can be stored at **0°C and 90-95% relative humidity** for up to 5-6 months.

Radish

- **Radish** is a **short-duration crop** that prefers **cool temperatures** for optimal growth.
- Susceptible to **Alternaria blight** and **white rust**, especially under moist conditions.
- Best grown in **light sandy soils** for tender roots.
- Requires a temperature range of **10°C-15°C** for rapid growth and better-quality roots.
- Popular varieties include **Pusa Desi** and **Japanese White** for diverse climatic conditions.

Turnip

- **Turnip** thrives in **cool, moist climates** with **sandy loam soils**.
- **Roots** are tender and flavourful when grown at temperatures around **10°C-15°C**.
- Sensitive to **bolting** in hot climates, which affects root quality.
- **Purple Top White Globe** and **Golden Ball** are well-known varieties.
- Turnip is a rich source of **Vitamin C** and can be harvested 60-80 days after sowing.

Beetroot

- **Beetroot** prefers **slightly alkaline soils** for uniform root formation and better color development.
- Ideal temperature for growth is between **18°C-22°C**.

- **Chioggia** and **Detroit Dark Red** are common varieties grown for high yield.
- Rich in **antioxidants** like **betalain** and **Vitamin C.**
- **Seed production** requires **vernalization**, ensuring roots are exposed to cooler temperatures.

Cabbage

- **Cabbage** is a heavy feeder, requiring **well-drained fertile soils** and **regular irrigation**.
- **Molybdenum deficiency** causes **whiptail**, especially in acidic soils.
- Varieties include **Pusa Mukta** and **Golden Acre** for different climates.
- **Temperature** range of **15°C-20°C** is optimal for compact head formation.
- Stored at **0°C and 90-95% humidity**, cabbage can last for up to **5 months.**
- Anticancer properties due to **Indole-3-carbinol.**
- Botanical name ***Brassica oleracea var capitata***, Inflorescence **Catkin**, Edible part **head**.
- **Cruciferae (family)** belongs to all cole crops.
- Flavour in cabbage leaves Due to glucoside '***sinigrin***'. Optimum pH range **5-6.5.**
- Major pest DBM (***Plutella xylostella***).
- Seed rate **500-750 gm**.
- **Tip burn** disease is due to **Calcium** deficiency.

Cauliflower

- **Cauliflower** prefers **cool, moist climates** with well-drained, fertile loam soils.
- Common disorders include **chlorosis** due to **magnesium deficiency** and **hollow stem** caused by **boron deficiency**.
- **Blanching** is an important practice to avoid curds turning yellow when exposed to sunlight.
- Popular varieties include **Pusa Snowball K-1** and **Early Kunwari**, developed for Indian plains.
- **Ideal temperature** for curd initiation is **12°C-16°C**, and the crop is sensitive to **frost**.
- All Cole crops are **Protogyny**.
- **Blanching** is an important process of cauliflower.
- **Blindness** disorder occurs due to **Low temperature** and **frost**.

Buttoning occurs due to **Nitrogen** deficiency.

- Botanical name ***Brassica oleracea* var *botrytis***, Native **Cyprus**, Edible part **curd.**
- Browning in cauliflower is due to **Boron** deficiency.
- Chlorosis occurs due to **Mg** deficiency.
- Hollow stem in cauliflower occurs due to **Excess Nitrogen** and **boron** deficiency.
- In the world, India **2nd** rank in Cauliflower production.
- Introduced in India by **Dr. Jemson** in 1822.
- The pH of the soil for maximum production should be **5.5 - 6.6**.
- The process of removal of the central portion of curd for earlier initiation of the **flower stalk** in cauliflowerknown as **Scooping**.
- ***Pusa Himjyoti & Pusa Snowball*** having self-blanched habits.
- Seed rate of Cauliflower 450-700 gm.
- Whiptail in cauliflower due to **Mo** deficiency.

Knolkhol (Kohlrabi)

- **Knolkhol** thrives in a **cool, moist climate** with temperatures of **15°C-20°C.**
- The **edible part** is the **knob**, which forms from the thickened stem above ground.
- Requires **sandy loam soils** for early crops and **silt loam** for higher yield and later crops.
- **King of North** and **Early White Vienna** are well-known varieties for better yield.
- Sensitive to **vernalization**, early bolting occurs if exposed to low temperatures during early growth.

Broccoli

- **Broccoli** prefers **well-drained soils** and grows best at **15°C-20°C.**
- Harvest the **flower heads** before buds open for best quality.
- Rich in **Vitamin C** and **beta-carotene**, it is widely used in health diets.
- Popular varieties include **Calabrese** and **Green Comet** for high yield and better quality.
- **Moderate irrigation** is required to avoid disorders like **hollow stem** caused by boron deficiency.

Brussels Sprout

- **Brussels Sprout** thrives in **cool climates** around **15°C-18°C** for best sprout formation.
- The **small lateral heads** or buds are harvested when they are firm and

2-4 cm in diameter.

- Requires **frequent irrigation** during sprout development to ensure firm heads.
- Varieties like **Jade Cross** and **Oliver** are popular for their compact and high-quality sprouts.
- Sensitive to **aphids** and **cabbage worms**, which need to be managed for better crop quality.

Chinese Cabbage

- **Chinese cabbage** prefers **cool, moist climates** with temperatures between **15°C-20°C.**
- It has two main types: **heading** (Napa) and **non-heading** (Pak Choi), widely used in Asian cuisine.
- **Light sandy soils** are preferred for early crops, with moderate nutrient requirements.
- **Popular varieties** include **Michihili** and **Grain Head** for heading types.
- Sensitive to **bolting** if grown in hot temperatures, reducing quality and yield.

Pea

- **Pea** prefers a **cool climate**, thriving at temperatures between **10°C-18°C.**
- It is sensitive to **frost** during the flowering and fruiting stages, which can affect yield.
- The crop requires **well-drained loamy soil**, and liming is necessary if the soil is acidic.
- Varieties like **Arkel** and **Bonneville** are commonly cultivated for fresh markets and processing.
- **Green pod yield** can vary between **2.5-10 t/ha**, depending on the variety.
- **Canada** has the highest production of peas in the world
- Shelling percentage of peas is **49%.**
- **U.P.** is first in pea production in India followed by Madhya Pradesh.
- Weed management by two-hand weeding at **30** and **45 days after sowing.**

Potato

- **Potato** is a **cool-season crop**, requiring **well-drained sandy loam soils** for optimal growth.
- Ideal temperature for **tuber formation** is around **20°C**, with higher temperatures reducing tuber quality.
- **Kufri Jyoti** and **Kufri Chandramukhi** are widely cultivated for their

high yields and disease resistance.

- The crop is sensitive to **frost** and **water stress**, especially during the tuberization period.
- **Seed tubers** are planted using the **ridge and furrow method**, ensuring proper aeration and soil temperature.

Other Vegetables

- Andra Pradesh, reports maximum production of **chili**.
- **Aphid** is the vector of the cucumber mosaic virus.
- ***Arka Ajit*** & ***Rachna*** (P. mildew resistant) is a variety of peas.
- **Arka Nishant is a** variety of radish (**multi-disease** resistant).
- ***Arka Rajhans,*** is good for the transportation of musk melon.
- Bolting in onion occurs as a result of **low temperature**.
- Brinjal has its **origins** in **India**.
- Brinjal is an excellent source of **vitamin B.**
- Brinjal under as **ripe fruit**.
- Brown heart of radish occurs due to Deficiency of **Boron**.
- Bud necrosis in watermelon is due to Aphids (***Aphis Craccivora***).
- Carrot variety with the greatest vitamin A found in ***Pusa Meghali.***
- **Chantenay** variety of carrots is suitable for preservation and storage.
- Chili seeding rates between 1.0 to 1.5 kg/ha.
- **Cowpea** is used as a vegetable as well as a fodder crop.
- The cucumber is a non-climacteric vegetable fruit.
- Cucumber pillow disease results from **Ca** deficiency.
- The daily requirement of vegetables 300 gm/day/capita.
- ***Durgapura Kesar*** is a Yellow-fleshed variety of watermelon.
- Extra early variety of Pea, **Harbhajan**.
- The first dwarf variety of peas is ***Aparna***/ HFP-4.
- The first hybrid of bottle guard is ***Pusa Meghdoot***.
- The first hybrid Onion by **IARI** in 2002 with a potential for increasing yield by **20%**.
- The flower color of the Chili, pointed gourd and bottle guard is **white**.
- The flower color of cruciferous is Yellow.
- Green leafy vegetables are rich sources of **Folic acid**.
- Heavy, dull sound at the time of harvesting of Watermelon shows Maturity.

- High temperature at the time of fruit maturity of muskmelon will result in **Increased sweetness.**
- In India, the country is the largest producer of okra at **4.8 Mt.**
- **India** is the largest chili producer worldwide.
- ***Kanji*** beverage is prepared from **black carrots.**
- **Key pest** of cucurbits also known as Red pumpkin beetle (Both adult & grab).
- Little leaf of brinjal due to **Mycoplasma** (transmitted by **Leaf hoppers**).
- Main pigment in brinjal crop **Anthocyanin.**
- **Market gardening** was an Intensive method of vegetable cultivation.
- Musk melon is harvested at the stage of **Full slip stage.**
- The Musk melon variety, ***Hara Madhu*** (Late variety) is not harvested at the full slip stage.
- The mutant variety of Palak is **Jobner greens.**
- Okra mosaic in the yellow vein is transmitted by the whitefly.
- Onion is an important source of vitamin **B.**
- Onion sowing is made by Seeds (**10-12 kg**) & bulbs (**750 kg/ha**).
- Pea is a rich source of **Protein (25%).**
- Powdery mildew in cucurbits caused by ***Erysiphae cichoraaceearum.*** Downy mildew in cucurbits due to ***Pseudoperanospora cubensis.***
- Powdery mildew of pea caused by ***Erysiphe polygoni.***
- Pungency in Chili is dyed to **Capsaicin.**
- Pungency in onion is due to **Allyl propyl di sulfide.**
- ***Pusa banana*** is a seedless hybrid variety of watermelon.
- ***Pusa Chikni*** and ***Arka Candlean*** are sponge protectors (*Turai*).
- ***Pusa Himani*, an** All-weather variety of radishes.
- ***Pusa viswas*** is a variety of **pumpkins.**
- Radish stinging is due to **Isothiocyanate.**
- Rajasthan was, first to production of cluster beans.
- The richest source of riboflavin **Radish- leaves**, Thiamine - **Giant chilies**, fat and vitamin **C- Drumstick**, carbohydrate - **Tapioca.**
- Roots of radish prepared for seed production are known as **stacking.**
- **Samara,** Highest highest-yielding variety of bottle guard.
- The seed rate for capsicum annually to **250 gm/ha.**
- The seed rate of the bottle guard is **6 kg/ha.**

- Seed rate of musk melon is **5-2. 0 kg/ha.**
- **Shoot** and **Fruit borer** is the serious pest of brinjal vegetable.
- Sweet potato, ginger & Garlic are examples of Perennial vegetables.
- Sweetest variety of Watermelon Sugar baby (**11-13% TSS**).
- The anti-bacterial substance in garlic is **allicin**.
- The **carrot fork** occurs because of the **hardness of the soil**.
- The external skin color of the onion is caused by **Quercetin.**
- The red color of chili is due to **Capcyanin**.
- **Thrips** are the primary pest of chile.
- **Truck garden**, Extensive method of vegetable cultivation.
- Vegetables can be processed" at a temperature of **115-121°C**.
- Vegetable crop is used as vegetables, fodder, and industrial use **Cluster bean**.
- **Vegetable forcing** is an off-season vegetable.
- The water content in watermelon is **92-95%**.
- **West Bengal** is the largest producer of Brinjal.
- Whiteflies are responsible for transmitting the chili mosaic virus.

Tuber Crops

Potato

- **Potato** thrives in **cool climates**, preferring **well-drained loamy soils** with pH 5-6.
- **Kufri Chandramukhi** and **Kufri Jyoti** are major high-yield varieties with disease resistance.
- Tuber formation is optimal at temperatures between **18°C-20°C** for quality.
- **Golden nematode** and **potato tuber moth** are major pests affecting tuber quality.
- Potato is rich in **carbohydrates** and contains **solanine**, which can be toxic if exposed to light.

Sweet Potato

- **Sweet potato** is a **drought-tolerant crop**, best grown in **sandy loam soils** with clay subsoil.
- **High carotene content** in yellow-fleshed varieties provides nutritional value.
- Propagated through **stem cuttings**, as seeds are highly **heterozygous**.

- Varieties like **Sree Nandini** and **Sree Ratna** are known for high yield and disease resistance.
- **Sweet potato weevil** is the major pest affecting vines and tubers, causing **bitterness.**

Arrowroot

- **Arrowroot** thrives in **warm, humid climates**, and is valued for its **starch-rich rhizomes.**
- Requires well-drained soils with **neutral pH** for optimal growth and starch extraction.
- Harvested **8-10 months** after planting when leaves turn yellow and wither.
- Commonly processed into **arrowroot flour** used in **baby food** and **gluten-free diets.**
- Arrowroot is sensitive to **waterlogging**, requiring careful **irrigation management.**

Cassava (Tapioca)

- **Cassava** is a **starch-rich tuber crop**, tolerant to **drought** but sensitive to frost.
- Widely used in making **sago, vermicelli**, and as an ingredient in **animal feed.**
- Grows best in **well-drained sandy loam soils** with a neutral pH.
- **Bitter varieties** contain **cyanogenic glucosides** that must be processed to remove toxins.
- Harvesting is done **8-12 months** after planting, depending on market demand.

Colocasia (Taro)

- **Colocasia** prefers **warm humid climates** and well-drained **sandy loam soils.**
- **Blight** is the major disease affecting **leaves**, controlled by fungicides like **mancozeb.**
- Harvesting begins **5-6 months** after planting, once the leaves **yellow.**
- Used in traditional dishes like **curries** and **stews**, with **side corms** used for propagation.
- Varieties like **Sree Rashmi** and **Sree Pallavi** are popular for high yield and resistance to diseases.

Xanthosoma (Tannia)

- **Xanthosoma** thrives in **tropical climates**, requiring **well-drained soils** for uniform corm formation.
- The corms are rich in **carbohydrates** and commonly used in **cooking**

and starch production.

- Harvesting is done **8-10 months** after planting, depending on corm maturity.
- Corms and leaves are used in traditional recipes and as **animal feed.**
- Sensitive to **root rot**, requiring careful **soil management**.

Amorphophallus (Elephant Foot Yam)

- **Amorphophallus** grows in **tropical climates** and requires **sandy loam soils** with high organic matter.
- Known for its **medicinal uses** in **Ayurveda**, including treatment for women's health issues.
- **Collar rot** is a major disease, controlled with **bio-control agents** and improved drainage.
- Harvested **8-9 months** after planting when leaves wither, yielding **30-40 t/ha.**
- **Sree Padma** is a popular variety for its high yield and quality.

Dioscorea (Yam)

- **Dioscorea** requires **warm humid climates** and grows best in **well-drained sandy loam soils.**
- Yams are commonly used as **staple food** in tropical regions due to their **carbohydrate-rich tubers.**
- **Propagation** is done through **tuber pieces**, and harvesting takes place **9-10 months** after planting.
- Varieties like **Sree Keerthi** and **Sree Roopa** are known for their **high yields.**
- **Yams** are sensitive to **water stagnation**, requiring careful **irrigation management**.

Jerusalem Artichoke

- **Jerusalem artichoke** is a **perennial tuber crop**, requiring **cool climates** for optimal tuber growth.
- Rich in **inulin**, it is used for **diabetic-friendly foods** and **health supplements.**
- Requires well-drained soils and can be harvested **120-150 days** after planting.
- Tubers are highly perishable, requiring prompt **storage at low temperatures.**
- Commonly used in **pickling** and as a **feedstock for biofuels** due to high starch content.

Horse Radish

- **Horse radish** thrives in **temperate climates**, producing long **taproots** used as a spice.

- Requires **well-drained fertile soils**, and proper spacing for **optimal root development**.
- Harvesting is done **150-180 days** after planting, depending on root size.
- Used in making **condiments** like horseradish sauce due to its **pungency**.
- Sensitive to **root rot**, requiring careful **soil management**.

Coleus

- **Coleus** is a **medicinal tuber crop** grown for its **starchy tubers** and **ornamental leaves**.
- Requires **warm climates** and **well-drained soils** with high organic matter.
- Harvesting is done **6-8 months** after planting, once the leaves **start to yellow**.
- The tubers are used in **Ayurvedic medicine** for digestive and respiratory ailments.
- Sensitive to **pests like aphids**, requiring regular **monitoring and control**.

Yam Bean

- **Yam bean** is grown for its **sweet edible tubers** and requires **warm climates**.
- Best grown in **well-drained loamy soils**, with **regular irrigation** for uniform tuber growth.
- Harvesting is done **5-6 months** after planting, when leaves start to yellow.
- Tubers are rich in **starch and inulin**, making them suitable for **diabetics**.
- Known for its **dual-use** as both a **vegetable** and a **fodder crop**.

Flower Crops

- Leading flower-producing country **Netherlands**.
- Flower capital of the world **California (U.S.A.)**.
- **Tamilnadu** has maximum production under floriculture.
- **Karnataka** has max area under floriculture.
- W. Bengal produces max cut flowers. Germany leading in the cut flowers market.
- In India, Jasmine has max area in the Flower crop. Japanese flower

arrangement is known as ***Ikebana.*** India is the largest producer of loose flowers in the world. The largest importer of floriculture products from India is the **U.S.A.**

- Mughal garden & Pinjore garden is a type of garden **Formal style garden.**Japanese & English gardens style is **Informal style**.
- Rose Garden, Chandigarh is an example of a Freestyle garden. The book, Beautiful Garden is written by M.S. Randhawa.
- The queen of flowers is the **Rose.**
- In India is Brindavan Garden (Mysore).
- Mughal Garden is situated at **Pinjore (Haryana).**
- The National Botanical Garden is situated at Lukhnow. Rockery & Lawn are the key elements of an English garden.
- Example of a Japanese garden in India- Buddha Jayanti Park, New Delhi. Rastrapati Garden is an example of an English garden.
- The key difference between formal and Informal Gardens is **Symmetrical** and **Asymmetrical**. The origin place of the rose in India.
- The Baradari & Terminal building is a key element of the Mughal Garden. Garden Lanterns & dry landscapes are key elements of Japanese gardens. Biggest formal garden.
- Best and fastest method of lawn development **Turf method.**
- The commercial method of propagation of rose is T- T-T-Budding.
- The best time of budding **Nov. to Feb**.
- The best time for planting roses is **September To October**.
- The rose is a national flower of **England.**
- Fruit of rose called **hips**.
- Thorn less variety of rose ***Suchitra & Pusa Mohit.***
- Dr. B.P. Pal is associated with **rose breeding**.
- Tushar is a variety of **White roses**.
- **Crimson glory** is a variety of red roses.
- Gulkand is prepared by Rose Petal & Sugar (11 ratio).
- Mexico is a Native of marigold.
- **Iridaceae** is a Family of Gladiolus.
- Gladiolus is commercially propagated by **Corms.**
- Botanical name of Chrysanthemum, ***Dendranthema gradiflora***, Family **Compopsiteae**.
- **Guldaudi** is a Common name known as Chrysanthemum.
- Origin of Chrysanthemum **China.**

- Propagation method of chrysanthemum **Root suckers**.
- Shrub planted, and grown on boundary fencing is known as **Hedge**.
- ***The Rafflesia amoldii*** plant produces the **largest flower** in the world.

Rose

- **Roses** are propagated by **T-budding** and **cuttings**, suited to a wide range of climates.
- **Hybrid Tea Roses** are valued for their **long-lasting cut flowers**.
- **Pruning** during **October-December** promotes better flowering in tropical regions.
- **Rose oil** is a major product used in the **perfumery industry**.
- **Die-back disease** caused by **Diplodia** is a serious issue in rose cultivation.

Jasmine

- **Jasmine** is mainly grown for **garlands** and **essential oil production**.
- **Propagation** is commonly through **semi-hardwood cuttings** for species like **Jasminum sambac**.
- **Boric acid spray** extends the **post-harvest life** of jasmine flowers.
- Jasmine oil is widely used in the **cosmetic industry** for its fragrance.
- **Pruning in mid-December** improves **flower yield** in jasmine cultivation.

Carnation

- **Carnations** are propagated via **cuttings**, with **NAA treatment** to enhance rooting.
- Ideal temperature for **flowering** is between **15°C-18°C**.
- **Disbudding** improves the size and quality of the flowers.
- Commonly grown in **greenhouses** to meet market demand for cut flowers.
- **Powdery mildew** is a major fungal disease affecting **carnation plants**.

Chrysanthemum

- **Chrysanthemum** flowers are used for **cut flowers, garlands, and religious offerings**.
- **Pinching** and **staking** improve plant architecture and **flower yield**.
- Thrives in **well-drained sandy loam soils** with a pH of **6.5**.
- **Short-day plants**, requiring fewer daylight hours for **flowering**.
- **Root rot** and **aphids** are common problems in chrysanthemum cultivation.

Gladiolus

- **Gladiolus** is propagated by **corms**, requiring a **cool climate** for optimal growth.

- Grown for **cut flowers**, ideal for **floral arrangements** due to long spikes.
- Gladiolus requires **well-drained soil** with a **neutral pH** for best results.
- **Corm rot** is a major issue, managed through the use of **Fungicides.**
- **Pinching** of the first spike is recommended to improve **flower quality**.

Marigold

- **Marigold** is a popular crop for **ornamental use**, and widely grown for **garlands.**
- **African and French marigolds** are the two primary types cultivated.
- **Pinching** is essential to encourage **bushy plant growth** and **increase flower yield.**
- Marigold is also used as a **natural pesticide** due to its **nematicidal properties.**
- The flowers are a source of **pigments used in poultry feed.**

Tuberose

- **Tuberose** is known for its **fragrant flowers**, widely used in the **perfume industry**.
- It thrives in **warm climates**, with temperatures between **16°C-30°C.**
- **Propagation** is done through **bulbs**, with flowering occurring **8-10 months** after planting.
- **Rajanigandha** is a common variety grown for its high **flower yield.**
- Tuberose requires **regular irrigation** to prevent **flower drop** in hot climates.

Cut Foliage Crops

- **Cut foliage crops** like **Philodendron** and **Dracaena** are valued for **indoor decoration.**
- These crops are used primarily for **floral arrangements** and **landscaping.**
- Propagation is generally through **cuttings** or **division of roots.**
- **Good foliage management** is key to maximizing market value.
- **Ornamental foliage** plants are tolerant of a wide range of environmental conditions.

Medicinal Crops:

Ashwagandha (Withania somnifera)

- **Ashwagandha** is used for its **adaptogenic properties**, enhancing stress resistance and stamina.
- Thrives in **dry, subtropical climates** and requires **well-drained sandy loam soils.**

- It is primarily grown for its **roots**, which contain **withanolides**, key active compounds.
- **Propagation** is done through seeds, and **harvesting** occurs **150-180 days** after sowing.
- Commonly used in **Ayurvedic medicine** for its **anti-inflammatory** and **anti-cancer** properties.

Costus (Costus speciosus)

- **Costus** is known for its **rhizomes**, used in the treatment of **diabetes** and other ailments.
- It requires **tropical, humid climates** and prefers **well-drained loamy soils** for optimal growth.
- The plant contains **diosgenin**, a precursor to **steroid drugs**, used in modern medicine.
- Propagated via **rhizomes**, and it flowers best under **partial shade**.
- **Harvesting** is typically done after **10-12 months** when rhizomes mature.

Isabgol (Plantago ovata)

- **Isabgol** is widely used for its **mucilaginous seeds**, which act as a natural **laxative**.
- Best grown in **cool, dry climates**, with **light sandy soils** aiding seed production.
- **Irrigation** is crucial during flowering for maximizing seed yield.
- Seeds are rich in **fiber**, especially **psyllium**, beneficial for **digestive health**.
- The crop matures **120-130 days** after sowing, and harvesting is done when **spikes turn brown**.

Mint (Mentha spp.)

- **Mint** is grown for its **essential oils**, particularly **menthol**, used in pharmaceuticals and cosmetics.
- Requires **well-drained loam soils** with a pH of **6.5-7.5** for vigorous growth.
- **Propagation** is done through **stem cuttings**, and the plant needs **frequent irrigation** for high oil content.
- **Harvesting** is done **90-100 days** after planting, with peak oil content just before **flowering**.
- **Mint wilt** and **rust** are common diseases affecting crop yield, requiring **integrated pest management**.

Genetics and Plant Breeding

- The power house of cell **Mitochondria.** The term Mitochondria was coined by **Carl Brenda in 1898.**
- **Friedrich Meves (1904)** first observed mitochondria in plant cells.
- Rediscovery of Mendelian principles in the year **1900.**
- Chromosomal theory of inheritance (1903) by **Sutton** & **Bovery**. It is a fundamental unifying theory of genetics, that identifies chromosomes as the **Carriers of genetic material.**
- The term genetics was given by **Betson (1905**).
- Chromosome named by **Waldayer (1888).**
- Muller Was the First to use of **X-rays** as a **mutation.**
- Allo - Hexaploidy found in **Wheat.**
- Auto-polyploidy is found in **Sugarcane, cotton, and Brassica.**
- Autotetraploidy is found in **Potato, and coffee.**
- **Chloroplast** is the Kitchen of the cell.
- Autotriploidy found at **Banana.**
- Two lines different for a single locus called is **Isogenic line.**
- Change in the genome concerning individual chromosomes called **Aneuploidy.**
- If a single gene governs multiple traits, it is called **Pleiotrophy.**
- Embryo development without fertilization is called **Apomixis.**
- The first interspecific cross was made by **Thomas Fairchild.**
- **E. Borlaug** was awarded the Nobel Prize in **1970.**
- Father of Hybrid Cotton (H - 4) **Dr. C.T. Patel.**
- The first hybrid of rice was developed by **Y.L. Ping (China**).
- The first transgenic plant was developed by **Fraley (1983)** in **Tobacco.**
- Laws of heredity were first discovered by **Mandel.**
- **Tift-60** is an important source of male sterility in **Sorghum.**
- The term **Germplasm** was first used by **Weismann (1834 -1914**).
- Centre of origin was first given by **Vavilov.** Vavilov recognized eight. Main countries of origin China; Hindustan; Central Asia; Asia Minor; Mediterranean; Abyssinia; South America; Central America.
- NBPGR was established in **(New Delhi) in 1976.**
- The term genomics was coined by **Tom Roderick (1986**).
- The term pathogenesis (reproduction without fertilization) was coined

by **Richard Owen (1849)**.

- The concept of pure line theory was developed by **Johnson (1952)**.
- The term heterosis was coined by **Shull (1914).**
- A nullisomic individual is represented by **2n - 2**.
- The chromosome was discovered by **Strasburger (1875)**. It was made up of **nucleic acids** and **proteins**.
- DNA and RNA were first synthesized by **A. Kornberg in 1953** & **S.Ochoa in 1969**.
- The nucleus was the Largest Organelle in the Eukaryotic cell.
- Term Protoplast was coined by Purkinje (1840).
- The Longest Phase of Mitosis is **Prophase**.
- The Golgi complex was described by **Camillo Golgi (1822).**
- Flexibility in plants is due to Collenchyma.

- The "Pusa Jay Kisan" variety developed by somaclonal variation by IARI is associated with **Mustard.**
- 13% moisture is ideal for certified Rice.
- Colchicine was discovered by ***Blackslee.***
- 1927, - Muller working with ***Drosophila*** provides proof of mutation induction by X-rays.
- In 1928, Stadler published the first results of mutation induction in crop plants, barley, maize, wheat, and oats.
- In 1936, The first induced mutant variety was released, tobacco var. **'Chlorine'** using X-rays in Indonesia.
- 1942, First report of induced disease resistance in a crop plant; X-ray induced mildew resistance in barley (Freisleben and Lein, 1942).
- 1944, First reports of chemical-induced mutation (Auerbach and Robson, 1944).
- 80-90% water in protoplasm.
- A cell contains genetically identical two copies of each chromosome **Double haploid**.
- "Germ Plasm" theory given by **Weisman (1889).**
- A cell is a structural & functional unit of life.
- A chart that traces the flow of genetic information from generation to generation is **Pedigree.**
- **Harrington** proposed the Mass Pedigree method in cotton in **1937**.
- A common crop of natural auto-tetraploids grown in India is **Potato.**

- A fiber of greatest commercial importance derived from the epidermis of seed is Cotton.
- A sequence of DNA used to "**mark**" or track the position of the gene is a **Genetic marker**.
- A stage in cell division in which DNA synthesis/replication takes place is **Interphase**.
- A stage of the spindle using cell division during chromosomes are arranged at the equatorial plate is **Metaphase**.
- A stage of the spindle using cell division during which chromosomes become shorter and thicker is **Prophase.**
- A type of asexual reproduction in which embryo development and seed formation take place without fertilization and with or without meiosis **Apomixis**.
- A stage of the spindle using cell division during chromosomes/chromatids move toward opposite poles is **Anaphase.**
- A stage of the spindle using cell division in which the chromosomes reach opposite poles is **Telophase.**
- A variety resistant to more than one race of pathogen is due to **Horizontal resistance.**
- A virus that infects bacteria is Bacteriophage An exact genetic replica of a specific gene or an entireorganism is **Clone.**
- Adaptation of introduced variety to the new environment is called **Acclimatization**.
- Cytoplasmic genetic male sterility (CGMS) system includes **A-line, B-line** & **R-line**.
- The term pure line, genotype & phenotype was coined by **Johansson**.
- Adventive- Development of embryo from the diploid cells of the ovule.
- After **6-8 Backcross**, progeny is identical to the **Recurrent parent.**
- All the plants in the pure line have thesame **Genotype**.
- Allopolyploidy is found in **Sugarcane** and **Cotton**.
- bgenetic base is found in **Mass selection**.
- Autotriploidy is found in **bananas.**
- An alternative form of a gene is known as an **Allele.**
- An agent that causes gene mutation is called **Mutagen.**
- An individual having both male and female reproductive organs is known as a **Hermaphrodite.**
- The breeding method generally used to improve the specific character of

a well-adapted variety is **Backcross.**

- An organism's genotype is characterized by two identical alleles of a gene is a **Homozygote**. Apple, watermelon, and sugar beet are **Triploids**.
- **Apogamy-** Development of embryo from synergids or antipodal cells of embryo sac.
- **Apomixis-** Development of seed without sexual fusion (fertilization).
- **Apospory-** Development of embryo from nucellus or integument cells of embryo sac.
- Aseptic conditions mean **Pathogen pathogen-free environment.**
- **Atlas-66** is an important source of high protein in **Wheat**.
- Erucic acid is found in **Mustard.**
- Auto-tetraploidy is found in **Potato and Coffee.**
- **Autotriploidy is** found in **Banana, Watermelon** & **Sugar beet**.
- The development of fruit without fertilization is called **Parthenocarpy**.
- Back cross- Crossing of F_1 with either of its parents. It is commonly used for the transfer of disease resistance, male sterility, development, lines, and multiline varieties.
- The Backcross method of crop improvement was suggested by **Harlan & Pope**.
- **The backcross method** used for the development of disease-resistant variety.
- backcross breeding, the parent used repeatedly for crossing is ***Recipient***.
- Bacteriophages are **Single-stranded DNA (virus).**
- Bajra is a cross-pollinated crop due to **Protogyny conditions**.
- Bajra is a rich source of Vit. A & B.
- **Better parent,** It is over the best commercial cultivar of a locality is Useful heterosis.
- ***Brassica juncea*** is an **amphidiploid** between ***B. nigra & B. campestris.***
- ***Stadler*** first used X-rays for induction of mutation in **1928** in **Barley**.
- Bt. cotton was first released for commercial cultivation in the world in **1996.**
- The bulk method is an Evolutionary method of crop improvement.
- A genic balance theory of sex determination was given to Bridges.
- The bulk method was proposed by **Nilsson Ehle, in 1908**.
- Bulk breeding is used for the development of high-yielding varieties having wider adaptability.
- The capacity of a pathogen to incite a disease is called **Virulence.**

- The cell wall of fungi is chiefly made up of **Chitin.**
- **The centrosome** is present only in **animal cells**.
- Change in the base sequence of a gene is **Gene mutation**.
- Chromosome number doubled in crop plants by using Colchicine.
- Changes in the genome concerning individual chromosome **Aneuploidy**.
- The chromosomal theory of inheritance (1903) was given by **Sutton & Bovery**.
- Chromosome is a **Nucleoprotein**. Chromosome was discovered in 1875 by **Strasburger**.
- Characters that express in one sex only are **limited traits.**
- Cleistogamous flowers prevent **Cross-pollination**.
- Cross-pollinated species are highly Heterozygous.
- Cytoplasmic-genetic male sterility (CGMS) was first reported in **Onion** by **Jones & Davis, in 1944.**
- Clonal selection is mostly in the crop **Ginger.**
- Clones are said to be immortal but deteriorate due to Viral, infections and Mutations.
- Combine **Kafir-60** is an important source of male sterility in **sorghum.**
- Common bread wheat is **Allohexaploid.**
- Complete failure of vertical resistance leads to a disease epidemic called as **Vertifolia effect**.
- Composite varieties are developed in **cross-pollinated crops.**
- The concept of ideotypes was developed in Wheat by McDonald.
- In England, Thomas Fairchild made 1st interspecific cross in Dianthus in 1717.
- The concept of pure line theory was developed by **Johansson.**
- Constant performance of a variety after repeated reproduction is called **Stability.**
- Continuous inbreeding (selfing) leads to **Homozygosity.**
- Cotton and tobacco crops are **Allotetraploid.**
- A cross between two genetically different homozygote plants is **Hybrid or F_1.**
- Cross-pollinated species are also known as outbreeders or **Allogamous species.**
- **Cybrid** is a hybrid formed by cell fusion containing the nucleus of one species and the cytoplasm of both theparental species.

- **Cytoplasm** includes all the structures outside the nucleus.
- The theory of acquired characteristics was proposed by ***Lamarck.***
- The cytoplasmic Male Sterility (CMS) line is maintained by the **'B' line**.
- The development of fruit without fertilization is **Parthenocarpy.**
- Development of seed by self-pollination is Autogamy.
- The development of a plant from a single cell is known as **Tissue culture.**
- Differences within the pure line are due to **Environment.**
- Diploid Apomixis- Recurrent Apomixis
- Discovery of Nucleus by Robert Brown.
- DNA was first synthesized by **A. Kornberg.**
- Dominance theory was proposed by **Devenport in 1908**.
- **Dr. H. B. Singh** was a famous Indian plant explorer.
- Drought tolerance in plants is increased due to **High proline.**
- Effective selection can be made in **Multilines.**
- **Epistasis-** Interaction between alleles of two or more different loci.
- ***Ethidium bromide*** has been found effective in inducing cytoplasmic male sterility in **pearl millet** and barley.
- Examples of prokaryotes **cells of Mycoplasma, Bacteria,** and **Blue-green algae**.
- Exotic varieties of rice are **TN-1, IR-8, IR- 36** and **IR-24.**
- Exotic varieties of wheat are **Sonara 64 &Lerma Rojo**.
- The father of Drosophila (fruit fly)/Modern genetics is ***T.H. Morgan.***
- The father of genetic engineering is **Paul Berg**.
- Father of plant tissue culture ***G. Haberland.***
- Father of Botany ***Theophrastus***.
- Father of Genetics ***G.J. Mendel.***
- Father of Zoology ***Aristotle.***
- The first gamma garden was built in Long Island, New York (USA).
- In India, the First gamma garden was in Calcutta at Bose Research Institute (1959).
- In 1960, 2nd garden IARI, New Delhi. The source of Y-garden was 6g of 60 co in small pellets.
- The first inter-specific hybrid of cotton was ***Varalaxmi.***
- The first man-made cereal is **Triticale.**
- For biograss production - ***Eicchorina crassipes*** (**Water Hyaunth**) is used.

- For every generation of selfing heterozygosity is reduced at a rate of 50%.
- For induction of polyploidy, colchicine was first used in 1937 by **Blakeslee.**
- **Ginger & turmeric** are examples of modified stems of **Rhizome.**
- ***Francis Crick's*** seminal concept that in nature genetic information generally flows from DNA to RNA toprotein is called **Central Dogma.**
- Functional gametes are formed Alternate only due to alternate segregation.
- Functions of chromosomes in the transmission of heredity were given by **T. H. Morgon.**
- Gamete is a Sexual unit.
- The GATT agreement came into force in 1948.
- Genetic variations originated in pure line due to **Natural hybridization**.
- **Gregg-399** is an important source of genetic male sterility in **Cotton**.
- **Guha** and **Maheshwari** developed another cultural technique by working with **Datura (1967)**.
- The polymerase Chain Reaction (PCR) technique was developed by **Kary Mullis, in 1985.**
- H4 was the first hybrid variety of cotton developed by Gujarat Agriculture University in 1970.
- Hand pollination during commercial seed production is practiced in **Cotton**.
- Hybridization is common in crop **Cotton**.
- Haploids are developed by Anther culture.
- Heterosis is estimated over **Mid, Better parent** & **Best local cultivar**.
- The highest uniformity is observed in a **Single cross**.
- Holandric genes are located on the Y-chromosome (Allosome) responsible for **Maleness.**
- Hybrid varieties were first commercially exploited in maize.
- HYVP was stated in 1966.
- If a single gene governs multiple traits, it is called **Pleiotropy.**
- In 1909, Johnannsen coined the terms **Gene, Genotype, and Phenotype.**
- In ***1944, Avery, MacLeod, and McCarty*** demonstrated that DNA was the genetic material.
- In CAM plants transpiration is negligible since stomata are closed during the day.

- In England, Knight 1st used artificial hybridization in fruit & vegetable crops.
- In India, Bt. cotton was released for commercial cultivation in the year **2002.**
- In India, the first hybrid variety of Jowar (***S. bicolor***) was CSH-1 by using Cytoplasmi Genetic Male Sterility **Combine Kafir 60** as a parent.
- In India, the First hybrid variety of Bajra (***P. americanum)*** was lasmic HB-1 released in 1965 by using cytoplasm genetic male Sterility of Tift 23 A.
- In India, hockey sticks are generally made from ***Morus alba***.
- In India, Hybrid cotton is produced by hand pollination.
- the first country to exploit hybrid cotton.
- All the hybrid varieties have been vigor commercially developed in tetraploid cotton.
- in India, the Seeds Act came into effect in the year **1969.**
- In India, the Seeds Act was enacted by the parliament in **1966.**
- In mitochondria only 70s types of **Ribosomes.**
- In pedigree breeding after F8, homozygous plants are known as **Strain**.
- In plants, meiosis takes place in **Anthers** and **Ovaries**.
- In plants, mitosis takes place in **Somatic organs.**Interphase lies between **Telophase & Prophase.**
- Largest organelle in eukaryotic cells is **Nucleus.**
- In rice, seed dormancy is observed in Indica Maize is a cross-pollinated crop due to **Protandrycondition.**
- **Inbreeding depression** loss or decrease in vigor and fitness due to inbreeding. Highest- **Carrot,** Moderate - Onion, cole crops.
- **Inbreeding** Mating between closely related individuals such as selfing, and sib mating.
- In India, the Seeds Act was enacted in **1966** by the parliament.
- India 1st in the world to have developed a hybrid of **cotton, Pear millet, Castor, and Pigeon peas.**
- The initial idea of recurrent selection was given by ***Hayes & Garber***.
- Isolation of hybrid and developing haploids by anthers/ovary.
- It can be fully exploited in the form of a **Hybrid**. It leads to an increase in **Yield,**
- **general vigor and adaptation.** Heterosis results due to **Dominance, Over-dominance & Epistasis.**
- Jawahar is a composite variety of **Maize.**

- Lines, **Isogenic lines** are identical in their genotype, except for one gene.
- Isogenic lines are **A-line & Bline.**
- Isogenic lines are developed by the **Backcross method.**
- A mixture of isogenic lines is termed a **Multilines.**
- There are **6 to 10 isogenic lines that** are usually mixed to constitute a multiline variety.
- **locus (ml-o)** located on the short arm of chromosome 4H in barley-induced mutations at resistance to powdery mildew and barley yellow mosaic virus.
- Lysosome was discovered by **Duve,** in **1956.**
- Male sterility in plants was first reported by **Koelreuter, in 1763**.
- Flowering in sugarcane requires **High temperature during the night**.
- Mass selection is more commonly used in **cross-pollinated crops.**
- Maximum mutant varieties were evolved in **Rice.**
- Medicine to check high blood pressure is obtained from *Rauwofia serpentine.*
- Mitochondria was discovered by ***C. Benda.***
- Most mutant tolerant are **Polyploids.**
- Movement of chromosomes during cell division is controlled by **Centromere.**
- The structure of chromosomes can be best observed during **Metaphase.**
- Multiline breeding is exploited widely in **Wheat.**
- Mutagens generally induce a high frequency of chromosomal changes and **meiotic** and **mitotic**.
- The mutant gene responsible for high lysine content in maize is **Opaque 2.**
- Non-edible oil-yielding crop is **Castor.**
- **N. I. Vavilov** was a famous Russian plant explorer.
- **NaOH** test used for testing the Karnal bunt disease of wheat.
- NBPGR was established in **1976.**
- Negative interference is observed in Viruses.
- Non Non-hybridization methods include **Introduction, Pure line selection,** and **Mass selection**.
- The pedigree method is more commonly used in **Self-pollinated crops**.
- NSC was established in 1963.
- Seed Act-1966 (NSC National Seed Corporation)

- Nucleolus disappears at the end of **Prophase.**
- Nucleolus reappears at the end of **Telophase.**
- Often cross-pollinated crops are ***Sorghum, Arhar, and Cotton.***
- One gene One enzyme theory was given by **Beadle.**
- Only about **0.1%** of the induced mutations are useful in crop improvement.
- The enzymes associated with the Krebs cycle are also present in the **Matrix.**
- Life was first originated in water the theory of genes in the chromosomes was introduced by **Morgan.**
- Openings are left at plants between the adjacent cells known as **plasmodesma** and thread-like lining between two cells is known as **Plasmodesmata.**
- Parthenogenesis Development of embryo from the egg cell without fertilization.
- **PCR techniques provide** Several copies of specific **DNA sequences.**
- The science of identifying the sequence of DNA in species is **Genomics.**
- Phenotypic ratio of Monocross hybrid **3:1.**
- Photosynthesis inhibitor is DCMU.
- The physical basis of life is the **Protoplasm.**
- Onion is a modified form of **Leaf** Onion & garlic are examples of **Bulb.**
- Plants showing less than 5% cross-pollination are considered **Self-pollinated.**
- Plants that produce seeds that germinate before they detach from the parent are **Viviparous plants.**
- Plants that owe their resistance to avoidance are called **Water savers.**
- Plasma membrane is **absent** in **viruses.**
- Pollination and fertilization occur before the opening of the flower is termed as **Cleistogamy.**
- popular mutant cultivars of chickpea developed in India; Variety Pusa-408 (Ajay) 1985, Resistant to Ascochyta blight, Pusa-413 (Atul) 1985, Resistant to Fusarium wilt, stunt virus & foot rot, Pusa-417 (Girnar) 1985, High resistance to Fusarium wilt & moderate resistance to Ascochyta blight, stunt virus.
- Potato and alfalfa are **Autotetraploid.**
- Progeny of artificially selfed homozygous plant in the cross-pollinated crop is known as the **Inbred line.**
- The Progeny test is also known as the **Vilmorin isolation principle.**

- The progeny test is developed by ***Louis Vilmorin.***
- Proteomics is the large-scale study of proteins concerning their **structure** and **function**.
- Protogyny & Protandry conditions promote **Cross-pollination**.
- **Quantitative character** is considerably affected by the environment.
- The chemically induced male sterility is **Not heritable**.
- The reciprocal recurrent selection method is 1st developed by Comstock, Robinson, and Harvey.
- Reciprocal recurrent selection method is 1st developed by **Robinson** and Harvey.
- **Recurrent selection** is a modified form of Progeny selection.
- Re-discovery of Mendel laws in 1900 by **Hugo de Vries, Carl Correns & Tschemark.**
- RNA synthesis is in which organ **Nucleolus.**
- Robert Hooke discovered the cell in 1665.
- Segregation occurs during **Meiosis only.**
- Self-pollinated species are also known as Autonomous species.
- Semi-conservative replication was postulated by Watson and Crick.
- A single gene affecting more than one character is known as **Pleiotropy.**
- Repeated crossing of a hybrid progeny back to one of its parents **Backcross.**
- RNA was first synthesized by S. Ochoa, in **1969.**
- Sunflower has a **Protandrous flower.**
- Terms prophase, metaphase, and anaphase were coined by **Strasburger.**
- Test cross used to determine the **Linkage**.
- Linkage in plant (pea) was discovered by ***Bateson &Punnet*** (1906).
- Linkage in animals was reported by Morgan in 1910 working with ***Drosophila***.
- The best method for developing disease-resistant plants is **Backcrossing**.
- The bread wheat is **Hexaploid.**
- The Cell is a ***Latin*** word that means little room.
- The central portion of the chromosome to the spindle fibres attached during mitotic and meiotic division is **Centromere**.
- The Central Seed Testing laboratory is in ***Varanasi***.

- The color of the tag prescribed for foundation seed Source of male sterile.
- The concept of multiline varieties was first given by **Jensen in Oat (1952).**
- The Brinjal also known as "**Egg plant**".
- The crop also known as "**Pungent pepper**" is Chilli.
- ***Ethidium bromide*** is found effective in inducing male sterility.
- **Mutation breeding** is the quickest method of plant breeding.
- The term **self-incompatibility** was coined by **Stout**.
- The crossing of F_1 with one of its parts is called **Back Cross**.
- The double helix model of DNA was proposed by **Watson** and **Crick (1953)**.
- **The first artificial** hybrid developed by **Thomas Fairchild** in **1717** popularly known as Fairchild Mule is produced by crossing **Carnation x Sweet William**.
- The first transgenic plant was developed by **Fraley in Tobacco (1987)**.
- The first transgenic cotton was developed in **1987** by **Monsanto company**.
- The greatest use of hybrid varieties has been made in maize.
- Four hybrids of maize i.e., Ganga 1, Ganga 101, Ranjit & Deccan were released in 1961 in India.
- The inflorescence of banana is known as **Spadix.**
- The longest mitotic phase is the **Prophase.**
- The male sterile line used as the female parent in hybrid seed production is the **A-line**.
- The male sterility that is commonly used in hybrid seed production programs is **Cytoplasmicgenetic male sterility (CGMS).**
- The method that provides information about the mode of inheritance of various qualitative characters isknown as the **Pedigree method.**
- The most abundant form of RNA is- **RNA (80%)**.The total nitrogenous bases are **Four.**
- The most appropriate method for the transfer of oligogenic characters is the **Backcross method.**
- The natural genetic engineer is ***Agrobacterium tumefaciens***.
- First use of X-rays as mutagens was done by **H.J. Muller, in 1927**.
- The newer method for crop improvement is **Mutagenesis**.
- The oldest selection method for crop improvement is **Mass selection**.
- The parent used only once in the back cross-breeding method is Donor or non-recurrent.

- The breeding method not appropriate for cross-pollinated crops is **Pure line selection.**
- The process of producing mRNA from DNA coding sequences is called **Transcription.**
- The process of producing a protein from its mRNA coding sequences is called **Translation.**
- The progeny of a single self-pollinated homozygous plant is the **Pure line**.
- The resistance of the host to the race of a pathogen is known as **Vertical resistance.**
- The scientist, ***Koelreuter*** produced successful hybrids in tobacco through artificial crosses.
- The general breeding method is **Introduction.**
- The self-progeny of $\mathbf{F_1}$ and the subsequent generations are termed as **Segregating generations**.
- The artificial hybridization in fruit and vegetable crops was first used by ***T. A. Knight***.
- The study of interactions between antigens and antibodies is called **Serology.**
- The term chromosome was coined by **Waldeyer**.
- The term 'Genetics' was coined by **W. Bateson**.
- The term Lysosome was 1st used by Duve (1955).
- The term meiosis was coined by ***Farmer & Moore*** **(1905)**.
- The term mitosis was coined by ***Flemming*** (1882).
- The term mutation breeding was first coined by Freisleben and Lein (1944).
- 1901-1904 - de Vries suggests and promotes radiation to induce mutations in plants and animals.
- The term mutation was described by ***Hugo de Vries.***
- The term protoplasm was given by ***J. E. Purkinje.***
- The theory of inheritance was proposed by **G.J Mendel.**
- The shortest phase of all the mitosis phases is **Anaphase**. The site of protein synthesis is the **Ribosome.**
- The theory of natural selection was proposed by **Charles Darwin.**
- Ribosomes are small cellular particles that are the sites of **Protein synthesis.**
- The closest form of inbreeding possible in self-incompatible species is **Sib-mating.**

- Physical chromosomal exchange (crossing over) takes place in **Pachytene.**
- The **Tift23-A** and **Combine Kafir- 60** are the important sources of male sterility in pearl millet and sorghum.
- The toxic compound in Lathyrus is **BOAA.**
- The use of synthetic varieties for commercial cultivation was first suggested in maize by **Hayes &Garber in 1919.**
- Thermosensitive GMS is found in Rice.
- Top cross used to determine **general combining ability (GCA).**
- Toxic substance in alfalfa is **Goitrogenic**.
- Transfer of genetic material from one cell to another cell using a viral vector known as **Transduction.**
- Transgenic male sterility is found in Brassica.
- Triangle for the origin of ***tetraploid spp***. of Brassica was proposed in **1935** by **Nagaharu, U.** **"Thomas Andrew Knight"** was a famous **Fruit crop breeder**.
- Triplet sequences **tRNA** anticodon.
- Two successive spindle using divisions reduce the chromosome number from diploid to haploid in Meiosis.
- Type of male sterility used in hybrid seed production in pearl millet **Cytoplasmic genetic male sterility.**
- The vacuole organelle of the cell is known as the dustbin of the cell.
- Varalaxmi was the First interspecific hybrid variety (cotton).
- Varietal purity is checked by the **Grow Out test.**
- Wheat variety resistant to all three rust is **Sparrow, Chhoti lerma**.
- The world's first superfine grain aromatic rice hybrid is **Pusa-RH 10**.The powerhouse of the cell is the **Mitochondria**.

Soil Science

- According to USDA, Soils have been divided into 10 orders generally 12 orders. (Entisol Vertisol Inceptisol, Acidisol, Mollisol Spodosol, Alfisol, Ultisol, Oxisol and Histosol).
- The acid tolerant crop is **Rice**.
- Ammoniacal fertilizers should be applied in the **Reduced zone**.
- A balance sheet of nutrients was given by **Boussingault**.
- Best pH range for bacteria and fungi growth is **6.5 to 8.0** & **4.5 to 6.5**.
- Black soils found in **Maharashtra**.
- Block delivery scheme (BDS) for fertilizer was launched in **1980-81.**
- Brittle leaf occurs due to **Ca** deficiency.
- C N ratio for normal soils is **10-12 1.**
- Cabbage Crop is highly sensitive to **Boron toxicity**.
- Capacity **(1/3 ATM)** and wilting coefficient **(15 ATM)** are known as **Available water**.
- Central fertilizer pool was started in the year **1944.**
- The chief constituent of Sandy fraction **Quartz**.
- **Chlorosis** in between the veins and veins remains green showing a Deficiency of **Mg**.
- Complete interveinal chlorosis occurs due to **Mn** deficiency.
- Criteria of essentiality were given by **Arnon & Stout (1939).**
- **Crumby structure** is best for cultivation.
- The desired soil sample size of soil is **0.5 kg.**
- The diameter of fine sand particles is **0.02-0.2** mm, silt particles- **02 - 0.002 mm**, and clay particles- Less than **0.002 mm.**
- Dieback of citrus occurs due to **Cu** deficiency.
- Electrical Conductivity is used to express the Salinity of the soil.
- Erosion is caused by **excessive grazing** & **deforestation** it is called **Anthropogenic erosion**.
- An example of free-living aerobic bacteria is ***Azatobactor chroccum***.
- Excess of **Ca** in soil, then availability of phosphorus **Decreases.**
- Excess vegetative growth is due to a High supply of **N**.
- Failure of terminal bud & root tip due to **Ca** deficiency.
- The fastest N-fixing plant is ***Sesbania rostrata***.
- The Fertilizer Control Act (FCO) was introduced in the year **1957.**

- The fertilizer prices committee was constituted in Jan **1976**.
- Fertilizers supply only one major plant nutrient called **Straight fertilizer** (Urea), two or more **Complex fertilizers** (DAP), and three fertilizer Complete fertilizers (NPK).
- **Fine texture** soils are most sensitive to Water erosion.
- The first manufactured fertilizer in India is **SSP (Single Super Phosphate).**
- The functional nutrient was proposed by **D. J. Nicholas (1963)**.
- Gneiss & Marble are types of **Metamorphic rocks**.
- Granite & Basalt are types of **Igneous rocks**.
- Gully erosion **cannot be** removed by normal tillage operations.
- **Gypsum** and **Limestone** are used for the reclamation of Alkali soils and Acidic soils.
- High lime requirement crops are **Soybean** & **Sugarbeet**.
- Highest acidic soils are found in **Assam< West Bengal< Bihar**.
- The highest SSP producer plants are in **Rajasthan**.
- Highly salt-tolerant crops are **Barley and sugarbeet**.
- Humic acid is soluble in **Alkali solution.**
- Ideal NPK ration for Cereals **421** & Pulses **121.**
- If, EC < 4 (ds/m), ESP > 15%, > pH 8.5 the soil will be Alkali.
- If, EC > 4 (ds/m), ESP < 15%, pH < 8.5 the soil will be Saline.
- If, EC > 4 (ds/m), ESP > 15%, pH < 8.5 the soil will be Saline alkali.
- Indian Institute of Soil Science (ISS) is situated in **Bhopal (M.P.)**.
- Indicator plant for Nitrogen deficiency **Cauliflower, cabbage**, Phosphorus deficiency **Mustard**, Potassium deficiency **Potato**, Sodium deficiency **Sugar beet** & **Turnip**, and Boron deficiency **Sunflower.**
- The insoluble fraction of soil organic matter is **Human**.
- **Interveinal chlorosis** occurs due to **Fe** deficiency.
- **K*** & **Na*** are determined by a **Flame photometer**.
- ***Kankar*** nodules are found mostly in **Laterite** and **Red soils**.
- Kaolinite is a type of mineral **11 type**, Montmorillonite **2 1 expanding type**.
- The law of minimum was proposed by **Von Liebig (1840)**.
- Liebig Law of Minimum was restated as the **Barrel concept**.
- Limestone, Dolomite, and stone are a type of **Sedimentary rocks.**
- Little leaf of cotton occurs due to **Zn** deficiency.
- The major constituent of chlorophyll is **Mg**.

- Major source of Mg - **Dolomite**, P- **Apatite**, B- **Tourmaline**, Mo- **Olivine**, K- **Orthoclase.**
- A major source of **Mn**- Pyrolusite.
- The maximum Eluviation horizon is **E**-horizon.
- Mechanical analysis of soil separation is done by the **Hydrometric method**.
- **Mn** Nutrient availability increases in rice fields due to water logging.
- Most & least resistant to weathering **Quartz** & **Calcite**.
- The most dominant mineral on Earth's crust is **Feldspars (48%).**
- The most essential function of **K** is **Stomata regulation**.
- Most of the exchange of gases in soils is due to **Diffusion**.
- The most outstanding green manure crop *is **Sunhemp.***
- The most serious form of water erosion is **Sheet erosion**.
- Most soil erosion is caused by **Saltation**.
- **Na** is essential for **Sugarbeets.**
- ***Nif gene is*** responsible for N fixation.
- Nitrate fertilizers should be applied in the **Oxidized zone.**
- Nitrogen Analyzing process for determination of available through Alkaline permanganate method.
- Nitrogen is an essential constituent of protein.
- horizon is absent in **Arable soils.**
- On the number basis population of microbes in soils - **Bacteria** > **Actinomycetes > Fungi > Algae**.
- The optimum temperature & pH for Nitrifying bacteria is **30-35°C** & **6.5- 7.5.**
- Organic carbon is determined by **Walkey** & **Black method** 2. **Morgan's method**.
- Organic matter content in Indian soils is **<0.5%.**
- **P** Nutrients essential for energy transformation.
- Particle Density is **2.65 g/cm3** and Bulk Density is **1.33 mg/cm3**.
- Phosphorus is extracted by **Olsen's method** & **Bray No. 1 method**.
- The physical property of Soil texture **cannot be changed.**
- Problems of Alluvial soils are highest in **Uttar Pradesh**.
- The process of mixing soils is known as **Pedoturbation**.
- The process of moving out of sesquioxide is known as **Podzolization**.
- The recently formed soil order is ***Entisols.***
- Red soils are mostly found in **Tamil Nadu**.

- **Rhizobium** is an Example of a symbiotic nodule forming aerobic & heterotrophic bacteria.
- Rosetting & excess gumming occurs due to **Cu** deficiency.
- **S** is essential for Oil seed crops.
- **Sandy loams** are the most suitable for most of the crops.
- Sickle leaf disease occurs due to **P** deficiency.
- Silicon is essential for **Rice and maize**.
- Size of soil colloids Less than **1 ppm**.
- Sodium (Na) is essential for **Osmo-regulation**.
- Soils having at least **20% organic matter** are known as Organic soils.
- Soils have the highly decomposed organic matter known as **Muck soils**.
- Source of phosphorus in acid soil **Bone meal**.
- The study of soils about higher plants is called **Edaphology**.
- Tea-yellow disease occurs due to **S** deficiency.
- A fertilizer having less than **25%** of the primary nutrients is known as an analysis fertilizer.
- The **Nitrate form** of N is preferable for saline soils.
- The **Paddy** & **Potato** absorbs the ammoniacal form directly.
- The smallest volume of soil is called **Pedon.**
- The soils that have pH < **4.0** are known as **Cat soils**.
- Tip burn, and margin scorching show the deficiency of **K+.**
- The top most mineral horizon is the **'A'** horizon.
- The top sickness of tobacco occurs due to **B** deficiency.
- Urea is a type of **Organic fertilizer**.
- **V-shaped** yellowing at the tip of the lower leaves shows **N** deficiency.
- Water held up to the tension of about ***31 ATM*** is known as the **Hygroscopic coefficient**.
- Weight of soil furrow slice **2 x 10^6 kg/ha**.
- **Whiptail** of cauliflower occurs due to **Mo** deficiency.
- White tip & white bud of maize occur due to **Zn** deficiency.
- Wood is mainly decomposed by **Actinomycetes**.
- Zinc is required for the biosynthesis of hormones.

Agricultural chemistry

- **Nucleic acids** are composed of nucleotides.
- **DNA** is a double-helical structure, while **RNA** is typically single-stranded.
- **Nucleosides** are formed by a base attached to a sugar.
- **Nucleotides** consist of a base, sugar, and phosphate group.
- The **pyrimidines** are **cytosine, thymine**, and **uracil**.
- The **purines** are **adenine** and **guanine**.
- **DNA** has a **deoxyribose** sugar, whereas **RNA** contains **ribose**.
- **Phosphodiester bonds** link nucleotides together in nucleic acids.
- **DNA replication** is semiconservative.
- **Transcription** is the process of forming RNA from a DNA template.
- **Enzymes** act as biological catalysts in biochemical reactions.
- **Substrate specificity** is a unique property of enzymes.
- **Lock and key hypothesis** explain enzyme-substrate specificity.
- **Induced fit model** suggests enzymes change shape to fit substrates.
- **Enzyme kinetics** studies reaction rates involving enzymes.
- **Michaelis-Menten equation** explains enzyme kinetics.
- **Km** represents the substrate concentration at half of the maximum velocity.
- **Lineweaver-Burk plot** is a graphical representation of enzyme kinetics.
- **Competitive inhibition** occurs when an inhibitor resembles the substrate.
- **Non-competitive inhibition** occurs when an inhibitor binds to a site other than the active site.
- **Uncompetitive inhibition** involves the inhibitor binding only to the enzyme-substrate complex.
- **Allosteric enzymes** regulate enzyme activity by binding at sites other than the active site.
- **Isozymes** are enzyme variants that catalyze the same reaction.
- **Coenzymes** are non-protein molecules assisting enzymes in catalysis.
- **Apoenzyme** is the protein portion of an enzyme, requiring a cofactor for activity.
- **Cofactors** can be inorganic ions like Fe^{2+}, Mg^{2+}, or organic coenzymes.
- **Enzyme activity** is highly dependent on **pH**.
- Most enzymes have an **optimum temperature** for activity.
- Enzyme activity is often maximal at a specific **pH value**.

- **Hydrolases** catalyze hydrolysis reactions.
- **Ligases** catalyze the joining of two molecules with ATP hydrolysis.
- **Isomerases** catalyze structural rearrangements within a molecule.
- **Transferases** transfer functional groups between molecules.
- **Oxidoreductases** catalyze redox reactions.
- **Lyases** break bonds without hydrolysis, forming double bonds.
- **Temperature** increases reaction rates up to a certain point, beyond which enzymes denature.
- **Substrate concentration** affects enzyme activity and follows a hyperbolic curve.
- Enzyme **denaturation** occurs at extreme pH or temperature.
- **Enzyme assay** measures enzyme activity under specific conditions.
- **Catalase** breaks down hydrogen peroxide into water and oxygen.
- **Pepsin** works in acidic environments to break down proteins.
- **Trypsin** is active in the small intestine and cleaves peptide bonds.
- **Lactate dehydrogenase** converts pyruvate to lactate in anaerobic conditions.
- **Glucose-6-phosphate dehydrogenase** is involved in the pentose phosphate pathway.
- **Phosphorylation** of glucose by **hexokinase** is a critical step in glycolysis.
- **DNA polymerase** catalyzes the formation of DNA strands.
- **RNA polymerase** transcribes DNA into RNA.
- **Reverse transcriptase** synthesizes DNA from an RNA template in retroviruses.
- **Telomerase** adds repetitive sequences to the ends of chromosomes.
- **Ligase** joins fragments of DNA together during replication and repair.
- **Amino acids** are the building blocks of proteins.
- **Peptide bonds** link amino acids to form polypeptides.
- **Primary protein structure** refers to the sequence of amino acids.
- **Secondary structures** include **α-helix** and **β-pleated sheets**.
- **Tertiary structure** results from interactions between amino acid side chains.
- **Quaternary structure** involves the arrangement of multiple polypeptide chains.
- **Hemoglobin** is a protein with quaternary structure consisting of four polypeptide chains.
- **Myoglobin** stores oxygen in muscle tissues and has a single polypeptide chain.

- **Fibrous proteins**, like collagen, provide structural support.
- **Globular proteins**, like enzymes, are functional proteins.
- **Denaturation** causes the loss of protein function.
- **Protein folding** is essential for correct enzyme function.
- **Chaperones** assist in protein folding.
- **Enzyme-substrate complex** is an intermediate in enzyme catalysis.
- **Transition state theory** explains how enzymes lower the activation energy of reactions.
- **Ribozymes** are RNA molecules with catalytic activity.
- **Allosteric regulation** controls enzyme activity via conformational changes.
- **Feedback inhibition** is a common regulatory mechanism for enzymes.
- **Proenzymes** or **zymogens** are inactive precursors of enzymes.
- **Isoenzymes** exhibit different kinetics but catalyze the same reaction.
- **Km** reflects the enzyme's affinity for a substrate; low **Km** means high affinity.
- **Vmax** is the maximum rate of an enzyme-catalyzed reaction.
- **Temperature optima** vary across different enzymes.
- **pH optima** are specific for each enzyme, influencing their ionization state.
- **Acidic pH** may protonate enzyme active sites, reducing activity.
- **Basic pH** may deprotonate substrates or enzyme active sites, affecting activity.
- **Allosteric inhibitors** bind at sites other than the active site.
- **Competitive inhibitors** can be overcome by increasing substrate concentration.
- **Non-competitive inhibition** cannot be reversed by increasing substrate concentration.
- **Allosteric activators** stabilize the enzyme's active form.
- **Lock and key** model emphasizes the specific fit between enzyme and substrate.
- **Induced fit model** suggests enzymes are flexible, adapting to substrates.
- **Suicide inhibitors** irreversibly inactivate enzymes.
- **Isoenzymes** are found in different tissues with specific roles.
- **Carboxylase** adds CO_2 to substrates.
- **Decarboxylase** removes CO_2 from organic compounds.
- **Enzymes** can have **metal ions** as cofactors.
- **ATP** serves as an energy source in many enzymatic reactions.
- **NAD^+** and **NADH** are electron carriers in metabolic pathways.

- **FAD** and **$FADH_2$** are involved in redox reactions.
- **Thiamine pyrophosphate** is a coenzyme in decarboxylation reactions.
- **Coenzyme A** is involved in acyl group transfer reactions.
- **Biotin** is a cofactor in carboxylation reactions.
- **Vitamin B12** is required for **methionine synthase** activity.
- **S-adenosylmethionine** donates methyl groups in biosynthetic reactions.
- **Protein stability** depends on temperature, pH, and solvent conditions.
- **Renaturation** is the process of refolding denatured proteins.
- **Proteolysis** breaks down proteins into smaller peptides or amino acids.
- **Ubiquitin** marks proteins for degradation in cells.
- **Chymotrypsin** is a digestive enzyme that breaks down proteins in the small intestine.
- **Phosphatases** remove phosphate groups from molecules.
- **Kinases** add phosphate groups to proteins, often regulating activity.
- **Aminotransferases** transfer amino groups between amino acids and keto acids.
- **Maltase** catalyzes the hydrolysis of maltose into glucose.
- **Invertase** breaks down sucrose into glucose and fructose.
- **Gluconeogenesis** is the process of synthesizing glucose from non-carbohydrate precursors.
- **Glycolysis** is the breakdown of glucose to pyruvate.
- **Pentose phosphate pathway** generates NADPH and ribose-5-phosphate.
- **Krebs cycle** generates ATP, NADH, and $FADH_2$.
- **Oxidative phosphorylation** produces ATP via the electron transport chain.
- **Photosynthesis** converts light energy into chemical energy stored in sugars.
- **Chlorophyll** is the primary pigment involved in photosynthesis.
- The **light reactions** occur in the **thylakoid membranes** of chloroplasts.
- The **dark reaction (Calvin cycle)** happens in the **stroma** of chloroplasts.
- **ATP** and **NADPH** produced in light reactions power the Calvin cycle.
- **CO2** is fixed into organic compounds during the Calvin cycle.
- **RuBisCO** catalyzes the carboxylation of ribulose-1,5-bisphosphate in the Calvin cycle.
- **Hill's reaction** demonstrates the splitting of water and oxygen release in light reactions.

- **Photorespiration** occurs when RuBisCO fixes oxygen instead of CO_2.
- **C3 plants** undergo photorespiration due to the inefficiency of RuBisCO at high O_2 levels.
- **C4 plants** minimize photorespiration by spatially separating carbon fixation and the Calvin cycle.
- **C4 plants** like maize have higher photosynthetic efficiency under hot, dry conditions.
- **CAM plants** like cacti fix CO_2 at night to reduce water loss.
- **CO_2 fixation** in CAM plants occurs during the dark, while the Calvin cycle occurs during daylight.
- **Malate** is a temporary storage molecule in C4 and CAM plants.
- **CO_2 concentration** increases photosynthesis up to a saturation point.
- **Temperature** affects photosynthetic rates, with an optimal range for most plants.
- **Carbohydrate metabolism** begins with **glycolysis**, the breakdown of glucose into pyruvate.
- **Glycolysis** occurs in the cytosol and does not require oxygen.
- **Pyruvate** enters the **TCA cycle** (Krebs cycle) in the mitochondria under aerobic conditions.
- The **TCA cycle** generates **NADH, $FADH_2$**, and ATP.
- The **electron transport chain (ETC)** occurs in the inner mitochondrial membrane.
- **ATP synthase** generates ATP using the proton gradient from the ETC.
- **Oxidative phosphorylation** is the main method of ATP production in aerobic organisms.
- **Beta-oxidation** breaks down fatty acids to produce acetyl-CoA.
- **Fatty acids** enter the **TCA cycle** after conversion to acetyl-CoA.
- **Fatty acid biosynthesis** occurs in the cytoplasm, opposite to its degradation in mitochondria.
- **Secondary metabolites** in plants include **phenolics, terpenoids**, and **alkaloids**.
- **Phenolics** provide plant defense against herbivores and pathogens.
- **Terpenoids** play roles in plant growth regulation and defense.
- **Alkaloids** are nitrogenous compounds with medicinal properties.
- **Phenolics** include **flavonoids** that contribute to the color of flowers.
- **Salicylic acid**, a phenolic, plays a role in plant defense mechanisms.
- **Shikimate pathway** is involved in the biosynthesis of phenolic compounds.
- **Lignin**, a phenolic, provides mechanical support in plant cell walls.

- **Monoterpenes** and **sesquiterpenes** are volatile compounds involved in plant defense.
- **Steroids** and **carotenoids** are examples of terpenoids.
- **Alkaloids** like **morphine** and **quinine** are used in medicine.
- **Glycolysis** results in the net production of **2 ATP** molecules per glucose molecule.
- NAD+ is reduced to **NADH** during glycolysis and the TCA cycle.
- **Oxygen** is the final electron acceptor in the **electron transport chain**.
- **C4 pathway** separates initial CO2 fixation and the Calvin cycle into different cells.
- **Photorespiration** is a wasteful pathway that decreases photosynthetic efficiency.
- **Pyruvate kinase** catalyzes the final step of glycolysis.
- The **TCA cycle** produces **3 NADH**, **1 FADH2**, and **1 GTP** per acetyl-CoA molecule.
- **Succinate dehydrogenase** is part of both the TCA cycle and the ETC.
- **ATP** is synthesized by **ATP synthase** using the proton gradient generated by the ETC.
- **Malate-aspartate shuttle** transports electrons from NADH into mitochondria for ATP production.
- **Oxaloacetate** is regenerated at the end of the TCA cycle to continue the cycle.
- **NADPH** is used in **fatty acid biosynthesis** as a reducing agent.
- **Triacylglycerols** are stored fats and broken down during beta-oxidation.
- **Acetyl-CoA carboxylase** regulates fatty acid biosynthesis.
- **Malonyl-CoA** is a precursor in fatty acid biosynthesis.
- **Phenolics** also function as antioxidants, protecting plants from oxidative stress.
- **Flavonoids** protect plants against UV radiation.
- **Anthocyanins**, a type of flavonoid, contribute to red, purple, and blue colors in plants.
- **Phenolic acids** are involved in the plant's response to biotic and abiotic stress.
- **Terpenoids** like **gibberellins** are plant hormones that regulate growth.
- **Carotenoids**, another group of terpenoids, play roles in photosynthesis.
- **Alkaloids** often act as **antifeedants** against herbivores.
- **Alkaloids** such as **atropine** and **nicotine** are toxic to animals.
- **Secondary metabolites** are not directly involved in plant growth but

serve ecological functions.

- **Pyruvate dehydrogenase** converts pyruvate into acetyl-CoA.
- **Fumarate** is converted into **malate** in the TCA cycle.
- **Citrate synthase** catalyzes the first step of the TCA cycle.
- **Aconitase** converts citrate into isocitrate in the TCA cycle.
- **Hill reaction** is the photochemical splitting of water in photosynthesis.
- **Chloroplasts** are the site of photosynthesis in plant cells.
- **P680** is the reaction center of **Photosystem II** in light reactions.
- **P700** is the reaction center of **Photosystem I** in light reactions.
- **Plastoquinone** and **plastocyanin** are electron carriers in the ETC of photosynthesis.
- **Photosystem II** splits water to release oxygen.
- **Calvin cycle** regenerates ribulose-1,5-bisphosphate for continued CO2 fixation.
- **Triose phosphates** are products of the Calvin cycle used for starch and sucrose synthesis.
- **Pyruvate carboxylase** replenishes oxaloacetate in the TCA cycle.
- **Malate dehydrogenase** converts malate to oxaloacetate in the TCA cycle.
- **Gluconeogenesis** produces glucose from non-carbohydrate precursors.
- **Phosphoenolpyruvate** is a high-energy intermediate in glycolysis.
- **Phosphofructokinase** is the key regulatory enzyme in glycolysis.
- **Glyoxylate cycle** is a variation of the TCA cycle in plants that bypasses decarboxylation steps.
- **Beta-oxidation** produces **acetyl-CoA**, which enters the TCA cycle for energy production.
- **Oxidative phosphorylation** is the process of ATP synthesis using the proton gradient.
- **Malonyl-CoA** inhibits carnitine acyltransferase, regulating beta-oxidation.
- **Acetyl-CoA** is a central metabolite in both carbohydrate and lipid metabolism.
- **Citric acid cycle** connects the metabolism of carbohydrates, fats, and proteins.
- **Hill reaction** involves electron transfer from water to NADP+.
- **Glucose-6-phosphate** enters glycolysis or the pentose phosphate pathway.
- **ATP** is the primary energy currency in all living organisms.
- **Chloroplast ATP synthase** synthesizes ATP during photosynthesis.

- **Hexose monophosphate shunt** generates NADPH for biosynthetic reactions.
- **CAM plants** conserve water by opening their stomata at night.
- **Glycogen** is the storage form of glucose in animals, while **starch** serves this function in plants.
- **Fructose-1,6-bisphosphate** is an intermediate in glycolysis.
- **Lactic acid fermentation** occurs in the absence of oxygen in plants.
- **Alcoholic fermentation** is used by some plants under anaerobic conditions.
- **Proton gradient** drives ATP synthesis in both mitochondria and chloroplasts.
- **Electron carriers** such as **ubiquinone** and **cytochrome c** play roles in the ETC.
- **Decarboxylation** steps in the TCA cycle release carbon dioxide.
- **Phenolics** are biosynthesized through the **shikimate pathway**.
- **Glycolysis** splits glucose into two molecules of pyruvate.
- **Isocitrate dehydrogenase** is a key enzyme in the TCA cycle.
- **Oxidation of NADH** in the ETC releases energy for ATP synthesis.
- **Citrate** is the first molecule formed in the TCA cycle.
- **Oxaloacetate** is regenerated at the end of the TCA cycle.
- **C4 plants** include important crops like sugarcane and sorghum.
- **PEP carboxylase** is a key enzyme in C4 and CAM plants for CO2 fixation.
- **Starch** is synthesized from glucose during photosynthesis in plants.
- **Tricarboxylic acid (TCA) cycle** is essential for cellular respiration.
- **Photosynthesis** is regulated by environmental factors like light, CO2, and temperature.
- **Flavonoids** also act as signaling molecules in plant-microbe interactions.

Agriculture Engineering

- An average man can develop maximum power of about **0.1 hp** for doing farm work.
- Power developed by an average **pair of bullocks** about **1 hp (0.5+ 0.5)** for usual farm work.
- The thermal efficiency of diesel engines varies from **32 to 38 percent** whereas that of petrol enginesvaries from 25 to 32 %.
- Compression ignition engine air is compressed and rises to **700-900** C.
- The stroke engine cycle is completed in **two revolutions** of the crankshaft and the stroke enginecycle is completed in **one revolution** of the crankshaft.
- Air-fuel mixture inside the engine cylinder is called **suction.**
- Injection of fuel in compressed air for ignition of the fuel by an electric spark to produce thermal powerinside the cylinder is called power.
- Removal of the burnt gases from the **cylinder** to receive fresh charge is called **exhaust**.
- Diesel engine has got valves for controlling the inlet of charge and outlet of exhaust gases.
- The diesel engine has a high compression ratio ranging from **141 to 221.**
- In the Diesel engine, an external spark. maintains higher torque for a longer duration of time at a lower speed.
- Only air is sucked into a cylinder in a suction stroke.
- Compression pressure inside the cylinder varies from 35 to 45 kg/cm2 and temperatureis about 500°C. kg/cm2.
- Compression pressure varies from 6 to 10 kg/cm2 and tempeṙature is above 260°C.
- Power S.I. unit of a watt. Watt = Joule/sec. (4.2 Joules = 1 Calorie). In metric units, the power can beexpressed in kg.m/sec.
- The PTO hp is around **80-85%** of tractor engine power.
- in India, Tractor manufacturing was started by **M/s Eicher Good Earth** (1960).
- on the basics of Landholding **20-25 hp** tractor is suitable for a **40-hectare farm.**
- on the basics of Cropping pattern 30-35 hp tractor is suitable for **40**

hectares of land.

- In India, the tractor is required for agricultural operations on 25-80 hp. Walking-type tractors are fitted with 8-12 hp engines.
- ASAE standards PTO speed is 540+ 10 rpm. the new standard has been developed to operate a **1000rpm** PTO drive machine.
- power tiller wheels inflation pressure ranges from 1.1 to 1.4 kg/cm2.
- **Primary tillage** mold-board ploughs, disc ploughs, heavy-duty disk harrows, and chisel ploughs.
- **Indigenous plow** field capacity is around **0.4 ha** per day of **8 hours**. The functional components include **share**, body, shoe, handle, and beam.
- Mould board that **pulverizes the soil slice**.
- Disc harrow is a circular **concave disc size 35-70 cm.** Gang bolt is the range between thediscs on the gang bolt from 15 to 25 cm harrows.
- A manual rice planter power harrow width of the operation is 2000 mm. and the field capacity is **1.5 ha/day.**
- The rotary tiller or rotary cultivator is widely considered as the most important implement for soilpulverization and the rotor is operated at **180- 200 rpm.**
- The automatic potato planter plant in 2-4 rows. Capacity is **6000-14000 potatoes/hr. it** is over 0.25 ha/ day and the mat seedlings of age 15-20 days, prepare100 m2 nursery for each 1 ha to be planted.
- Power teller came into the world in **1920.** Introduced in **India in 1963**.
- In India, walking-type tractors are fitted with **8-12 hp** engines.
- In India, **75%** of farm holdings belong to small and marginal formers.
- **1000 hectares** of cultivated lands by bullocks' requirements 500 pairs, Power tiller power tiller 200 and tractors are generally required tractor 67.
- Studies have shown that about **54% of energy** in crop production comes from a direct source like mechanical powers, electrical, and human power brought by animals, and 46% of power comes from indirect sourceslike fertilizer, chemicals seeds farm yard manures.
- MB plow, tractor full work **2.5-3.0 ha/day**.
- Rotavator work capacity of five hours per hectare.
- In India, the level of form mechanization stands at **40-45%.**
- In the world, the level of form mechanization stands at **U.S. (95%),** Brazil (75%), and China (57%).
- Sub-mission on agriculture mechanization (SMAM) launched by the

Ministry of Agriculture and Farmers Welfare in the **year 2014- 15** for five years.

- First commercial tidal energy power station in **France (1965).**
- The flywheel is mounted on the rear end of the crankshaft.
- The speed of the camshaft is exactly **half the speed** of the crankshaft in **four-stroke engines.**
- The fuel pressure at the feed pump must be in a range of **1.5 to 2.5 kg/cm3.**
- The cross-sectional area of one cylinder of the engine multiplied by its stroke is swept volume.
- Rotary tillage used as **primary and secondary operations**. PTO of the tractor operated at **180-200rpm.**
- The concept of minimum Tillage is started in the **USA.**
- The optimum range of soil moisture for effective ploughing is 25 to 50 % depletion of available moisture.
- Central Research Institute for Dryland Agriculture (CRIDA), Hyderabad according to deep ploughing **25-30 cm**, medium **15 - 20 cm.**
- Indigenous Plough/country plough is form **'V' shaped** furrows with a 15-20cm top width and depth of 12-15 cm, its field capacity is around **0.4 ha Per day of 8 hours**. Form walks **65-66 km** on foot while ploughing 1 ha land having 15 cm furrow width.
- Disc harrow have **concave discs** of size varying from 35-70 cm in diameter.
- Capacity of volume sprayer is **(high -400, low 5-400, ultra-low** <5) liters/ ha.
- Knapsack sprayer tank capacity is 10-15 litres. Its average pump pressure is up to 3 to 12 kg/cm2, Discharge rate ranges from 500 liters/ha.
- 3 hp power required for power sprayer.
- The cheapest source of energy is **renewable energy.**
- PTO was introduced in 1915-1919.
- Chisel plough work up to **60-70 cm depth** and 10-15 Hp per will be Required.
- **type greenhouse** is placed against the **side of the existing building.**
- It faces typically the **Southside** and total width of 7-12 feet.
- **Even span-type** greenhouse standard type **two roof slope** or equal pitch and width.
- Single span size is 5-9m and length 24m.

- Sawtooth-type greenhouses are like side and furrow types of natural ventilation type.
- Uneven span type treehouse is constructed on a hilly area.
- Visible and white light was wavelength of **400 - 700 nm**.
- For most of the crops are acceptable range of relative humidity is between **50-80%**.
- Most crops cell responses favourably to CO_2 at **1000 -1200** ppm
- Glass and acrylic sheet life span greenhouse are ideal for **10-20 years**.
- Power requirements are usually water pressure of 0.5kg/cm2 to 10kg/cm2.
- The **emitter's** discharge rate is usually from **2-10 liters per hour**.
- Threshing in manual range 30-50 kg /h and power thrashing range 300 -500kg/h.
- Traditional storage structure is ***Bukhari* type** storage capacity 3.5 - 18t. Examples are wheat, paddy, maize, and sorghum. ***Kothar* type** capacity 9-35 t. Examples are paddy, maize, and sorghum.
- Surveying is the art of determining the surface of the earth by measuring the horizontal and vertical distances between them and by preparing a map to any suitable scale.
- Gunter chain comes in **standard 66ft**.
- square Gunter's chains = 1 Acre, Gunter chains = 1 mile.
- Engineers' chain comes in 100ft length.
- The average force that a draft animal can exert is approximately **1/10** of its body weight.
- Percent of methane gas in biogas varies from **45 to 70%**.
- Better biogas production, the pH of slurry should be between **7 to 8**.
- Thermal efficiency of biogas is about **60%.**
- Thermal efficiency of cow dung is about **11%.**
- The **horizontal distance** between the front and rear wheels of a tractor is called wheelbase.
- Ground clearance of the tractor is measured under **maximum permissible load conditions**.
- In tractors, the weight transfer is affected by wheelbase and hitch height.
- The desi plough cuts the soil in the shape of **'V'** and the M.B plough cuts the soil in the shape of **'L.'**
- The diameter of the disc plough in standard disc plough Rise from **60 to 90 cm.**
- Disc angle of a quality disc plough varies from **43 to 45°**.

- A good quality disc plough, the tilt angle varies from 15 to 20°.
- The soil mass, which is cut, lifted, and thrown during ploughing is called a **furrow slice.**
- The top portion of the turned soil mass is called the **crown.**
- An open trench left between two adjusted strips of land after ploughing is called a **dead furrow.**
- Un-ploughed land left at the end of the field for turning the tractor is called **headland.**
- One-way ploughing is done by the **reversible plough.**
- Where the wind velocity is more than 32 km/hr windmills can be used for lifting water.
- The average capacity of a windmill would be about **0.5 HP.**
- The engine is a mechanical device that generates thermal energy and transforms it into **mechanicalenergy.**
- Diesel engine develops more torque when it is **heavily loaded while petrol.**
- Disc plow is not suitable for covering surface trace and weeds effectively.
- Blade Harrow popularly known as **Bakhar.**
- Power-operated sprayer suitable for treating a large area. they are operated at a pressure ranging from **20 to 55kg/cm2.**
- The efficiency of even the best heat engines is low usually below 50%.
- 4500 kg m of work /minute = 1.0 hp; 75 kg m of work /second = 1.0 hp;
- The word tractor appeared first on record in a patent issued on a tractor or traction engine invented by **George H. Harris of Chicago** (1890).
- Tractor manufacturing was started in India by the first manufacturer M/s **Eicher Good Earth (1960-1961).**
- Speed range of Low-speed engine less than 350 rpm, High-speed engine greater than **1000 rpm.**
- Sandy and hard compacted soil is not suitable for operating rotavators.
- Depth of penetration of disc harrow is altered by gang angle.
- The working life of a tractor-drawn cultivator is **2500 hours.**
- Mechanization level is measured in terms of kW/ha.
- capacity of tractor-drawn harrow in **1 - 2.0 ha/hr.**
- An average man can develop maximum power of **about 74.6W.**
- In the tractor, the three-point hitch is operated by the Hydraulic

system.

- MB PLOUGH, tractor pull can work in 1.5 to 2.0 ha. /Day.
- The crankshaft converts the **reciprocating motion** of the piston into the rotary motion of the **flywheel**.
- BHP (Brake Horse Power) It is horse Power available at the **end of the crankshaft**.
- BHP = IHP - FHP.
- IHP (indicated Horse Power) = BHP + FHP (Frictional Horse Power).
- The IHP of an engine is **always more than** its BHP.
- Two-stroke engines can be operated in both directions IHP > BHP > FHP.
- **Stroke bore ratio** It is defined as the ratio of the length of the cylinder to the diameter of the cylinder.
- **Firing order** It is defined as a sequence of power strokes in a multi-cylinder engine.
- **Traction** (The tendency of the wheel to grip the ground surface is called Traction) in the tractor can bereduced by **Wheel ballasting**.
- Ignition in the diesel cycle is a constant pressure process.
- The average force a draft animal can exert is nearly **1/10th of its body weight**.
- **Octane** and **Cetane** numbers indicate the ignition quality of fuel (Petrol and diesel respectively).
- **Compression ratio** It is the ratio of total cylinder volume to the clearance volume of an engine.
- **Thermal efficiency** The ratio of the horse output of the engine to the fuel horsepower input of the engine and expressed in percentage.
- **DBHP** It is defined as the power required to pull the engine.
- IHP (Indicated Horse Power) It is power generated in the engine cylinder and available at the top of the piston.
- Frog is part to which other components of the plow bottom are attached.
- Gutter is a stanchion barn that has a minimum slope of 2%.
- **Vertical section** of mould board plough is responsible for the depth of ploughing. While **horizontal section** for the width of ploughing.
- Residential building on the farm is the heart of the farmstead.
- Feed manger space may be between **70 to 75 cm** wide for each cow.
- In the deep litter system of the poultry house the floor area for each **bird is 0.36 m2**.

- The ideal fencing for poultry houses. Rabbits and goats are **close mesh type**.
- The dimensions of the cage house for one bird may be **0.6x0.2x0.45m**, placed it at **75-90 cm** from the floor, and for **400 birds** may be **23 x 5.5 m.**
- Normal silage ratio is **14 to 18 kg/cow/day**.
- 1 HP = 75 kg m /sec. = 746 watt.
- The Heart of the diesel engine is an injection, system, injector, and fuel pump.
- Specific fuel consumption of diesel engine 0.2 kg / BHP/hr.
- Specific fuel consumption of petrol engine 0.29 kg / BHP/ hr.
- The cooling system of an IC engine. maintains the engine temp **88-90°C** for heavier fuel. The cooling system of the IC engine maintains the engine temp at **71 to 82**°C for a petrol engine.
- **Magneto** is used to supply spark for ignition.
- Use of Tractor is considered economical when it is utilized for **1000 hrs/yr.**
- **Bore** is the diameter of the engine cylinder.
- The velocity of the stream of the river is measured directly by the **Current meter.**
- 0.15% carbon steel is most weldable.
- **Tacnometer** to measure revolution.
- Calorific value of Petrol 11,100 Kcal/kg. Biogas = 4500 Kcal/m3, Calorific value of High-speed diesel 10550 Kcal / kg.
- Horizontal suction of M.B. Plough is 5 mm, and Vertical suction is 3-6 mm.
- Indigenous Plow is used for multi-Purpose.
- The power used to perform various agricultural works on the farm is called **Farm Power.**
- Work that is done by pulling power by moving from one place to another is done by, is called Tractive Work.
- Those works that are done by humans, bullocks, or machines by remaining fixed in one place arecalled **Stationary works**.
- A horse has a horsepower of **0.65 to 1.25** horsepower.
- Water power is mostly used with the help of which to generate electricity **Water Wheel and Turbines.**
- **Canada and America** countries are completely mechanized countries.
- mechanization is not possible in India because of small farm holdings.
- One who changes or tries to change the conditions of stability or

motion of an object is called Force.

- The motion of the object is called **Kinetic energy.**
- That energy is due to the position of the object is called **Potential energy.**

Entomology

- Any species that interferes with human activities, property, or health or is objectionable is called Pest.
- A chemical that gives an adaptive advantage to the receiver but not to the emitter is **Kairomone.**
- A good trap crop for ***Spodoptera litura*** is **Castor**.
- A multiple insect and disease resistance variety of rice grown on more than 11 million ha. in the world is **IR-36.**
- A particular plant condition or environment that makes a plant resistant to pests under other circumstances is known as **Induced resistance**.
- Adult of ***Lytta spp***. feed on the inflorescence part.
- ***Amsacta moorei*** is the scientific name of the **Red hairy caterpillar.**
- An allelochemical beneficial to emitter only is **Allomone.**
- An insecticide having both fumigant and penetrative action **DDVP (Dichlorvos)**.
- An insecticide used as a seed treatment for sucking pests is **Imidacloprid.**
- Anamorphosis is found in the insect order **Protura**.
- Antennae is absent in **Protura.**
- A parasitic species grows parasitically on other parasitic species and this phenomenon is **Hyperparasitism.**
- ***Aphelinus mali*** has been a successful parasitoid in controlling **Apple wooly aphids**.
- Aphids in mustard can be controlled by **Imidacloprid**.
- ***Apis mellifera*** is the most suitable species for bee culture.
- ***Appis mellifera, the*** best suitable spp. for bee culture.
- **An aspirator** is used for Collecting small insects.
- The author of the book "Silent Spring" is **Rachel Carson.**
- ***Autocidal*** technique of insect control Release of sterile male.
- *Avermectins* are derived from **Bacteria**.
- ***Bacillus thuringiensis*** was first isolated from diseased larvae of Silkworm.
- The mode of action of (Bt) ***Bacillus thuringiensis*** is a **Stomach poison**. It is available in the market as **Dipel, Delfin** & **Thuricide**. It is discovered by ***S. Ishiwata.***

- Bacteria is produced at a commercial level for pest control ***Bacillus thuringiensis.***
- Bagging of fruit is recommended for the control of **Anar butterfly** & **fruit-sucking moth**.
- The binomial system of nomenclature was first given by **Carl Linnaeus.**
- Biological control of rice borer is ***Trichogramma japonicum***.
- Bipectinate antennae are present in the **Tasar silk moth**.
- The blackish appearance of safflower plants is due to the incidence of **Aphids.**
- **Blister beetle** undergoes ***Hyper metamorphosis*** type of metamorphosis.
- The body and wings are covered by overlapping scales found in **Lepidoptera.**
- **Bromadiolone** (0.005%) is an effective **Rodenticide**.
- Bt. cabbage is developed against the **Diamondback moth**.
- Bt. formulation is used for **Early instars** of **bollworms.**
- Bud necrosis in groundnuts is transmitted by **Thrips**.
- Bud necrosis in watermelon and muskmelon is transmitted by **Aphids**.
- Bunchy top in sugarcane is due to **Sugarcane top shoot borer.**
- ***Callosobruchus chinensis*** is a major store grain pest of **Gram**.
- ***Callosobruchus chinensis*** is a storage pest of **Pulse.**
- Celphos tablets are used for the management of Storage pests.
- Central Insecticides Laboratory (CIL) is located in **Faridabad.**
- Central Silk Board is located in **Bangalore.**
- Certain secretions attract the opposite sex of the same species termed **Pheromones.**
- **The cervix** is located between the **Head** & **prothorax.**
- Chaffy grains with black spots in rice are due to the Gundhi bug (***Leptocorisa acuta***).
- Chemicals used for the control of rats are called **rodenticides.**
- Chemically chitin is a **Polysaccharide**.
- Chewing and lapping type of mouth parts are present in **Honey bees**.
- The chief producer of *lac* is **Female**.
- A common molluscicide is **Metaldehyde**.
- Conservation of frogs is suggested for pest management in **Paddy crops.**

- Control of ***tundu*** disease Hot water treatment at 50 °C for 2 hrs.
- Control of weeds by a biological agent known as Parabiological control.
- ***Corcyra cephalonica*** is a **Primary** and **Secondary** store grain pest.
- ***Cryptobiosis*** is a phenomenon when insects become quiescent due to adverse climatic conditions and show no visible sign of **metabolic activity**.
- Cultivation of resistant variety is the **Cultural method** of pest control.
- Damaging stage of armyworm (***Mythimna separata***) is **Caterpillar.**
- Damaging stage of citrus psylla is **Nymph**.
- Damaging stage of thrips is **Both Nymph** and **Adult**.
- DDT was banned due to **Prolonged persistence in soil**.
- DDT was first synthesized by **Ziedler (1874).**
- DDVP is an insecticide that has **fumigant** and **penetrating action**.
- Deformities in Okra fruit are due to the infestation of ***Earias vitella.***
- **Diflubenzuron** is the chitin synthesis inhibitor.
- Directorate of Plant Protection & Quarantine is located in **Faridabad.**
- Division of the insect's body i.e. **Head, Thorax,** and **Abdomen** is called **Tagmosis.**
- Double seed formation in cotton bolls is due to pink bollworm.
- Eco-friendly insecticide is Nimbecidine.
- Egg laying site for ***Holotrichia serrata*** is **Compost pits**.
- **Elytra wings** are present in **Coleoptera.**
- **Endosulfan** is the safest insecticide for honey bees.
- Enforcement of laws for the control of insect pests in India is governed by Destructive.
- ***Epiricania melanoleuca*** is a lepidopteron parasitoid effective against ***Sugarcane pyrilla.***
- Eri silkworm is reared on **Castor.**
- An example of an insect order having an aquatic nymphal stage is **Odonata**.
- The family of whitefly is **Aleyrodidae.**
- Females of red cotton bugs lay eggs in **Soils**.
- The first chemical pesticide used in India was **DDT.**
- The first part of the antennae is **Scape.**
- Flaring of squares in cotton is due to Spotted bollworm (***Earias vitella***).

- Flooding of the field will help to control **White grub, Termites & Cutworms.**
- Fore legs are modified for catching prey in **Mantid.**
- Fumigants are **Respiratory poison.**
- Galleries in the seed of pigeon peas indicate the damage of **Tur Pod Fly.**
- Gizzard helps in the **Crushing of food.**
- Grasshoppers lay eggs in the soil of **fallow lands** and **bands.**
- Grease painting (tree banding) in mango tree is done to control the **Mealy bug.**
- **Hamulate wing** coupling is present in **Honey bees.**
- ***Ha*NPV** is used against **American bollworms.**
- ***Helicoverpa armigera*** is an international polyphagous pest.
- Highest consumption of pesticides in the crop **Cotton.**
- The hind legs of honey bees are also known as **Corbicula.**
- Hopper burn symptoms in rice due to BPH (***Nilaparvata lugens***).
- House fly spread the disease **Cholera.**
- **Housefly**, insect possesses halters.
- The ideal trap crop used for control of tomato fruit borer is **Marigold.**
- If a pest is confined to a particular area and **occurs regularly**, its infestation is termed as **Endemic.**
- **Imidacloprid** belongs to the group of insecticides called **Neonicotinoids.**
- The immature stage of insects is Juvenile.
- In Bt-cotton, **10,000 plants/ha** is the optimum plant population.
- In the case of order **Isoptera** the damage is caused by the **Worker.**
- In Cockroaches, a **Hypognathous** type of head position is observed.
- In the digestive system of cockroaches, **Malpighian tubules** are present at the **Junction of the mid & Hindgut.**
- In honey bee pollen basket is present in **Hind leg.**
- In paddy, the formation of onion-like silvery shoots in place of normal ear head is due to **Gall midge.**
- In rice, Gundhi Bug causes damage during the **Milky stage.**
- In sorghum zonal sowing is recommended against **Midge fly.**
- Insects that can survive at higher temperatures and low humidity are the **Khapra beetle.**
- Insects pass through four stages Egg, Larvae, Pupa, and Adult under

Complete metamorphosis.

- Insecticidal properties of DDT were discovered by **Paul Muller**.
- Insects and Pests Act **(1914).**
- Insects are the most abundant and diversified of all animals due to their 3 Pairs of legs.
- International Institute of Biological Control located in West Indies, 1927.
- International Organization for Biological Control Zuriec Switzerland.
- **Inundative release** is associated with **Biological Control**.
- **Jassids** produce the hopper burn symptoms in cotton.
- Juvenile hormone secreted by **Corpora allata**.
- **The Kusum tree** is associated with the **Lac insect.**
- Ladybird beetle is a **Predator.**
- Ladybird beetle represents the **Third tropic level** in the agroecosystem.
- In the world, the largest consumer of silk is **India**.
- The largest size of the honey bee is ***Apis dorsata***.
- Leading producer of lac in the world **China.**
- **Leaf tip clipping** at the time of transplanting is recommended for **Paddy stem borer.**
- Light trap is used to attract the **Nocturnal pest.**
- Light traps are used for the collection of **Positively phototrophic insects.**
- **Limnetic zone,** the open water zone to the depth of effective light penetration.
- Major pests cause damage to more than 10% of the field.
- Mango stone weevil is the monophagous pest of **mango.**
- Metaldehyde is a **Molluscicide**.
- **Methyl eugenol** acts as an **Attractant**.
- Mining and skeletonization of cabbage leaves are the characteristic damage symptoms of the **Painted bug.**
- **Monoculture** is responsible for the pest outbreak.
- Most cosmopolitan polyphagous insect is **Locust.**
- Mustard sawfly is classified in the order **Hymenoptera.**
- **Bark-eating caterpillar** is managed by probe method.
- **Nephrocytes** are related to **Excretion**.
- ***Nosema bombycis*** causes a disease in silkworms Pabrine.

- ***Nosema apis*** of honey bees is caused by protozoa.
- Nozzle is a part of **Sprayer**.
- NPV is mostly used to control **Lepidopteran insects**.
- One egg/second laid by termite.
- **6** segments in insect head.
- Pebrine is the **transovarian disease** of **mulberry silkworm**.
- Peritrophic membrane is present in **Solid feeders**.
- Pest population should be kept below the **Economic Threshold Level (ETL).**
- "National pest" is White grub.
- 'International pest' is Desert locust (***Schistacera gregarea***).
- Pheromone trap attracts **Males.**
- Pheromones are also known as **Ectohormones.**
- Phorate 10 G is a granular insecticide HaNPV acts as a **Stomach poison**.
- Phytosanitary certificate is related to **Legal control**.
- Piercing and sucking types of mouth parts are present in **Red cotton bugs**.
- Pipronyl butoxide is an example of **Synergist**.
- Ploughing of the field is a cultural control method.
- Honey bees are **Beneficial insects**.
- Protein hydrolysate is used as an attractant for the control of **Fruit flies**.
- Pyrethrum is extracted from ***Chrysanthemum.***
- ***Rangeeni*** and ***Kusumi*** are the strain of ***Laccifera lacca.***
- ***Rangeeni*** strain is related to **Lac insect.**
- A recent method of control of bollworms is Bt. Transgenic plants.
- Resetting of cotton flowers due to Pink bollworm (***Pectinophora gossypiella***).
- Rice stem borer (***Scirpophaga incertulus***) is an absolute/monophagus pest of rice.
- The right mandible is absent in insect **Thrips**.
- ***Rodolia Cardinalis*** has been a successful predator in controlling the **Cottony cushion scale.**
- Scientific name of Brinjal shoot and fruit borer is ***Leucinodes orbonalis.***
- A secondarily wingless insect is the **Head louse**.

- A serious pest of wheat is **Termite**.
- Silver shoot & onion leaf in rice is caused by **Gall midge** (***Orseolia ooizae***).
- SINPV is used against which pest **Tobacco leaf eating caterpillar**.
- A specific pest of wheat nursery is Ghujhia weevil (***Tenymecus indicus***).
- Spotted bollworm, ***Earias vitella*** is a pest of **Cotton** & **Okra**.
- Sterile insect technique (SIT) developed by **E.F. Knipling** & **Bushland (1937).**
- A sticker that is used along with insecticide for better spread is **Teepol.**
- Sucking pests (aphids, jassids, whiteflies, and mealy bugs) are effectively controlled by **Systemic insecticide.**
- **Sulphur** is recommended to control **mites.**
- **Supra esophageal ganglion** is also called **Brain**.
- Termite control can also be done by **Irrigation.**
- Termite is known as an "Egg laying machine".
- Termites live in a social colony.
- The acaricide widely recommended for mite management is ***Kelthane*** (Dicofol).
- The anticoagulant used for the control of rats is Warfarin.
- The appropriate time for insecticide application to control damaging pests ETL.
- The caste of honey bee Workers is useful in **collecting honey**.
- The chief excretory organ in insects is the **Malpighian tubules**.
- The damaging stage of ***Eudocima materna*** is **Adult**.
- The dwelling place of termites is the **Mound/Termitarium**.
- The first commercial formulation of NPV was **Elcar**.
- The forewing of Coleoptera is called **Elytra.**
- The granular insecticide having a long residual effect is **Phorate**.
- The headquarters of the Directorate of Plant Protection, Quarantine, and Storage is located at Faridabad,Haryana.
- The infestation of which insect starts from the field **Angoumois grain moth**.
- The insecticide belonging to the organophosphate group is **Malathion.**
- The insects are ***poikilothermic*** i.e. they have no precise mechanism in the body temperature so also called cold-blooded organisms.

- The integument comprises of **Cuticle epidermis + basement.**
- The Johnson's organ is present on **Pedicel.**
- The lowest pest density causing economic damage is referred to as the **Economic Threshold Level (ETL).**
- The main characteristic feature of an insect is **Three pairs of legs**.
- The major excretory product of insects is **Uric acid**.
- The major insect enemy of honey bees is ***Galleria mellonella***.
- The male reproductive organ of the insect is present in the **9th segment**.
- The most effective molting hormone in insects is **Ecdysome.**
- The most suitable fumigant for quarantine purposes is **Methyl bromide.**
- The nozzle used for spraying herbicides is **Flat fan type**.
- **Four** primarily wingless/apterygote insect orders.
- The pest which attacks all the parts of the plant is **Termite**.
- The recommended trap crop for IPM of diamondback moth in cabbage is **Indian mustard**.
- The scientific name of maize stem borer is ***Chilo partellus.***
- The site of pupation of ***Helicoverpa armigera*** in Soil.
- The total heat required for the completion of physiological processes in the life history of a species isconsidered a Thermal constant.
- The toxin produced by ***Bacillus thuringiensis*** interferes with the insect's Digestive system.
- The young dragonfly is called a **Naiad.**
- Trap cropping is an example of a cultural method of **pest control.**
- Tree banding is useful for the control of **Mango mealy bugs.**
- ***Trichogramma chilonis*** is an **Egg parasitoid**.
- **Trichomes** present on leaves are associated with **Antixenosis**.
- The vector of the cotton leaf curl virus is Whitefly (***Bemisia tabaci***).
- The vector of rice 'Grassy stunt' disease is Brown Plant Hopper (***Nilaparvata lugens***).
- Wax moth (***Galleria melonella***) is the most serious pest of apiculture.
- Wheat stem borer (***Sesamia inferens***) attack at Night.
- **Wingless saprophagous** insects with the lowest number of six abdominal segments are present in **Collembola.**
- Yellow sticky trap is used to attract the pest **Aphids & Whiteflies**.
- **Zinc phosphide** is used against **Rat** non-insect pests.

Plant Pathology

- **Anton de Berry** was the Father of Pathology.
- Father of microbiology **Louis Pasteur**.
- Father of Mycology **P. A. Mitchell**.
- Father of Indian pathology **E. J. Butler**.
- Father of modern plant pathology **J. F. Dastur**.
- Exanthema disease caused by **Bacteria**.
- **ELISA** (Enzyme-linked immunosorbent assay) test is done to detect **Virus disease**.
- **Ooze test** is done to detect **Bacteria**.
- **Fire blight** of Pear was the **first** bacterial disease discovered.
- White rust of cruciferous caused by ***Albugo candida***.
- Most of the plant virus is single-stranded RNA.
- **Vitavax (Carboxin)** is an effective fungicide for **Smut disease**.
- Hot water treatment was developed by **J. L. Jensen** (1887) (Used for loose smut of wheat).
- **Bavistin** is a Systemic fungicide.
- The downy mildew of pearl millet is suppressed by **Chlorine**.
- Incidence of blast rice can be reduced by the application of **Silicon**.
- Agar- Agar is produced by **Red Sea algae (Nostoc)**.
- Mycoplasma is sensitive to **Tetracycline**.
- In the world, the first transgenic plant developed in **Tobacco.**
- Most common vectors of plant viruses are **Aphids**.
- The degree of infectivity of a given pathogen called **Virulence**.
- Iris famine is related to the Potato (1845). The disease occurred due to the Late blight of potatoes(***Phytophthora infestans).***
- Disease responsible for Bengal famine brown spot (***Helminthousporum oryzae)*** disease of Rice.
- Examples of **endemic disease**- Early blight of potato, **Epidemic disease** - Late blight of potato, Red rotof S. cane, Wheat rust disease.
- Copper sulfate was discovered by Prevost (1807). Father of Nematology Nathan Augustus Cobb.

- Death of tissues and cells, is the symptom of **Necrosis**.
- Increase in size of plant organ due to increase of cell **size** known as **Hypertrophy.** An increase in the size of plant organs due to an increase in the **number** of cells is known as **Hyperplasia**.
- Ufra disease of rice occurs due to Nematode (***Ditylenchus angustus***).
- **Ditylenclius** and **Anguina** are a type of nematode, both are **Ecto** & **Endo** parasite nematode.
- First plant parasite nematode Anguina tritici discovered by J. T. Needham (1743). Mentake disease of rice caused by Rice root nematode.

Important Crops Diseases

Rice

- Blast disease is due to ***Pyricularia Oryzae*** (**airborne**).
- Brown spot disease is due to ***Helminthosporium Oryzae*** (seed-borne).
- Bacterial blight disease is due to ***Xanthomonas campestris* pv. *Oryza***.
- ***Kresek*** symptom found in Bacterial blight (**Seedling stage**).
- Foot rot disease due to ***Fusarium moniliforme***.
- Sheath blight disease is due to ***Rhizoctonia solani***.
- Vector of rice ***tungro*** virus Green leaf hopper (***Nephotettix virescens***).
- Khaira disease of rice is due to **Zinc** deficiency.
- Ufra diseases of rice are due to ***Ditylenchus angustus* (Nematode)**.

Wheat

- Black stem rust disease is due to ***Puccinia graminis tritici***.
- Brown rust is due to ***Puccinia graminis triticina.***
- Loose smut is due to ***Ustilago tritici***, (**Internally seed borne**).
- Ear cockle disease is due to ***Anguina tritici*** (nematode).

Agricultural Economics

- (NCUI) National Co-operative Union of Warehousing Board was established in 1956.
- 14 major commercial banks were nationalized in 1969 as per the **RBI** norms, and **18 percent** of the Net Bank Credit should be deployed in agriculture.
- A fall in the market price increases the **Consumer's surplus.**
- A market structure with many producers selling the same product is known as **Perfectcompetition.**
- A National Bank, NABARD provides indirect finance to rural communities or farmers.
- A rise in the general price level of goods and services in an economy over a period is called **Inflation**. A indicating the financial condition of the farmer at a point in time is known as a **Net worth statement.** After the inflection point, the TPP curve increases at a **decreasing rate.** An erosion in the purchasing power is known as **Inflation**. The first stage of the production function is known as **Irrational**.
- ***Adam Smith*** is a father of economics.
- ***Adam Smith*** is the author of the book "**Wealth of Nations.**"
- AGMARK is an indicator of **Purity.**
- Agricultural cost and price commission was established in the year **1965.**
- Agriculture Insurance Company of India *Ltd.* started on **December 20, 2002.**
- Agriculture year **1 June** to **31 May.** Financial year **1 April** to **31 March.**
- All possible combinations of two inputs capable of producing the same level of output are referred to as **Isoquant.**
- All possible combinations of two inputs **Iso-cost line** can be purchased with a given amount of funds. Appropriate agronomic practices reduce **Production risk.**
- All possible combinations of two inputs that can be purchased with a given amount of funds are referred to asiso-cast line.
- **An oligopoly market** is more than two but still a few sellers of a commodity.
- **An open auction system** is the most common method that exists in a

regulated market.

- Anything that can satisfy human wants is called **Goods.**
- **APEDA** (1986)- Agricultural & Processed Food Products Export Development.
- As per Dalton, the optimum production is that which gives the **Maximum income per head**.

- B C ratio means **Gross return/Total cost** Consumption means **Destruction of utility.** Crop loans are an example of **Current liabilities.**
- BIRD (Bankers Institute of Rural Development) was promoted by **NABARD** in **1983** for Training,Research, and Consultant at Lucknow in (U.P).
- BIS (Bureau of Indian Standards) was set up on **1st April 1987**.
- Business is done by the rules and regulations and is called a **Regulated market**.
- **CACP** (1965)- Commission for Agriculture Cost & Price. CACP recommends the minimum support prices(MSP) for **23 crops**.
- Central Warehousing Corporation was started in the year 1957 (Corporate office New Delhi).
- Community Development Program was started on **2nd October 1952**.
- Co-operative movement in India started in **1904.** The Co-operative Credit Society Act was passed in **1904.**
- Crop farming and milk production is an example of **Complementary enterprise**.
- Demand for luxurious goods is **more elastic**.
- Demand for necessary commodities is **Inelastic.**
- The demand for agricultural products in general is **Inelastic.**
- The price elasticity of demand for 'food' is **Relatively inelastic**.
- **The negative** is the income elasticity of demand for inferior goods.
- The income elasticityof demand for Giffen goods.
- When demand does not change because of a price change, such elasticity is a case of **Inelastic demand**.
- Demand for wheat is **Inelastic**.
- DMI (Directorate of Marketing & Inspection, Setup 1935).
- ***F. Nicholson (1904)*** was ***the*** father of the cooperative movement in India.

- **Farm budgeting** is the most important component in farm management.
- Farm building value can be re-valued by the **Depreciation method.**
- Farm management is generally considered to fall in the field of **Microeconomics.**
- Father of economics, Modern economics, Agriculture economics, Adam Smith, Paul Samuelson.
- Fertilizers and seeds are examples of **Variable costs**. Sales tax is an example of **Indirect tax**.
- First crop loan wags given to **Cotton** (Maharashtra).
- 'Giffen' goods refers to **Inferior goods.**
- Govt. of India signed the WTO agreement in **1994.**
- If the marginal rate of substitution is smaller than **zero** the enter price relationship is **Competitive**.
- If the price of a commodity increases its demand will **Decrease**.
- If the price of its product is less than the average variable cost (AVC). Then the firm should **close** theoperation.
- If the rise in the price of one good leads to a fall in the demand for another good, the two goods can be called **Complementary goods.**
- In case of relatively inelastic (or less elastic) demand means **Ep < 1.**
- Perfectly inelastic demand is presented by Ep=0.
- Unitary (unit) elastic demand is presented by **Ep= 1.**
- The measure of the demand to the change in price of inter-relative goods is known as **Cross elasticity.**
- In economics any work done for earning money is called **wages.**
- In economics cash is a **Working capital.**
- In India, **Capitalistic farming** is restricted to the crops **Tea, Coffee** & **Rubber**.
- In India, **NABARD** is the apex body in **institution finance** for agriculture.
- In India, the first cooperative bank was situated in Greater Bombay (Co-operative of Bank Ltd.,) in **1952.**
- In India, the marketed surplus is greater than the marketable surplus.
- In India, the maximum agricultural area is irrigated by the **Canals**.
- In India, the maximum number of tube wells or pumping is found in **Tamil Nadu**.

- In market life blood is known as **Market information**.
- In the case of fruits and vegetables the marketed surplus is nearly **80%.**
- In the case of fruits and vegetables the marketed surplus is nearly **80%.**
- In three zones of production, Zone-I- **Increasing return**, Zone-II- **Decreasing return**, Zone-III- **Negative return**.
- **Keynes** is the father of modern economics.
- Land Development Bank Finances **Long-term loans.**
- Land holding for the **marginal farmer** is Less than 1 ha., small farmers 1-2 ha., Medium farmers 2-10.
- **Land rent** is one of the important fixed costs on farms.
- Liquidity preference theory was given by **M. Keynes.**
- Marginal cost always **Zero**.
- Medium-term Loan is given to purchase Agri equipment & Animals. Example- **Tractor Loan**.
- Monopoly market is only one buyer of the product.
- There are many buyers and sellers and they have perfect knowledge of demand, supply, and prices termed as the **Perfect market**.
- **Mr. Osporne A. Smith** was the first governor of RBI. **C. D. Deshmukh** was **the** first Indian governor of RBI.
- **NABARD** was established on **12 July 1982** with the recommendation of the ***Shivaraman committee***.
- **NAFED**- National Agricultural Cooperative Marketing Federation, New Delhi was established on **2nd Oct1958.**
- **NAIS (1999-2000)** - The National Agriculture Insurance Scheme was introduced in the country from Rabi.
- Name two types of wages (i) Nominal wages or money wages and (ii) Real wages.
- **NIAM (1988)**- National Institute of Agricultural Marketing is located at, **Jaipur** (Rajasthan).
- **Passive factor** is called farm production capital. **The active factor** is known as Labor in farm management.
- Period for short-term loan **1- to 1.5 Years**, Period for long-term loan **5 to 30 Years**.
- Planning Commission established in the year **1950.**
- RBI-Reserve Bank of India came into existence on **1 April 1935** with the **RBI Act 1934** and was nationalized on 1 January **1949.**
- Regional Rural Banks were established in the year 2nd Oct. 1975 (Muradabad, Gorakhpur, Bhiwani,Jaipur and Malda).

- Regulated Marketing is the most effective way to overcome the defects of **agriculture marketing.**
- Relationship between cost function and production function is **Negative.**
- Retail markets are **Perfect markets.**
- Risk is minimized in **Diversified farming.**
- Risk-bearing ability depends on **Net worth** When total utility is maximum then marginal utility is **Zero.**
- SBI came into existence on **1 July 1955.** RRB-Regional Rural Bank was established on 2 Oct 1975 (RRB Act 1976) Share capital of RRB was subscribed by the Central govt. 50%, state govt. 15%, and sponsored bank 35%.
- Short-term credit facility is given for **Crop production**.
- Short-term credit is given for **Crop production**.
- Stage 1 of production is also called the stage of **Increasing return**. In the monopoly market, there is **one seller of the produce**.
- Supplementary is one enterprise that neither adds nor hinders the production of another enterprise, the enterprise relationship.
- The 'AGMARK' (Agricultural Produce Grading and Marking) Act was enforced in **1937** and amended in 1986. The laboratory was situated in **Nagpur**.
- The addition made to the total utility by consuming one more unit of a commodity is called Marginal utility.
- The agriculture census is taken every **5 years.**
- The Agriculture Produces (Grading & Marketing) Act was passed in **1937**.
- The balance sheet of farmers exhibits the **financial position of a farmer**. Finance management at the farm level is called **microfinance management**.
- The central laboratory of AGMARK is located in **Nagpur,** Maharashtra.
- The cost involved in moving the product from the point of **production** to the point of **consumption** is called **Marketing cost.**
- The difference between consumers' and producers' prices is called **Price spread.**
- The father of the cooperative movement in India was **Nicholson**.
- The first crop loan was given to cotton at Berar in **Maharashtra**.
- The first function performed in the marketing of agricultural

commodities is **Packing.**

- **The** First Nationalization of commercial banks took place in the year **19 July 1969.**
- The first ***RuPay*** Kisan Card was established at the Bank of Maharashtra in Pune in November **2012.**
- **The gestation period** is the time gap between investment and return.
- The highest per capita income of farmers is in **Panjab.**
- The income that could have been received, if the input has been used in its most profitable alternativeuse is called **Opportunity cost**.
- The Indian economy is a **mixed type** economy.
- The law of diminishing returns operates when **One input is variable.**
- The law of diminishing returns was a most important principle in farm management.
- The **least cost combination** of production of the crop can be minimized by using economic principles.
- The line or curve connecting the least-cost combination of inputs for all output levels is known as **Isocline**.
- The Market where permanent/ durable commodities are traded is known as the **Secular market**.
- The measure of quantity demanded to a change in price is known as **Price elasticity of demand.**
- Less demand at a higher price means Contraction of demand.
- The measure of the reactivity of demand to changes in income is **Income elasticity.**
- A decrease in demand means less demand at the **Same price**.
- More demand at a lower price means an **Extension of demand.**
- A great rise or fall in the price of the commodity, its demand remains unchanged is known as **Perfectly inelastic demand.**
- The most limiting factor of production in Indian agriculture is **Capital**.
- The National Center for Agricultural Economics and Policy Research is located in **New Delhi.**
- The number of **Five** divisions of agricultural economics.
- The organization that promotes a universal standard for facilitating the international exchange of goods & Services is ISO (International Organization for Standardization) Estd. On 23rd Feburary, 1947.
- The percentage expenditure on luxurious commodities increases as

Income increases.

- The Planning Commission of India was established in **March 1950.**
- The first Five-Year Plan started on **1 April 1951.**
- The presence of a **single buyer** for the products, produced by the firm is called **Monopsony**.
- The principle of Equi-marginal returns is applied when Resources are limited. The price of resources is high.
- The most important principle of farm management is the **Law of diminishing return**.
- According to the law of diminishing return, the economically relevant zone is **Zone II**.
- The reward for entrepreneurial function is called **Profit.**
- The Rural Bank takes a loan from the **Lead Bank**.
- The share of capital is referred to as **Interest.**
- The state first accorded the status of Industry to Agriculture, **Maharashtra** in **1997**.
- The tax, SGST is collected in Intra State sales.
- The technique that protects the trades from extreme falls in price is called **Hedging**.
- The technique which protects the traders from extreme falls in price is known as **Hedging**.
- The theory of profit was given by **Walker**.
- The wholesale business of wheat in India was nationalized in the year **1973.**
- Three Tier Co-operative Credit Structure finances the **short- and medium-term loan**. Two Tier Co-operative Credit Structure finances the **Long-term loan**.
- VAT (Value added tax) is an **Indirect tax.**
- Want the satisfying quality of good is called **Utility, the** Transportation function creates Place utility, Storage function creates **Time utility.**
- Human wants are **unlimited**.
- When total utility is maximum then marginal utility is **Zero**.
- When marginal utility is zero, total utility is **Maximum**.
- When marginal production is equal to average production, then the elasticity of production is equal to **One**.
- When MPP=0, then TPP is **Highest**. When MPP is greater than APP

then elasticity of production is **E=1.** Marginal utilization of resources is attained where **MR=MC.**

- To get the maximum profit keep adding the variable resources in the production process till **MR=MC.**
- When the percentage change in quantity supplied equals the percentage change in price, then the supply is called **Unitary Elastic supply**.
- When the supply of commodity increases to infinite quantity or unlimited quantity even though the rise in price and the elasticity supply is said to be **Perfectly elastic**.
- World Bank located in **Washington, D.C.**

Extension Education

- The basic operational unit for rural development is **Block**.
- Block consists of **100 villages**.
- The basic unit of society/Civilization is the **Family.**
- Best method of selection of leader is **Sociometry**
- The central element in the effective learning situation is the **Learner**.
- Yong Farmers Association of India was started by **P. S. Deshmukh.**
- Concept & Father of the demonstration was given by ***Dr. Seeman A. Knapp.***
- The concept of a model village was given by ***Daniel Hamilton*** **(1903)**.
- The Lab to Land programme was launched in India on 16 July **1979.**
- The concept of T & V is given by ***Daniel Benor***.
- Country where the T&V system originated **Turkey** (1973).
- The father of extension education is ***J. Paul Leagens.***
- The father of extension in India is ***K. N. Singh***.
- The father of modern sociology is ***R. K. Maston.***
- The father of rural sociology is ***August Compte.***
- The father of the university extension is ***James Stuart.***
- The first KVK was started in Pondicherry, **TNAU (1974).**
- For one talk, the number of flashcards used is **10-12.**
- KVK is recommended by the ***Mohan Singh Mehta*** Committee.
- National Extension Service **2nd Oct 1953.**
- **Laggards** is traditional and the last to adopt an innovation.
- Number of KVK till March 731 2023.
- Puppet shows are included in **Audio-visual aid**.
- Radio is an example of **Hot media.**
- Result demonstration is conducted by **Farmers.**
- The basic unit of development under IRDP is **Family.**
- The basic unit of rural society is the **Village.**
- The first agriculture university, G. B Pant University of Agriculture & Technology, Pant Nagar (Uttarakhand) established in **1960**.
- the first time T & V was introduced in India in **1974** in **Rajasthan**.
- Result demonstration is the **Individual contact method**.
- The rule that one must marry within one's caste is called Endogamy.
- Exogamy-Marriage outside a group or **caste**.

- The word extension was used first time in the **USA.**
- Two-tier system of Panchayat raj was recommended by the Ashok Mehta committee. 2 tier Panchayat raj was first adopted in Karnataka.
- The tier system of Panchayat Raj was recommended by the ***Balvantraj Mehta*** **committee.**
- **Three-tier** Panchayat Raj was first adopted in **Rajasthan (2nd Oct, 1959).**
- Village is the first unit in the development of the **country.**
- When a woman marries more than one man, it is known as a **Polyandrous family**. S-M-C-R-E model of communication was developed by **Rogers** & **Shoemaker.**
- extension word used for the first time, **1873.**
- Father of extension education **James Stout J.**
- In India, the Father of extension education **K.N. Singh.**
- Rural Reconstruction Institute started by **Shanti Niketan, in 1921**.
- The Gurgaon Experiment was given by **F.L Brayne, in 1921**.
- Mazdoor Manzil was given by **SK. Dey, (1947).**
- In India, the first smart village ***chhatki*** (Angul), **Odisha.**
- Etawah pilot project was started by **Albert Mayer, (1948).**
- (C.D.P.) community development project was started in **1952**.
- (NES) National Extension Service, **1953 (S. K. Dey).**
- Panchayati Raj, was started in **1957-1958**. First state to adopt in **Rajasthan** (Nagaur District) on 2 October1959.
- (IADP) Intensive Agriculture District Program was started in the year **1960.** (IAAP) Intensive AgricultureAn area program started in **1964.**
- High high-yielding varieties programme started in **1966**.
- (MKP) Minikilt Programme for Rice **1971**.
- (DPAP) Drought Prone Area Programme **1970.**
- Administration Reform Commission, **1966 (GOI)**.
- (T & V) Training & Visit Programme was started by **Daniel Boner (1974)**.
- K.V.K. Was recommended by Mohan Singh Mehta Committee (1974), and it was established at TNAU.
- (TRYSEM) Training Rural Youth for the self-employment program was started in **1979.**
- Credit for the success of KVK"s goes to **Chandrika Prasad Yadav**.
- (IVLP) Institute Village Linkage Program, **1994**.
- Pradhan Mantri Gram Sadak Yojana (PMGSY) was started in the year

2000.

- Lab to land program started June **1979** (on ICAR Golden Jubilee celebrations).
- The first Department of Agriculture was established in **1881.**
- First Irrigation Commission appointed, 1901.
- Nation rural livelihood mission (2011).
- Imperial Lac Research Institute, (Ranchi), **1925**.
- 1st five-year plan started **1951-1956**.
- Food Corporation of India (FCL) Founded on 14th January **1965.**
- NABARD came into existence **12th July, 1982.**
- Gram Panchayat is a Basic unit of **local administration**.
- Food and Agricultural Organization is situated in **Rome.**
- In India, the term 'Vision' in 'Vision-2020' by **Dr. A.P.J. Abdul Kalam** means Articulation of desiredresults.
- The ratio of Central and State Governments in the MANREGA scheme i s **5050.**
- In Farm Management, the most important unit is the **Production unit**.
- The state which was electrified was rural first in **Haryana**.
- National Food Security Mission (NFSM) was started during the year **(2007-2008)**.
- 3 Tier Panchayat Raj was given by **Mehta Balwant Rai.**
- The First Agriculture University pattern was based on the **Land Grant System** of the U.S.A.
- The National Agricultural Insurance Scheme was started in the year **1999**.
- RBI was Nationalized in the year, January 1949.
- The Krishi television channel was launched in the year 2004.
- Father of method demonstration **Dr. Seeman A. Knap**.
- Highest percentage of Early majority (34%) & Late majority (34%).
- The most important element of communication is the **Receiver.**
- Method demonstration is a **short type of** demonstration.
- Panchayati Raj, the General body of the village Panchayat was Gram Sabha.
- The basic unity of civilization is the family.
- The T & V system was introduced in **Rajasthan** for the **Canal Area**.
- *Deen Dayal Upadhyaya Grameen Kaushal Yojana* (DDU-GKY) was launched on **25 Sep 2014**.
- Soil Health Card Scheme was launched on **7 Feb 2015** from **Suratgarh,**

Rajasthan.

- Pradhan Mantri Jan Dhan Yojna was launched on 28 August 2015.
- The Namami Gange project was launched in **October 2016**.
- National Nutrition Mission (***POSHAN Abhiyaan***) is an expansion of the '***Beti Bachao Beti Padhao***'Program.
- **Extension** means education for rural people, extending knowledge beyond schools.
- **Education's aim** in extension is changing knowledge, attitudes, and skills.
- **Extension education** synthesizes social and natural sciences for non-credit adult education.
- **Paul Leagans (1971)** described extension education as applied social science.
- **Extension services** improve rural welfare through practical programs.
- **Extension process** works with rural people to improve living standards.
- **Scope of extension** includes awareness creation and behavioral change.
- **Nine areas** emphasize agriculture, marketing, and community development.
- **Extension is essential** in India's agricultural and rural programs.
- **Educational principles** like "learning by doing" are key in extension.
- **Rural sociology's importance** is significant in agricultural societies like India.
- **Rural sociology** studies the structure and function of rural society.
- **Rural sociology assists** in addressing rural attitudes and behaviors.
- **Rural sociology** supports extension workers in understanding rural issues.
- **Indian rural society** is village-centric with caste-based social structures.
- **Village cooperation** is integral for both economic and religious activities.
- **Caste structure** often determines rural economic and social interactions.
- **Rural vs. urban societies** differ significantly in lifestyle and culture.
- **Women in rural India** often lack equality in various life aspects.
- **Land ownership** holds social prestige in Indian rural communities.
- **Panchayat system** plays a crucial role in rural organization.
- **Cultural traditions** influence village layout, dress, and behavior.
- **Rural-urban relations** are impacted by environmental and occupational differences.
- **Sociology** is the study of group interactions and social structures.

- **Max Weber** described sociology as understanding social human behavior.
- **Rural sociology** explores human relationships in rural settings.
- **Agrarian socio-economics** was self-sufficient until the British era.
- **British laws** changed traditional rural self-sufficiency.
- **Rural social processes** include cooperation and competition.
- **Rural planning** needs guidance from rural sociology.
- **Religion's role** is strong in shaping rural social life.
- **Community issues** require comprehensive rural sociology analysis.
- **Rural sociology** examines rural-urban social dynamics.
- **Government focus** on rural development highlights sociology's importance.
- **75% of India's population** lives in rural areas.
- **Rural reconstruction** aims to improve village life post-independence.
- **Extension workers** bridge research and rural application.
- **Supe (1987)** emphasized extension in translating research to rural contexts.
- **Intrinsic motivation** in rural programs fosters long-term interest.
- **Extrinsic incentives** can accelerate rural learning.
- **Need-based training** enhances effective agricultural outreach.
- **Realistic goals** improve farmer engagement in new practices.
- **Community involvement** boosts motivation in agricultural change.
- **Audio visuals** aid in engaging rural learners.
- **Local leaders** extend agricultural education within villages.
- **Group educators** share knowledge within rural communities.
- **Symbolism** plays a role in leadership within rural groups.
- **Demonstration plots** are crucial for showing new agricultural methods.
- **Latest technology** dissemination is vital in agriculture.
- **Credit assistance** is essential for small farmers.
- **Farmers' associations** promote community-led learning.
- **Leadership benefits** local agricultural education.
- **Community acceptance** increases with local leaders' support.
- **Local leaders' influence** can be both beneficial and limited.
- **Selection of leaders** is often based on popularity and competence.
- **Sociometry** helps identify community leaders.
- **Group support** facilitates leader-led activities.
- **Selection challenges** exist due to community size.
- **Local leaders' neutrality** may vary, impacting group cohesion.

- **Extension economics** offers indirect benefits via local teaching.
- **Self-sufficiency** defines rural economic structure.
- **Urban influence** brings change to rural areas.
- **Agricultural productivity** often depends on extension support.
- **Social change** in rural areas is slower due to traditionalism.
- **Social institutions** form the backbone of rural sociology studies.
- **Educational psychology** aids in understanding rural learning behavior.
- **Interpersonal dynamics** affect rural group interactions.
- **Group reactions** are fundamental in social behavior.
- **Rural sociology** explores societal tolerance and family influence.
- **Sense of belonging** is stronger in rural settings.
- **Rural solidarity** is typically informal and strong.
- **Income levels** are generally lower in rural communities.
- **Economic stratification** often divides rural and urban societies.
- **Family hierarchy** influences rural decision-making.
- **Religious influence** shapes rural values and practices.
- **Superstitions** are more common in traditional rural settings.
- **Motivation** is key to rural agricultural engagement.
- **Psychological understanding** aids in program effectiveness.
- **Cultural alignment** is necessary for new practices' success.
- **Social groups** play a role in agricultural learning.
- **Group roles** vary by community structure.
- **Paternalism** often governs rural leadership.
- **Agricultural seasons** impact training timing.
- **Off-campus training** better fits rural farmer needs.
- **New practices** should match current farmer knowledge.
- **Encouragement** drives rural adoption of new techniques.
- **Profit motivation** is crucial for rural farmer participation.
- **Hierarchy of needs** applies to rural learning approaches.
- **Panchayat** empowers local governance.
- **Social cohesion** supports rural agricultural projects.
- **Intrinsic values** sustain farmer learning interest.
- **Extrinsic rewards** help maintain rural training momentum.
- **Risk of change** affects rural acceptance of innovation.
- **Communication gap** between research and farmers exists.
- **Group membership** enhances rural educational impact.
- **Norms and rules** govern rural group dynamics.
- **Sociology** helps explain rural farmers' group behaviors.

- **Traditional roles** limit rural women's participation.
- **Cultural adherence** hinders certain rural advancements.
- **Group identity** is essential in rural cooperative projects.
- **Farmers' aspirations** may be lower without external influence.
- **Perceived status** impacts farmers' self-motivation.
- **Symbolic actions** reinforce rural group norms.
- **Extension success** depends on appropriate cultural adaptation.
- **Caste differences** influence rural group dynamics.
- **Village character** shapes agricultural practices.
- **Economic disparities** create diverse rural communities.
- **Caste conflict** sometimes hinders cooperation.
- **Agriculture's prestige** sustains rural social structure.
- **Traditional practices** shape Indian rural values.
- **Social distance** between classes affects agricultural roles.
- **Labor needs** often bridge caste divides in rural settings.
- **Scientific support** is required for new farming practices.
- **Urbanization** affects rural agricultural extension needs.
- **Faith in science** grows with effective extension programs.
- **Rural leaders** exemplify desirable agricultural techniques.
- **Acceptance of extension** depends on trust in leaders.
- **Cultural resistance** to new crops or methods is common.
- **Environmental factors** influence rural adoption rates.
- **Education alignment** with farmers' reality is vital.
- **Self-efficacy** boosts rural farmers' involvement.
- **Extension goals** focus on realistic rural changes.
- **New values** like productivity increase rural progress.
- **Role of panchayat** expands in rural development.
- **Paternalistic culture** persists in rural governance.
- **Farmers prioritize** profitability in practice adoption.
- **Leadership training** enhances rural teaching capacity.
- **Influence of religion** often impacts agricultural methods.
- **Public recognition** can support rural leaders' initiatives.
- **Self-confidence** grows with successful rural programs.
- **Secondary education** impacts rural acceptance of extension.
- **Community interest** often directs rural projects.
- **Primary contacts** reinforce trust in rural extension.
- **Group differentiation** affects training success.
- **Religion limits** certain agricultural practices.

- **Science integration** must consider rural beliefs.
- **Adapted messages** bridge research-farmer gaps.
- **Demonstration** engages rural learning processes.
- **Village self-sufficiency** supports rural traditions.
- **Economic changes** reshape traditional roles.
- **Societal cohesion** aids rural agricultural success.
- **Urban mobility** contrasts with rural stability.
- **Role models** impact rural behavior changes.
- **Community-based programs** better meet rural needs.
- **Cultural capital** aligns with rural improvement.
- **Research collaboration** supports rural program efficiency.
- **Trust in tradition** moderates rural adoption of changes.
- **Behavioral changes** are gradual in rural areas.
- **Social mobility** is less prevalent in rural settings.
- **Training adaptations** improve agricultural outreach.
- **Extension education's goal** is holistic rural development.
- **Social organizations** serve as structures that bring together individuals with common goals.
- **Organizational purpose** influences social decisions and stimulates change.
- **Formal membership** in organizations involves defined roles and status.
- **Social organizations** may be government-sponsored or independent.
- **Voluntary membership** drives participation in many social organizations.
- **Administrative structures** within organizations define roles and decision-making.
- **Goal orientation** is essential for organizational longevity and relevance.
- **Social control** refers to measures ensuring conformity within society.
- **Social control** maintains social order by regulating behaviors.
- **Formal and informal control** mechanisms guide individual actions.
- **Laws and regulations** act as formal tools of social control.
- **Social norms and values** are informal means of controlling behavior.
- **Social change** signifies the variation in societal structures over time.
- **Change theories** explain the causes and direction of social evolution.
- **Deterministic theory** suggests economic factors largely drive change.
- **Religious determination theory** sees religion as a prime change agent.
- **Social change impacts** include shifts in economic and political systems.
- **Technology** plays a key role in accelerating social change.
- **Leadership** is crucial in guiding social organizations and groups.

- **Leader qualities** impact their influence within the group.
- **Leaders act** as spokespersons and organizers for their groups.
- **Leadership selection** involves sociometric, participatory, and discussion methods.
- **Effective leaders** boost group morale and cohesion.
- **Educational psychology** aids in understanding rural learning patterns.
- **Psychology's goal** is to understand human behavior systematically.
- **Personality traits** affect individual participation in social groups.
- **Environmental factors** shape individual learning and behavior.
- **Intelligence factors** influence agricultural extension efficacy.
- **Educational psychology** examines factors like memory and perception.
- **Learning principles** guide effective agricultural training.
- **Group dynamics** support collective learning and action.
- **Social groups** form based on shared agricultural interests.
- **Formal education** in extension bridges knowledge gaps in rural areas.
- **Organizational goals** align with agricultural development objectives.
- **Group leaders** encourage agricultural innovation adoption.
- **Sociometry** helps identify popular leaders in communities.
- **Democratic leadership** promotes collective decision-making in extension.
- **Active participation** signals potential for rural leadership.
- **Social change dimensions** include shifts in values and norms.
- **Technological adoption** influences rural social structures.
- **Social mobility** affects class and status within rural settings.
- **Agricultural extension** relies on effective communication channels.
- **Training programs** support farmer education and self-sufficiency.
- **Cultural traditions** impact the acceptance of new practices.
- **Interpersonal relationships** shape rural social structures.
- **Organizational roles** help streamline agricultural activities.
- **Group cohesion** enhances rural agricultural outcomes.
- **Informal groups** in villages support agricultural learning.
- **Family units** remain strong in rural social frameworks.
- **Educational psychology scope** includes personality development.
- **Agricultural psychology** focuses on adapting teaching to adult learners.
- **Perception and memory** are key to rural learning retention.
- **Psychology of motivation** underpins rural group behavior.
- **Learning theories** support agricultural education frameworks.

- **Positive reinforcement** encourages new farming practices.
- **Social stratification** influences rural educational outreach.
- **Social control in extension** ensures conformity to group goals.
- **Training on-site** is effective for rural farmer engagement.
- **Intelligence measurement** assists in customizing rural education.
- **Social mobility** influences leadership within rural groups.
- **Motivation factors** drive farmer engagement in extension.
- **Social adaptation** is essential for effective agricultural extension.
- **Organizational types** vary by membership and operational structure.
- **Training flexibility** aligns with farmer seasonal schedules.
- **Environmental adaptation** supports rural educational psychology.
- **Learning aids** improve rural educational outcomes.
- **Organizational objectives** guide social group actions.
- **Self-initiated leaders** support rural extension goals.
- **Practical learning** through demonstration boosts farmer confidence.
- **Leadership in extension** involves acting as change agents.
- **Leader selection methods** include sociometry and participatory approaches.
- **On-the-job training** enhances agricultural extension reach.
- **Supportive structures** aid group-based agricultural extension.
- **Educational theories** guide rural teaching strategies.
- **Cultural barriers** impact rural social change.
- **Extension relies** on leaders within the local community.
- **Leader qualities** include empathy and decisiveness.
- **Social psychology** supports understanding group dynamics.
- **Educational approaches** vary to fit rural needs.
- **Community-based training** is crucial for extension success.
- **Leadership training** improves local leader efficacy.
- **Formal institutions** often support agricultural learning.
- **Group learning** builds solidarity in rural settings.
- **Psychological adaptation** aids rural extension success.
- **Training models** cater to adult learning styles.
- **Effective learning** combines theory with hands-on experience.
- **Supportive peers** influence farmer education positively.
- **Adult education models** fit rural agricultural needs.
- **Group cohesion** fosters effective agricultural change.
- **Cultural adaptation** is key to rural extension adoption.
- **Practical examples** facilitate rural learning.

- **Intrinsic motivation** sustains long-term rural engagement.
- **Community leaders** bridge rural extension gaps.
- **Learning situations** involve real-life applications.
- **Psychology explains** social behavior trends in groups.
- **Leadership models** include autocratic and democratic types.
- **Active group roles** empower rural community members.
- **Behavioral adaptation** is crucial in rural extension.
- **Practical demonstrations** reinforce agricultural knowledge.
- **Positive social reinforcement** encourages behavior change.
- **Communication skills** enhance rural teaching efficacy.
- **Educational settings** affect learning behavior outcomes.
- **Group support** in extension encourages new practices.
- **Social values** influence rural group interactions.
- **Community involvement** drives effective change.
- **Training adaptability** ensures rural education success.
- **Social systems** structure rural community actions.
- **Learning psychology** focuses on rural adaptability.
- **Educational aids** support agricultural teaching goals.
- **Social attitudes** guide rural learning experiences.
- **Group roles** enhance agricultural knowledge spread.
- **Community influencers** impact extension reach.
- **Educational principles** improve agricultural learning.
- **Extension builds** on rural social structures.
- **Group objectives** support agricultural goals.
- **Hands-on methods** are essential in rural settings.
- **Learning experiences** tie into rural practical needs.
- **Influential leaders** boost group learning outcomes.
- **Social motivation** supports rural educational uptake.
- **Social learning models** influence extension training.
- **Group leaders** foster agricultural innovation.
- **Leadership roles** vary by community structure.
- **Realistic goals** boost rural training efficacy.
- **Rural extension** builds on educational psychology.
- **Community acceptance** drives rural success.
- **Learning flexibility** supports rural outreach.
- **Supportive relationships** aid rural learning.
- **Motivational theories** apply in rural extension.
- **Peer learning** reinforces rural agricultural knowledge.

- **Practical demonstrations** promote new techniques.
- **Leader influence** supports rural adaptation.
- **Training content** meets rural learning needs.
- **Social theories** underpin agricultural psychology.
- **Extension involves** community-based approaches.
- **Educational methods** vary by rural need.
- **Social cohesion** strengthens rural learning.
- **Practical solutions** suit rural agricultural needs.
- **Role modeling** aids extension in communities.
- **Extension success** relies on community leaders.
- **Adaptation principles** drive rural learning.
- **Learning innovation** benefits rural outreach.
- **Agricultural goals** align with extension objectives.
- **Effective communication** is essential in rural extension.
- **Support structures** aid rural knowledge sharing.
- **Cultural sensitivity** improves rural program adoption.
- **Field demonstrations** suit rural learning.
- **Active involvement** enhances rural education.
- **Motivational factors** support agricultural extension.
- **Learning facilitation** boosts rural knowledge.
- **Cultural norms** shape rural group behavior.
- **Extension psychology** aids rural educational success.
- **Extension Education** provides non-credit educational services.
- Originates from **Latin** "ex" (out) and "tensio" (stretching).
- Central aim is to **reach people beyond formal education** institutions.
- **Extension Process** educates people outside formal structures.
- Focus on **economic and social betterment** of rural families.
- **Paul Leagans (1971)** defined extension as applied social science.
- Emphasizes **self-reliance** in rural communities.
- **Extension Services** use community engagement for rural welfare.
- Fosters **awareness and behavioral changes** in rural areas.
- **Kelsey & Hearne (1967)** identified agricultural extension scopes.
- Key areas: **agriculture efficiency, natural resource use, youth, leadership**.
- Extension education operates as a **two-way communication** system.
- **Extension Philosophy** relies on teaching people to think critically.
- **Democratic methods** in extension ensure inclusive planning.
- Encourages **cultural compatibility** with rural traditions.

- **Broad-based extension** focuses on integrating farming systems.
- Broadened scope includes **animal husbandry, forestry, fisheries**.
- **Village Extension Workers** help increase farm productivity.
- Emphasizes **"learning by doing"** for lasting knowledge retention.
- **Objective:** Increase farm income and **improve rural quality of life**.
- Advocates for **continuous training** of extension staff.
- **World Bank** supported Training & Visit (T&V) system since 1979.
- **Single Command Line** approach under Dept. of Agriculture.
- **Time-bound visits** to enhance productivity.
- **Field focus** ensures contact with farmers at set times.
- **Fortnightly training** keeps extension workers updated.
- Regular training helps address **field-specific challenges**.
- **Training workshops** involve multi-agency participation.
- **Farmers' input** is essential in technology dissemination.
- Agricultural **Technology Management Agencies (ATMA)** established.
- **ATMA** strengthens farmer-researcher links.
- ATMA pilot projects span **seven states** in India.
- New **methods in tech transfer** are ATMA's main goals.
- ATMA empowers **district-level decision-making**.
- **Research-extension-farmer** linkages improve through ATMA.
- **Women's participation** promoted in extension services.
- **Marthandam Project** in 1921 fostered community development.
- ATMA involves **NGO and private sector** partnerships.
- **National Watershed Development Programme** aids wasteland recovery.
- **Field visits** by VEWs ensure tailored guidance.
- Farmers grouped by **VEWs for regular outreach**.
- **Monthly zonal workshops** bridge research with field realities.
- **Extension's main role** is to bridge research and farmers.
- **National Extension Service (NES)** established 1953.
- NES fills gaps left by **Community Development Program**.
- **NES integrated** with CD blocks in 1963.
- **Formal education** is limited to fixed curricula.
- Extension provides **flexible, field-based learning**.
- **Objective-based education** shapes rural extension goals.
- Extension educates through **direct and interactive methods**.
- **Sriniketan Project** (1914) model focused on rural upliftment.
- **Marthandam Project** (1921) combined physical, spiritual, and

economic aid.

- **Gurgaon Project** used publicity to promote healthier practices.
- T&V model emphasized **close scientific support**.
- **Broad-based extension** incorporates diverse agri-services.
- **VEWs trained in workshops** for continuous improvement.
- **NAIP and NATP** include modern agri-tech dissemination.
- **Cyber extension** connects rural areas with tech support.
- **Market-led extension** focuses on market trends.
- **Farmer-led extension** empowers through local leadership.
- **National Agricultural Tech Project** promotes district autonomy.
- **ATMA Governing Board** includes district officials and farmers.
- Regular **district meetings** plan extension activities.
- **Evaluation step** checks extension goal progress.
- **NATP (1998-2003)** fosters local agri-research partnerships.
- **Knowledge-sharing workshops** address emerging challenges.
- **In-service training** enhances field worker skills.
- **Extension educators** work with local communities.
- **Problem analysis** in extension identifies improvement areas.
- **Extension philosophy** teaches methods, not instructions.
- **Experiential learning** through on-farm demonstrations.
- **Extension values community** participation.
- **Agricultural Research Services (ARS)** inform extension efforts.
- **NATP structure** decentralizes extension functions.
- ATMA enhances **farmer-centered extension planning**.
- **Evaluation data** guides future planning steps.
- **Multiple institutions** back up extension services.
- ATMA pilot areas adapted to **unique district needs**.
- **Core extension goals** guide rural development.
- **Personal growth** emphasized in extension outcomes.
- **Village extension training** benefits rural economies.
- **Linkage activities** with ICAR amplify outreach.
- **Focus on value-added** agri-products for farmers.
- Extension meets **cultural compatibility** standards.
- **Resource-based planning** adopted in extension systems.
- **Flexible curriculum** meets rural needs.
- **Farmers taught with cultural context** in mind.
- **VEW sessions promote continuous field** presence.
- **Village-specific programs** address unique needs.

- **Regular VEW-farmer meetings** maintain support.
- **Nodal points** identified in VEW scheduling.
- **Empowerment of rural families** through education.
- ATMA encourages **multi-stakeholder engagement**.
- **Adaptability of messages** to regional needs.
- **Evaluation reviews impact** on community.
- **Goals in each phase** provide clear direction.
- **Fortnightly visit system** allows timely tech advice.
- **Broad extension programs** cover multiple sectors.
- **KVKs** set up to streamline tech dissemination.
- **Community issues** addressed in zonal workshops.
- **Community integration** vital for program success.
- **Out-of-school education** principle in rural contexts.
- **Active farmer engagement** in planning steps.
- **Funding supports rural development programs.**
- **Workshops train VEWs on local challenges.**
- **Linkage with local leaders** enhances reach.
- **Informal education** supports lifelong learning.
- **Classified as experiential learning.**
- **Classroom-teaching adaptable** to rural settings.
- **Practical application in extension** ensures impact.
- **Outreach centers** provide agricultural advice.
- **Coordination with line departments.**
- **Integrated extension model** in each district.
- **Govt initiatives** support these programs.
- **Non-credit courses** serve adult learners.
- **Extension planning framework** for rural support.
- **Multi-disciplinary support** in farm tech.
- **Monitoring mechanisms** support field improvements.
- **Long-term goal** to improve rural standards.
- **Training by specialists** enhances crop production.
- **Village guides** enhance info delivery.
- **Tech modules** encourage local engagement.
- **Community support integral** to programs.
- **Formal courses structured** for rural residents.
- **Research backs extension** efforts.
- **ICAR** offers guidance to extension programs.
- **Workshops organized** per farming cycles.

- **Evaluation leads to refinements.**
- **Extension tech builds resilience.**
- **Problems addressed by specialists** in rural settings.
- **ATMA decentralizes decision**-making.
- **Structure tailored** to state needs.
- **Agri-services** linked to educational needs.
- **Agriculture committees oversee** pilot projects.
- **VEWs to meet farmer goals** effectively.
- **Policy reforms** bolster extension efforts.
- **Farm services promoted** by govt agencies.
- **Active community input** in extension planning.
- **Local support via VEWs** ensures success.
- **Extension teams** improve living standards.
- **Community planning teams** for each project.
- **Continuous rural support** in planning.
- **Specialized programs like Marthandam** promote all aspects.
- **ICAR** ensures rural service alignment.
- **Training and evaluations** guide field strategies.
- **Extension model prioritizes rural input.**
- **Field agents central to program success.**
- **Govt and private sectors work together.**
- **Pilot programs show the way** for others.
- **Extensive outreach networks** developed.
- **Goal of extension: self-reliant communities.**
- **Rural Development** focuses on elevating rural standards of living.
- **Development** implies progressive economic and social change.
- **Community Development** mobilizes local resources for improvement.
- **Agriculture** is central to rural development strategies.
- **Rural population** contributes to over half of national income.
- **Self-sufficiency** is a key goal in rural areas.
- **Community Development** is a participatory movement.
- **Objectives** include economic growth, justice, and democracy.
- **CDP (1952)** launched on Gandhi's birth anniversary.
- **NES (1953)** aimed for nationwide rural outreach.
- **Panchayat Raj** reinforces local governance in villages.
- **Panchayat Raj's** foundation in community empowerment.
- **Village panchayats** are primary governance units.
- **Block and district committees** guide rural initiatives.

- **Community Development Program** started in 55 blocks.
- **Panchayat Raj structure** includes three governance tiers.
- **Economic development** is an aim of community projects.
- **Social equity** promoted through community programs.
- **Agricultural productivity** boosts rural development.
- **Rural crafts** bolster local economic stability.
- **Health programs** in rural areas aim for disease prevention.
- **Adult education** strengthens community knowledge.
- **Educational programs** enhance rural literacy.
- **Block Development Officers** lead local projects.
- **Village leaders** encourage local initiative.
- **Gram Sevak** or village workers aid rural projects.
- **Women workers** address rural women's needs.
- **Public health** improvements vital for rural welfare.
- **Infrastructure** advances rural access and mobility.
- **Self-help** a principle of rural progress.
- **Cooperation** between villages enhances resilience.
- **Youth education** for continuity in rural areas.
- **Leadership** essential in rural organization.
- **Rural leaders** selected for community loyalty.
- **Leaders empower** village decision-making.
- **Democratic leaders** promote inclusive participation.
- **Effective leaders** inspire rural confidence.
- **Rural leadership** adapts to local needs.
- **Administration in Extension** is management-focused.
- **Principles of extension** guide implementation.
- **Extension workers** facilitate rural teaching.
- **Technology Transfer** crucial in rural transformation.
- **Training and Visit (T&V)** model popular in agriculture.
- **Continuous learning** emphasized in extension.
- **Capacity building** for rural change.
- **Leadership in extension** combines empathy and action.
- **Communication skills** central to extension success.
- **Education builds** self-reliance in villages.
- **Behavioral changes** are teaching objectives.
- **Teaching methods** adapted to rural learners.
- **Community integration** essential in extension.
- **Panchayat Raj** enhances village decision autonomy.

- **Objectives of extension** align with rural uplift.
- **Extension administration** streamlines rural services.
- **Leaders bridge** village needs with resources.
- **Community groups** foster rural cooperation.
- **Village unity** supports rural development.
- **Rural sociology** explores rural dynamics.
- **Adoption of innovations** spurs rural growth.
- **Diffusion theory** explains adoption spread.
- **Innovation diffusion** relies on social networks.
- **Rogers' Model** clarifies adoption steps.
- **Early adopters** drive village innovation.
- **Late majority** cautious about new methods.
- **Innovation attributes** affect adoption rate.
- **Relative advantage** influences adoption choice.
- **Trialability** crucial for rural innovation.
- **Observability** enhances adoption appeal.
- **Media** spreads innovation in rural areas.
- **Extension Teaching** tailored to rural needs.
- **Methods classified** by group or individual focus.
- **Field demonstrations** showcase new practices.
- **Training workshops** support hands-on learning.
- **Farm publications** extend rural knowledge.
- **Visual aids** support comprehension.
- **Role playing** enhances teaching effectiveness.
- **Feedback loops** assess learning impact.
- **Aristotle's model** roots in message delivery.
- **Shannon-Weaver model** focuses on noise reduction.
- **Berlo's SMCR model** emphasizes communication components.
- **Extension communication** needs cultural sensitivity.
- **Agricultural radio** educates remote farmers.
- **Visual communication** aids rural learning.
- **Capacity building** in ToT strengthens extension.
- **Monitoring and evaluation** vital for success.
- **Evaluation identifies** program weaknesses.
- **Systematic feedback** for continuous improvement.
- **Behavioral changes** indicate program success.
- **Training transfer** assessed through observation.
- **Adoption measures** rural program impact.

- **Follow-up visits** reinforce learning.
- **Evaluation tools** include surveys and interviews.
- **Community buy-in** ensures sustainability.
- **Youth education** for future rural leadership.
- **Group learning** reinforces information retention.
- **Teaching planning** aligns with community needs.
- **Curriculum flexibility** needed for rural relevance.
- **Feedback in training** aligns with goals.
- **Rural leadership** driven by community trust.
- **Success in extension** linked to grassroots input.
- **Formal communication** supports policy outreach.
- **Media and tech** expand rural access.
- **Field agents** implement extension on ground.
- **Program reviews** offer improvement paths.
- **Data collection** aids monitoring.
- **Surveys assess** adoption success.
- **Local leaders** foster trust in new ideas.
- **Extension impact** measured by rural progress.
- **Economic indicators** of program success.
- **Market growth** supports extension relevance.
- **Social equity** a rural development aim.
- **Informal learning** in community meetings.
- **Workshops provide** immersive training.
- **Sustainable methods** for long-term success.
- **Evaluation reports** on program efficacy.
- **Field visits** gauge program adoption.
- **Self-assessment** fosters program ownership.
- **Teaching aids** boost retention.
- **Impact analysis** identifies gaps.
- **Leadership training** supports local engagement.
- **Success metrics** align with program goals.
- **Structured evaluations** guide adjustments.
- **Follow-up** maintains program relevance.
- **Active community role** in evaluation.
- **Local extension offices** support engagement.
- **Feedback cycle** improves rural services.
- **Program goals** shaped by feedback.
- **Adoption rates** reflect learning effectiveness.

- **Community feedback** refines training.
- **Process evaluation** for ongoing updates.
- **Goal clarity** in training plans.
- **Communication mix** tailored to village needs.
- **Farmer leaders** advocate new practices.
- **ToT enhances** resource use in rural areas.
- **Needs assessments** shape program design.
- **Grassroots feedback** informs strategy.
- **Shared learning** in extension groups.
- **Group dynamics** aid rural motivation.
- **Leadership structure** in community projects.
- **Learning-by-doing** fosters hands-on skills.
- **Innovation spread** key to rural success.
- **New practices** drive rural productivity.
- **Diffusion relies** on social support.
- **Model choice** depends on context.
- **Group support** boosts morale.
- **Training improvements** follow evaluations.
- **Adoption challenges** shape training content.
- **Positive change** measured by rural standards.
- **Technical knowledge** for field application.
- **Program adjustments** based on real-time data.
- **Teaching effectiveness** linked to adaptability.
- **Feedback sessions** gather rural input.
- **Research-informed** training updates.
- **Stakeholder meetings** support mutual goals.
- **Communication channels** assess program reach.
- **Implementation schedules** align with cycles.
- **Program phases** structured for adaptation.
- **Rural context** guides teaching methods.
- **Socially acceptable** innovations adopted faster.
- **Training success** reflected in application.
- **Ongoing monitoring** strengthens extension programs.
- **Communication** is the mutual exchange of ideas to reach a common understanding.
- The **process of communication** includes source, message, channel, and receiver.
- **Berlo's Model** emphasizes skills, attitudes, knowledge, and culture

affecting communication.

- **Feedback** in communication ensures understanding between the source and receiver.
- **Shannon and Weaver Model** views communication as a linear process.
- **Noise** in communication refers to distortions in the transmitted message.
- **Aristotle's Model** (2000 years old) highlights speaker, message, audience, and effect.
- **Lasswell's Model (1948)** asks who, says what, in which channel, to whom, and with what effect.
- **Vertical Communication** can be upward or downward within organizational hierarchy.
- **Horizontal Communication** occurs among peers at the same hierarchical level.
- **Encoding** is converting the message into symbols or codes.
- **Decoding** is interpreting the received message.
- **Verbal Communication** uses spoken or written words to convey a message.
- **Non-verbal Communication** includes gestures, body language, and facial expressions.
- **Body Language** often communicates emotions and attitudes more accurately than words.
- **Linguistic Barriers** are caused by language differences and jargon.
- **Non-linguistic Barriers** include cultural differences and physical conditions.
- **Effective Listening** involves understanding and accurately interpreting the message.
- **Speaking Skills** are crucial for clear and impactful verbal communication.
- **Reading Skills** enhance knowledge and comprehension.
- **Writing Skills** aid in clear and structured message delivery.
- **Precise Writing** focuses on clarity and brevity, avoiding unnecessary details.
- **Summarizing** condenses information while retaining essential points.
- **Technical Communication** is tailored to specific fields and audiences.
- **Farm Journalism** focuses on agricultural issues and rural development news.
- **News in Farm Journalism** includes updates on pest outbreaks, crop conditions, etc.

- **Diffusion of Innovations** involves the spread of new ideas within a social system.
- **Innovation Attributes** include relative advantage, compatibility, and complexity.
- **Rogers' Convergence Model (1981)** describes communication as a cycle for mutual understanding.
- **Shannon-Weaver Model (1949)** was foundational in engineering and mass communication.
- **Osgood-Schramm Model (1975)** adds noise and personal influence to communication cycles.
- **Feedback Loop** is essential in adjusting communication based on responses.
- **Effective Communication** requires accuracy, brevity, and clarity (ABC's).
- **Audience Analysis** is crucial for message relevance and impact.
- **Horizontal Communication Challenges** arise from departmentalization in organizations.
- **Formal Communication** follows official channels and protocols.
- **Informal Communication** includes spontaneous exchanges like grapevines.
- **Personal Influence Model (Katz & Lazarfeld, 1955)** highlights opinion leaders in media.
- **David Berlo's Model (1960)** covers skills, attitudes, and the social system in communication.
- **Public Speaking Skills** involve voice modulation, gestures, and stage presence.
- **Farmers' Committees** play a role in the dissemination of agricultural innovations.
- **Organizational Communication** can be downward, upward, or horizontal.
- **Communication Overload** leads to reduced effectiveness and retention.
- **Visual Aids** enhance audience understanding and engagement.
- **Photojournalism** captures agricultural scenes to communicate rural realities.
- **Educational Background** affects message reception and comprehension.
- **Convergence Model** stresses mutual understanding through information exchange.

- **Symbol Variation** in communication enhances message clarity.
- **One-way Communication** (Lecture Method) provides rapid information delivery.
- **Listening Barriers** include distractions, biases, and emotional interference.
- **Group Discussions** promote active engagement and knowledge sharing.
- **Media Mix** in teaching methods combines verbal, visual, and experiential channels.
- **Audience Feedback** shapes future communication effectiveness.
- **Concept of Audience Response** includes mental and physical action.
- **Message Clarity** is essential for agricultural extension outreach.
- **Environmental Change** is a factor in adapting communication processes.
- **Cultural Sensitivity** enhances communication in diverse rural settings.
- **Formal Social Organizations** facilitate structured communication.
- **Grapevine Communication** fills informal information gaps within groups.
- **Electronic Communication** expands reach in rural extension programs.
- **Vertical Flow** ensures information consistency across organizational levels.
- **Effective Speech** requires coherence, confidence, and audience rapport.
- **Two-way Communication** is fundamental to feedback and learning.
- **Repetition in Messages** reinforces retention among rural audiences.
- **Feedback Mechanism** regulates and improves communication strategies.
- **Rural Leaders** serve as communication intermediaries in agricultural extension.
- **Communication Medium** selection is based on audience accessibility.
- **Transactional Model** emphasizes the dynamic exchange of messages.
- **Audience Perception** determines the impact of messages.
- **Cognitive Factors** affect audience reception in communication.
- **Communication Channels** vary in scope from personal to mass media.
- **Cultural Barriers** often hinder cross-regional communication.
- **Gestural Communication** complements verbal cues.
- **Shannon-Weaver's Noise Element** disrupts message clarity.
- **Sender's Credibility** influences message acceptance.
- **Transmission Barriers** include physical, psychological, and

environmental factors.

- **Collective Mindset** shapes group-based communication in rural settings.
- **Non-verbal Signals** reinforce message credibility.
- **Role of Communication Models** is to simplify and represent complex interactions.
- **Importance of Visuals** in rural extension helps illiterate farmers.
- **Eye Contact** builds trust in public speaking.
- **Team-based Communication** aids in collective decision-making.
- **Farm Extension Workers** act as mediators in the technology transfer process.
- **Channel Efficiency** enhances message delivery.
- **Social System** influences communication norms and expectations.
- **Awareness Programs** use multimedia channels for rural outreach.
- **Public Awareness Campaigns** utilize both direct and indirect channels.
- **Written Communication** allows for record-keeping and precision.
- **Reliability of Feedback** is crucial in adaptive communication.
- **Scientific Information** in agriculture needs simplification for rural audiences.
- **Decentralized Communication** promotes local decision-making.
- **Vertical and Horizontal Integration** in communication aids in resource sharing.
- **Participation Feedback** fosters inclusivity in program planning.
- **Human Expression in Communication** is often more impactful than technology.
- **Cognitive Dissonance** can reduce message effectiveness.
- **Communication Interference** from external noise weakens message strength.
- **Program Planning in Extension** requires clear communication of objectives.
- **Encoding Efficiency** directly impacts message comprehension.
- **Auditory Channels** are preferred for rural communities lacking visual literacy.
- **Language Simplification** increases agricultural message reach.
- **Noise Filtration** enhances communication accuracy in field outreach.
- **Social Networking** aids in quicker information dissemination.
- **Digital Platforms** support widespread rural information access.
- **Rural Social Organization** structures influence group decision-making.

- **Cultural Awareness** improves communicator credibility.
- **Visual Representation** simplifies complex agricultural concepts.
- **Feedback-Driven Communication** adjusts according to field conditions.
- **Shannon-Weaver Linear Model** is fundamental to agricultural communication.
- **Regular Audience Interaction** increases trust and information uptake.
- **Channel Diversification** avoids dependency on single communication means.
- **Hierarchical Structures** affect vertical communication flows.
- **Context Sensitivity** ensures message relevance in diverse rural areas.
- **Rural Communication Networks** enable effective agricultural outreach.
- **Rural Language Use** enhances cultural resonance.
- **Decoding Accuracy** enhances message fidelity in information transfer.
- **Social Ties** facilitate agricultural knowledge exchange.
- **Media Literacy** strengthens rural audience's understanding.
- **Traditional Media** remain effective in isolated areas.
- **Structured Presentation** aids in clear message flow.
- **Tailored Communication** ensures relevance to rural demographics.
- **Agricultural Extension Training** improves rural communication skills.
- **Community Radio** serves as a powerful communication tool.
- **Demonstration Method** simplifies complex agricultural practices.
- **Capacity Building** involves training on message creation.
- **Listening Exercises** improve understanding of rural perspectives.
- **Feedback Collection** helps in program adjustment.
- **Audience Inclusion** in planning stages ensures engagement.
- **Task-Oriented Communication** suits fieldwork planning.
- **Participatory Media** enables audience input.
- **Mutual Understanding** is key in technology adoption.
- **Cultural Storytelling** enhances agricultural awareness.
- **Audience-Specific Models** in communication boost effectiveness.
- **Field Research** aids in identifying communication gaps.
- **Communication as a Process** enables flexibility and adaptation.
- **Consistency in Communication** fosters audience trust.
- **Regular Updates** keep communities informed.
- **Feedback Loops** strengthen connection with rural audiences.
- **Peer Communication** among farmers aids in best-practice sharing.
- **Self-help Groups** enable agricultural extension.

- **Behavioral Insights** aid in tailoring communication.
- **Feedback Mechanisms** improve program effectiveness.
- **Cognitive Approach** to learning in rural settings.
- **Group Dynamics** affect the spread of innovations.
- **Behavioral Change Communication** targets adoption in agriculture.
- **Visual Cues** bridge literacy gaps.
- **Mobile Platforms** for timely information dissemination.
- **Learning Groups** promote agricultural innovation.
- **Audience's Experience** with technology influences adoption.
- **Simplified Messages** aid understanding among rural audiences.
- **Behavioral Modification** through targeted messages.
- **Content Prioritization** ensures message clarity.
- **Effective Presentation** impacts comprehension.
- **Interactive Sessions** improve engagement.
- **Customized Content** suits local contexts.
- **Field Training** boosts practical skills.
- **Follow-up Mechanisms** maintain momentum.
- **Contextual Models** aid in practical application.
- **Message Adaptation** to audience's existing knowledge.
- **Contextual Language Use** strengthens connection.
- **Simplicity in Design** boosts visual aid effectiveness.
- **Resourcefulness** in rural communication delivery.

Agricultural Biotechnology

- Father of Plant Tissue culture HaberLandt (1884 to 1945).
- Term tissue culture, coined by American Pathologist- **Montrose Thomas Burrows.**
- Term Biotechnology was coined by **Karl Ereky** (1919).
- DNA (deoxyribonucleic acid) molecule which encodes genetic information. It contains four bases
- Micropropagation is the vitro multiplication of plants from a small **tissue explant.**
- In vivo is a biological process or reaction taking place in a **living cell** or **organism.**
- ***E-coli*** is an ***Agrobacterium rhizogenes*** Bacterium used in genetic engineering for its **small size.**
- ***Agrobacterium tumefaciens*** Soil bacteria often possess the plasmid.
- **Allele** is a variant form of a **gene.**
- DNA was first synthesized by **Arthur Kornberg (1956**).
- **Paul Berg,** father of genetic engineering.
- RFLP (Restriction Fragment Length Polymorphism), APD (Random Amplified Polymorphic DNA), and PCR (Polymerase Chain Reactions) were developed by **Dr. Karl Mullis (1980**) and won the Nobel Prize (1993). PCR technique uses **Bacterial enzymes** for in vitro amplification of **DNA.**
- Gene pyramiding is a technique of combining **two** or **more major genes.**
- GUS (B-glucaronidase) Gene from Eschericha. coli. It is used in transformation as a reporter gene.
- Germplasm was discovered by **August Weismann.**
- Golden rice was developed by **Ingo Potrykus** and **Peter Bayer.**
- The molecular signal that binds to the receptor is called a **Ligand.**
- Golden rice provides **Higher B-carotene** than normal rice.
- Carotene is the Precursor of **Vitamin-A.**
- **m-RNA** is primarily used for the Transcription of DNA.
- **Chromosomes,** Thread-like bodies that carry genes.
- The insoluble RNA that constitutes the largest part of cellular.
- The height of the sugarcane plant can be increased by the application of **Gibberellins.**
- Lysosome was discovered by **Christian de Duve** (1955).

- The term DNA Fingerprinting was coined by **Prof Alec Jeffrey (1984)**.
- ***Flavr savors*** variety of tomatoes was the first transgenic plant product to touch the market.
- Invitro multiplication of plants from small tissue (Explants) is called **Micropropagation.**
- **Embryo culture** Overcome the post-zygotic barriers, shortening the breeding cycle &
- overcome seed dormancy.
- First successful embryo culture in Cherry embryo (1993).
- **Double haploids** Production of 100% homozygous plants.
- Haploid is a plant with the gametic or '***n***' **number** of chromosomes.
- Doubled haploids or diploids, are chromosome-doubled haploids or **2n plants.**
- Haploid plants develop from **another culture** either directly or indirectly through a Callus phase.
- Androgenesis is the process by which haploid plants develop from the **male gametophyte.**
- **Gynogenesis** Haploids are derived from the female gametophyte e.g. Sugar beet, onion, and gerbera.
- **Somaclones** Plants derived from any type of somatic cell culture.
- **Somaclonal variation** Creation of novel source variability by **regeneration** of **callus culture.**
- **Protoplast fusion or somatic hybridization** Fusion of two somatic cells of different species, genera, or families. To overcome the sexual incompatibility.
- **Cybrids** Nuclear genes from one species and the cytoplasm from both parents combine to produce cytoplasmic hybrids or cybrids.
- **Main application of cybrids** Direct transfer of CMS from donor to recipient lines.
- Cybrids (Cytoplasmic hybrids) e.g., **Citrus.**
- The basic concept of association of markers with quantitative traits was first proposed by **Sax in 1923.**
- The first genetic map was published by **T.H. Morgan** in 1911.
- To minimize the linkage, drag, need to identify of flanking marker Less than **5cM**
- 1st molecular marker RFLP (1980).
- PCR developed by **Dr.Karry Mullis**, (1985).
- PCR based marker is known as **RAPD, SSR, DAF, and AP-PCR.**
- **Single primer** marker is **RAPD. The pair of primers** is SSR.

- Sequence-based molecular marker is known as **SNP.**
- **Monomorphic markers** are not differentiated between genotypes.
- Polymorphic markers can differentiate between the **homozygotes** and **heterozygotes.**
- SNP (Single Nucleotide Polymorphism) is a third-generation marker based on DNA sequencing. A high throughput system is a specific feature.
- **RAPD** Dominance, low level of polymorphism, Diversity analysis. Second-generation markers based on PCR. **RAPD** (Random Amplified Polymorphic DNA) and AFLP (Amplified Fragment Length Polymorphism) both are **Gene tagging. RAPD** is a Random random-based marker.
- **AFLP** Dominance, low level of polymorphism, High resolution, RFLP (Restriction Fragment Length Polymorphism) is a first-generation marker based on restriction fragment detection. Using a Physical mapping of genes.
- **RFLP** Co- Dominance, low level of polymorphism, Construction of linkage maps, Hybridization-based marker is **RFLP.** It is the oldest marker.
- **SSR** Co-dominant, very high level of polymorphism Second-generation markers based on PCR. SSR (Simple sequence repeat (**microsatellite**) is a Highly informative marker.
- **Mapping Population** Plant mapping populations are usually created from F_1 lines that are derived from two parents that show differing phenotypes for a target trait
- **NIL** Near Isogenic Line which is developed through repeated random backcrossing.
- **NIL** Commonly used for mapping of QTLs.
- RIL Recombinant Inbred Lines are the homozygous selfed or sib-mated progeny of the individuals of an F_2 population up to F_7- F_8.
- A short method to detect the **QTLs** is BSA (Bulked segregants analysis).
- **Recombinant selection** Selections of **best back cross progeny** with the target gene, using flanking markers.
- **Linkage map/Genetic map** A genetic map is a representation of the genes on a chromosome arrayed in linear order with distances between ***loci*** expressed as percent recombination (map units, centimorgans). It is measured by centimorgans (cM). One linkage map unit (LMU) is 1% recombination. One map unit = one centimorgan (cM) = 1% recombination between loci.

- **Genome** the sum of all an individual organism's genes. Thus, genomics is the study of **all the genes of a cell**, or tissue, at the DNA (genotype), mRNA (transcriptome), or protein (proteome) levels.
- **Genomics** The study of all the **nucleotide sequences**, including structural genes, regulatory sequences, and non-coding DNA segments, in the chromosomes of an organism. The term 'genomics' was coined by **Dr. Tom Roderick.**
- **Structural genomics** describes the **3-dimensional structure** of every protein encoded
- by a given genome.
- **Functional genomics** Understanding the function of genes and other parts of the genome. **Proteomics;** A complete set of proteins present in s single cell. **Transcriptomics**; A complete set of mRNA present in a single cell. **Metabolomics**; A complete set of metabolites present in a single cell.
- 1st transgenic plant was developed in **tobacco, in 1983.**
- 1st transgenic engineering company Genentech established, in **1976.**
- 1st transgenic variety **"Flavr Savr"** in tomato developed by ***Calgene*** for enhancing shelf life.
- In India, 1st transgenic crop commercially cultivated Cotton, 2002.
- Transgenic Leading crops in the world **Soya bean> Maize > Cotton.**
- Leading traits in the world Herbicide tolerance > ***Bt***. insect resistance
- Leading countries in the world USA > Argentina > Canada
- **Vector gene transfer** Agrobacterium-mediated transfer, agro-injection, viral vector.
- **Direct gene transfer** Microinjection, particle bombardment.
- The Cartagena Protocol on bio-safety (CPB) originated from the Convention on Biological Diversity (CBD) in 2000 and came into force in 2003.
- Transgenic varieties are approved by **GEAC** (Genetic Engineering Approval Committee).
- **DNA** is the carrier of genetic information in plants and animals.
- **RNA** plays a key role in protein synthesis in plants.
- The discovery of the **double-helix structure of DNA** by Watson and Crick revolutionized genetics.
- **Genetic material** includes both **DNA** and **RNA** in living organisms.
- **Genetic engineering** allows manipulation of DNA for crop improvement.
- **Recombinant DNA technology** is used to introduce desirable traits

into crops.

- **Agrobacterium tumefaciens** is a natural vector used in plant genetic engineering.
- **Biotechnology** is essential for crop improvement, pest resistance, and disease control.
- **DNA cloning** is used to amplify genes of interest in plants.
- **Biotechnology in agriculture** improves crop yield and quality.
- **Gene cloning** involves isolating and replicating a specific gene for crop modification.
- **Vectors** like **plasmids** and **viruses** are used to transfer genes into plants.
- **Transgenic plants** carry genes from different species for improved traits.
- **Plant tissue culture** is used for in vitro propagation of plants.
- **Biotechnology** reduces reliance on chemical pesticides by creating pest-resistant crops.
- **DNA fingerprinting** helps in plant genome analysis.
- **Molecular markers** are used for **Marker Assisted Selection (MAS)** in plant breeding.
- **Biotechnology** helps develop **herbicide-resistant** crops.
- **Genomics** studies the complete set of genes in plants for crop improvement.
- **Proteomics** studies proteins to understand plant metabolism and stress responses.
- **Functional genomics** identifies gene functions important for agricultural traits.
- **CRISPR technology** is used for precise gene editing in plants.
- **Gene silencing** through **RNA interference (RNAi)** helps control gene expression in plants.
- **Antisense RNA** technology is used to block undesirable gene expression in crops.
- **Metabolomics** analyzes plant metabolites to understand plant responses.
- **Genetic diversity** in plants is important for breeding programs.
- **Plant tissue culture** supports the production of disease-free plants.
- **Somaclonal variation** generates genetic diversity for crop improvement.
- **Micropropagation** produces large numbers of identical plants rapidly.
- **In vitro fertilization (IVF)** is used for hybrid crop production.

- **Embryo rescue** techniques prevent abortion of hybrid embryos.
- **Haploid production** accelerates the development of homozygous crop lines.
- **Somatic hybrids** are produced by fusing plant protoplasts for novel traits.
- **Marker-assisted breeding** is faster and more precise than traditional methods.
- **Bioremediation** uses plants to clean pollutants from the environment.
- **Phytoextraction** involves plants removing heavy metals from contaminated soils.
- **Biopesticides** made from **microorganisms** control agricultural pests.
- **Bt crops** express bacterial toxins for insect resistance.
- **Genetically modified crops** are engineered to withstand **abiotic stress** like drought.
- **Nitrogen-fixing crops** reduce the need for chemical fertilizers.
- **Genetic markers** identify traits like drought tolerance in crops.
- **Tissue culture** supports conservation of endangered plant species.
- **QTL mapping** helps identify genetic regions linked to important agricultural traits.
- **DNA markers** assist in tracing disease resistance in crops.
- **Genome editing** enhances crop resistance to pests and diseases.
- **Functional foods** contain bioactive compounds that benefit human health.
- **Nutraceutical crops** are enhanced with vitamins and nutrients.
- **Biotechnology** improves the **nutritional quality** of staple crops.
- **Transgenic plants** produce **healthier cooking oils** with reduced saturated fats.
- **Golden Rice** is genetically engineered to produce vitamin A to combat deficiency.
- **Gene pyramiding** combines multiple disease-resistance genes in one crop.
- **DNA markers** are used in **marker-assisted backcrossing** for trait introduction.
- **Recombinant vaccines** are produced using plant biotechnology.
- **GMO crops** are regulated to ensure environmental and food safety.
- **Molecular breeding** accelerates the development of improved crop varieties.
- **Gene gun** is a method used to introduce foreign DNA into plant cells.
- **Microinjection** directly injects DNA into plant cells for genetic

transformation.

- **Cisgenesis** uses genes from the same species for crop improvement.
- **Antibiotic resistance genes** are used as selectable markers in genetic transformation.
- **Selectable marker genes** help identify successfully transformed plants.
- **Chimeric genes** are created to combine traits from different species in plants.
- **Gene silencing** suppresses the expression of undesirable traits in plants.
- **Knockout plants** lack specific genes for studying gene functions.
- **Biotechnology** supports the production of **biofuels** from plants.
- **Bioethanol** production from genetically engineered plants reduces carbon emissions.
- **Biodiesel** is produced from **genetically modified oilseed crops**.
- **Synthetic biology** designs novel plant functions for agricultural use.
- **Genetically engineered crops** are crucial for sustainable agriculture.
- **CRISPR-Cas9** allows for targeted gene editing in plants.
- **Genome-wide association studies (GWAS)** link traits to genetic variations.
- **Gene stacking** allows multiple beneficial traits to be added to crops.
- **Transplastomic plants** have foreign genes integrated into chloroplast DNA.
- **RNAi technology** is used to control viruses in crops.
- **Plant biotechnology** reduces **post-harvest losses** through better storage traits.
- **Biofortified crops** contain higher levels of micronutrients.
- **Molecular biology** tools help develop **salt-tolerant** crop varieties.
- **Agrobacterium** is used as a natural genetic engineer for crop transformation.
- **Cryopreservation** stores plant tissues for long-term conservation.
- **Cryogenic storage** of plant germplasm ensures genetic diversity.
- **Tissue culture techniques** help mass-produce **virus-free** planting materials.
- **Bioinformatics** analyzes plant genetic data for crop improvement.
- **GMOs** are engineered for enhanced **pest resistance**.
- **Genetic transformation** produces plants with improved **nutritional content**.
- **Transgenic crops** are engineered for **herbicide tolerance**.
- **Molecular breeding** enhances resistance to **biotic and abiotic stresses**.
- **Genetic engineering** reduces pesticide use by creating **pest-resistant**

crops.

- **Gene editing** increases **crop productivity.**
- **Agro-biotechnology** plays a critical role in **sustainable agriculture.**
- **Recombinant DNA technology** is essential for producing **high-yield crops.**
- **Plant biotechnology** aids in producing **disease-free** plants.
- **Virus resistance** in crops is achieved through genetic modifications.
- **Biotechnological crops** contribute to **food security.**
- **Genomic selection** accelerates breeding of **high-yielding crops.**
- **Genetically engineered plants** can grow in **saline soils.**
- **CRISPR-based editing** improves **crop tolerance** to environmental stress.
- **Plant biotechnology** enhances **fruit quality** and **shelf-life.**
- **Gene flow** from GM crops is monitored to prevent **cross-contamination.**
- **GM crops** increase **nutritional value** of staple foods.
- **Synthetic biology** develops crops for **pharmaceutical production.**
- **Genomics** identifies genes related to **plant disease resistance.**
- **Proteomics** helps understand **protein functions** in plant growth.
- **Secondary metabolites** in plants are studied for **pest resistance.**
- **Plant genomics** accelerates development of **stress-tolerant crops.**
- **Gene expression** analysis helps identify **key agricultural traits.**
- **RNA interference** controls **pests and pathogens** in crops.
- **Epigenetic modifications** in plants improve **crop resilience.**
- **Gene therapy** in plants helps develop **disease-resistant crops.**
- **Genetically engineered enzymes** increase **biofuel production** from plants.
- **Plant tissue culture** is used to regenerate **transformed plants.**
- **Gene knockout studies** in crops reveal important **metabolic pathways.**
- **Gene cloning** allows for **precise genetic modifications** in plants.
- **Biotech crops** enhance resistance to **herbicides and pathogens.**
- **Plant genome projects** reveal the **genetic basis of stress tolerance.**
- **Bioinformatics tools** manage **large plant genomic datasets.**
- **Transgenic plants** reduce the need for **synthetic fertilizers.**
- **Metabolomics** profiles **biochemical pathways** in plants.
- **Proteomics** identifies **stress-responsive proteins** in crops.
- **Plant breeders** use **genetic markers** for trait selection.
- **GM crops** produce **higher yields** under **adverse conditions.**

- **Gene editing** enhances **drought tolerance** in crops.
- **Bioengineered plants** produce **medicinal compounds.**
- **Hybridization** and **tissue culture** improve **crop varieties.**
- **Biotech seeds** offer better **germination rates.**
- **Transgenic crops** have longer **shelf life** and **better flavours.**
- **Biotechnological approaches** increase **resistance to pathogens.**
- **DNA sequencing** identifies genes related to **crop traits.**
- **Molecular biology** tools assist in creating **stress-resistant crops.**
- **Tissue culture techniques** ensure rapid propagation of **elite plants.**
- **Biotechnology** supports the **preservation of plant biodiversity.**
- **Synthetic biology** enhances crop productivity by **creating novel traits.**
- **CRISPR technology** in agriculture is transforming **plant breeding.**
- **Molecular markers** are tools for tracking specific genes in plant genomes.
- **RFLP (Restriction Fragment Length Polymorphism)** detects DNA polymorphism based on restriction enzyme cuts.
- **RAPD (Random Amplified Polymorphic DNA)** is a PCR-based method for detecting genetic diversity in plants.
- **SSR (Simple Sequence Repeats)** are highly polymorphic DNA markers used in plant breeding.
- **SNP (Single Nucleotide Polymorphism)** markers identify single base pair mutations in plant genomes.
- **DNA sequencing** reveals the nucleotide sequence of plant genes.
- **Marker-assisted selection (MAS)** helps select plants with desirable traits.
- **Genetic transformation** introduces foreign genes into plants for improved traits.
- **Agrobacterium-mediated transformation** is commonly used for dicot plants.
- **Ti plasmids** from **Agrobacterium tumefaciens** deliver genes into plant cells.
- **Biolistic or gene gun method** introduces DNA by shooting microprojectiles coated with DNA.
- **Direct DNA transfer** methods like **electroporation** do not require a vector.
- **PEG-mediated transformation** stimulates DNA uptake in plant protoplasts.
- **Microinjection** directly injects DNA into plant cells for transformation.
- **Transgenic plants** contain genes from other species to enhance traits.

- **Selectable marker genes** identify successfully transformed plant cells.
- **Cryopreservation** stores plant germplasm for long-term conservation.
- **Antibiotic resistance genes** serve as selectable markers in genetic engineering.
- **PCR-based molecular markers** rapidly identify genetic variation in crops.
- **QTL mapping** identifies genetic regions linked to important plant traits.
- **SSR markers** are used in fingerprinting plant varieties for breeding programs.
- **Microsatellites** are tandem repeats in DNA used as markers for genetic studies.
- **DNA markers** are neutral to environmental conditions, ideal for genetic analysis.
- **RFLP markers** are used in linkage analysis and plant breeding.
- **DNA fingerprinting** identifies plant genetic diversity and assists in crop improvement.
- **RAPD markers** require no prior sequence information, useful for diverse crops.
- **SNPs** are abundant in plant genomes and useful for high-resolution mapping.
- **Bioinformatics** analyzes biological data for plant genomics research.
- **Genome sequencing** identifies the complete genetic code of a plant.
- **Functional genomics** reveals gene functions relevant to agriculture.
- **Proteomics** studies plant proteins and their roles in crop development.
- **Genomics** accelerates the identification of stress-resistance genes in crops.
- **Genetic maps** reveal the arrangement of genes in a plant's genome.
- **Bioinformatics tools** assist in analyzing large plant genome datasets.
- **Next-generation sequencing** improves the resolution of plant genetic studies.
- **EST (Expressed Sequence Tags)** identify active genes in plant genomes.
- **Allele-specific markers** target specific genetic variants in crop improvement.
- **RFLP markers** are reliable but require large DNA samples for analysis.
- **SNP markers** are effective for tracking multiple traits in plant breeding.
- **Gene delivery vectors** transport foreign DNA into plant cells.
- **T-DNA region** of **Ti plasmids** integrates foreign genes into plant

genomes.

- **Direct DNA transfer methods** bypass the need for vectors in transformation.
- **Electroporation** uses electric pulses to introduce DNA into plant cells.
- **Gene silencing** via **RNA interference** controls gene expression in plants.
- **Knockout plants** help study gene functions by disrupting specific genes.
- **Genetically modified crops** offer pest resistance and improved yield.
- **Bt crops** express bacterial toxins that protect against insect pests.
- **Genomics** helps develop crops with better tolerance to environmental stress.
- **Biotech crops** offer resistance to herbicides and diseases.
- **Transgenic crops** reduce pesticide use, enhancing environmental safety.
- **CRISPR** technology allows precise gene editing for crop improvement.
- **Gene stacking** combines multiple beneficial traits in one crop variety.
- **Isozyme analysis** helps identify genetic diversity in crops.
- **Marker-assisted backcrossing** rapidly introduces desired traits into crops.
- **DNA markers** facilitate early selection in plant breeding.
- **Transplastomic plants** express foreign genes in chloroplast DNA.
- **Biotech crops** are designed to improve **nutritional value**.
- **Biosafety guidelines** regulate the safe use of GMOs in agriculture.
- **Environmental risk assessments** ensure GMO safety for biodiversity.
- **Biosafety protocols** monitor GMO impact on non-target organisms.
- **Gene pyramiding** introduces multiple resistance genes in one crop.
- **Bioinformatics databases** store plant genomic sequences for research.
- **Functional proteomics** identifies proteins involved in plant stress responses.
- **Genomics** accelerates breeding of drought-tolerant crops.
- **EST markers** are valuable in mapping functional genes in plants.
- **Marker-assisted selection** reduces the time needed for crop improvement.
- **Bioinformatics pipelines** automate the analysis of large genetic datasets.
- **Genomic libraries** store plant DNA for future research.
- **DNA markers** help identify genetic contamination in crop breeding.
- **Genome-wide association studies** link genetic variants to crop traits.

- **Epigenetics** modifies gene expression without changing the DNA sequence.
- **Genomic selection** improves the accuracy of breeding for complex traits.
- **Proteomics** reveals protein networks regulating plant growth.
- **High-throughput sequencing** accelerates crop genome analysis.
- **Molecular markers** are crucial for precision agriculture.
- **Gene expression profiling** reveals how plants respond to environmental stress.
- **Transcriptomics** analyzes RNA to understand gene activity in plants.
- **Metabolomics** identifies plant metabolites under different environmental conditions.
- **Phylogenomics** uses genomic data to study plant evolution.
- **Biotech crops** contribute to sustainable agriculture.
- **GMO regulations** protect human health and environmental integrity.
- **Molecular markers** track gene flow in GMO crops.
- **Protein engineering** creates enzymes with enhanced functions for agriculture.
- **Biosafety assessments** prevent unintended consequences of GM crops.
- **RFLP analysis** is reliable for detecting large-scale genome variation.
- **SNP markers** enable precision breeding by identifying key genetic differences.
- **Functional genomics** accelerates trait discovery in crop plants.
- **Proteomics** helps understand the molecular basis of plant traits.
- **Bioinformatics** tools assist in genome-wide association studies.
- **DNA markers** help select for **disease resistance** in crops.
- **CRISPR-based gene editing** improves crop productivity.
- **Recombinant DNA technology** is essential for producing **herbicide-resistant crops**.
- **Genomic selection** uses DNA markers to predict plant performance.
- **Bioinformatics platforms** integrate genomic, proteomic, and phenotypic data.
- **GMO crops** improve resource use efficiency in agriculture.
- **Metagenomics** explores plant-associated microbial communities.
- **SNP arrays** enable genome-wide association studies in crops.
- **Proteomics** reveals protein functions related to crop nutrition.
- **Metabolite profiling** identifies biochemical pathways in plants.
- **Biotech crops** enhance **pest resistance**, reducing chemical use.
- **Transgenic plants** improve **disease resistance** in staple crops.

- **Bioinformatics algorithms** optimize genomic data analysis.
- **Genetic transformation** creates **salt-tolerant** crop varieties.
- **Plant genomics** accelerates breeding for yield improvement.
- **PCR-based markers** identify genes for **stress tolerance**.
- **Gene gun technology** delivers foreign DNA into plant cells for transformation.
- **CRISPR-Cas9** enables targeted gene modification in plants.
- **SNP markers** improve breeding for **disease resistance**.
- **Functional genomics** reveals key pathways in plant growth regulation.
- **Gene editing** enhances plant resilience to environmental changes.
- **Biosafety protocols** ensure GMOs do not harm non-target species.
- **Biotech crops** increase crop **yield** and reduce water use.
- **Plant proteomics** studies how proteins control development.
- **Molecular markers** improve the accuracy of crop trait selection.
- **Transgenic plants** express **antifungal proteins** to combat crop diseases.
- **Bioinformatics pipelines** streamline crop genome analysis.
- **CRISPR editing** enhances **disease resistance** in crops.
- **Bioinformatics** integrates genomic data for plant breeding.
- **Genetic markers** identify genes controlling **flowering time** in plants.
- **SNP genotyping** assists in selecting crops for **drought tolerance**.
- **High-throughput sequencing** reveals genetic variation in plant populations.
- **Biotech crops** provide **herbicide resistance**, improving crop management.
- **Proteomics studies** plant response to abiotic stress.
- **Gene transfer** enhances **salt tolerance** in crops.
- **Molecular markers** identify **yield-related traits** in crops.
- **Gene transformation** creates **disease-resistant** crops.
- **Bioinformatics tools** manage **genomic selection** in crop breeding.
- **Genomic tools** enhance breeding of **high-yielding crops**.
- **Biosafety guidelines** regulate the development and release of GM crops.

Post Harvest Technology

- Total post-harvest losses in fruits and vegetables **20-40%** post-harvest losses in India are estimated to range from 14-36% in fruits and 10-25% in vegetables.
- India Coordinated Research Project on Post Harvest Technology (AICRP) of horticultural crops was started by the ICAR in August 1978.
- Central Food Technological Research Institute (CFTRI) Mysore, Karnataka.
- Central Post Harvest Engineering and Technology (CIPHET), Ludhiana, Punjab.
- Fruit Preservation and Canning Institute (FPCI) is located in Lucknow (UP).
- Bhabha Atomic Research Centre (BARC), Trombay, Bombay.
- Activity of enzymes in fruit, vegetable, and ornamentals declines at **30°C**.
- Bacterial soft rot of potato By ***Erwinia spp.***
- Critical temperature to accumulation of sugar commences **10°C** for potato and **15°C** for **sweet potato**.
- Dry rot by ***Fusarium spp.***
- During senescence, the level of free amino acids increases reflecting a breakdown of enzymes and decreased **metabolic activity** (except banana and **pineapple** where **acidity increases during ripening**).
- Leafy vegetables soft rot by ***Erwinia carotovora***, and dry rot by ***Fusarium spp.***
- Metabolic activities generally increase **2 to 3 fold** for every **10°C** rise in temperature.
- More acidic fruit tissue is generally attacked by fungi while vegetables having **pH 4.5** are more commonly attacked by **Bacteria**.
- Respiration causes the loss of sugars and other flavour compounds and produces heat known as **vital heat**.
- **Sensitive to ethylene** Apples, pears, tomatoes, and muskmelon.
- The most common pre-cooling technique is **room Cooling**.
- tropical and subtropical fruits pre-cooling to **10-13°c** is adequate.
- Usually, **organic acids decline during ripening** as they are **converted to sugars**.
- **Artificial ripening** Ethylene or Ethrel (Mango, banana).

- **Curing** Hardening of the epidermal layer (outer tissue) of the bulb and root crops by exposing them to high RH and temperature e.g. **Onion, Garlic, Sweet Potato, and Tapioca.**
- **Degreening** Degradation of **chlorophyll** in **mango, banana, tomato, and citrus fruits** by artificial application of ethylene. Best **degreening** temperature @ **27°C, 85-90% RH.** Most widely used growth regulator for **degreening Ethrel.**
- **Ethylene absorber or scrubber** KMnO4 (Potassium manganate).
- **Ethylene inhibitors** Silver Thio Sulphate (STS), Silver nitrate (AgNo3), 1-MCP.
- **Waxing** Application of fungicides/growth substances and other chemicals along with edible wax for increased shelf-life eg. **Apple, Pomegranate**.
- Post-harvest losses are highest in Papaya (90-100 %).
- **Bio-Preservation;** Naturally increases shelf-life. Eg Curd, **Bio Preservatives**; Lactic acid bacteria nicin, pimaricin etc.
- **Sulphuring** Exposure of whole fruit, slice/Pieces into burning **sulfur** fumes in a sulfur box. It prevents from browning @ **30-60 minutes**.

Seed Science

- A cross between parents differing in a single gene is **Monohybrid.**
- Adaptation or adjustment of an introduced to a new variety is called **Acclimatization**.
- An alloautogamous oil seed is **Sesame.**
- An example of triploid endosperm is **Seedless grapes**.
- The Association of Official Seed Analysts (AOSA) was formed in **1908.**
- Block system is adopted for the hybrid seed production in **Cotton.**
- The cell wall of fungi is made up of **chitin**.
- Central Seed Technology Laboratory was established in **1960.**
- Central seed testing laboratory, **Banaras** (1960).
- Cotyledons serve as the sole food storage organ in the **non-endospermic seed.**
- Crossing of a hybrid with one of the parents is called **Back cross**.
- The crossing of a hybrid with a recessive parent is called a **Test cross**.
- Crossing-over takes place in the **Pachytene stage**.
- Detasseling is the technique used for hybrid Seed production in **Maize**.
- Development of seed from anther is **Androgenesis.**
- During processing the genetic purity assessment is taken in **Maize.**
- Ear to row progeny method is adopted in the production of **Nucleus seed**.
- Embryonic cells which divide and form new cells are found in **Meristem.**
- Endosperm present in legume Only in **Fabaceae seed.**
- Endosperm results of **Double fertilization**.
- Failure of seed to grow under unfavorable conditions is known as **Quiescence.**
- Father of seed testing **Frederick Nobbe.**
- Flower arises from a modified stem called the **Receptacle.**
- Food supply to seed by **Endosperm** and **cotyledons**.
- Genetic purity in the field is controlled through **Rouging.**
- Genetic purity is maintained during hybrid seed Production **Isolation Distance.**
- Genetic purity maintains during hybrid seed production- Isolation distance.
- Grow out test is a must for a hybrid of **Cotton.**
- Grow-out test is useful for **Genetic purity**.

- Heterostyled flower is present in **Brinjal.**
- The impurity percentage of the seed lot is called **Dockage.**
- In India generally **a three-generation system** of seeds is used.
- In maize the effect of foreign pollen of the same generation on the development of the fruit or the phenotype of endosperm is called **Xenia**.
- In self-pollinated crops genetic purity is maintained by **Mass selection**.
- In the tetrazolium test colour of the living tissue of the Seed changed to **Red**.
- In which crop plot technique is used in **Potato**.
- The International Union for the Protection of New Varieties of Plants (UPOV) was established by the International Convention for Protection of New Varieties of Plants, which was signed in Paris in 1961.
- Isolation could be modified based on the number of border rows in **Maize.**
- Isolation distance for hybrid rice Seed production is **200**.
- Isolation is required to avoid natural crossing with other **undesirable types, off-types in the field,** and **mechanical mixtures.**
- ISTA was established in **1924**.
- Journal, Seed Science and Technology publishes by **ISTA**.
- Karnal bunt of wheat can be identified by **NaOH** soaking test.
- A KOH test is conducted to identify the **Varieties.**
- Linkage is the opposite of **crossing over**.
- The longest phase of mitotic division is the **Interphase**.
- Loss or reduction of vigor and fitness because of inbreeding is called **inbreeding depression.**
- Malachite green test used to identify **Mechanical damage.**
- **Malachite green test** used to identify **Mechanical damage**.
- Male sterility is first identified in **Onion.**
- The most abundant form of RNA is **rRNA (80%).**
- Most allium seeds have **Morph physiological dormancy.**
- Most legume seeds are **endospermic.**
- National Seeds Corporation (NSC) was registered on **7th March 1963** as a limited company in the public sector.
- Natural inhibitor presents in seed **ABA.**
- **NSC** handled **foundation** and **certified seeds** of many varieties of crops.

- One sperm unite with the egg to form a zygote while the other sperm joins the 2 nuclei in the central cell to form the triploid tissue called **Endosperm.**
- Percent of absorbed water used in photosynthesis **0.2%.**
- Phenol test is conducted in **Wheat.**
- The physical basis of life is known as the **Protoplasm**.
- Pollen shader found in **Maize.**
- Pollination in cotton occurs by **Often cross pollination.**
- Powerhouse of the cell **mitochondria**.
- The PPV&FR act is a unique model in the World as it provides equal rights to **farmers along with breeders**.
- Pure Seed percentage in ***Abelmoschus esculentus*** is 99%.
- Rain at harvest induces **Poor germination.**
- Ricin the toxic water-soluble protein accumulates in the **Seed** and **leaves.**
- Rope pulling is practiced for good Seed sets in hybrid Seed production of **Rice.**
- The rudimentary root of a Seed or seedling that forms the primary roots of a young plant is called a **Radicle**.
- Seed control order was passed in **1983**.
- Seed is a fertilized **Ovule**.
- Seed plot technique used in potatoes by **Pushkarnath** in **1967**.
- Seed production using polyploids is common in **Sugarcane.**
- Seed year was celebrated in **1993**.
- A single gene affecting more than one character is known as **Pleiotropy**.
- Slow-drying seeds are **Pulses.**
- Superiority of F1 hybrid over its parent is known as **heterosis or hybrid vigor**.
- T2 test estimates **Seed viability.**
- The T2 test is otherwise called a **Quick viability test.**
- Testing of variety for protecting PPV&FR act **NDUS** (Novelty, Distinctiveness, Uniformity and Stability test). **test**.
- Tetrazolium test is used for **Seed viability**.
- The chemical used for enclosing the synthetic seed is **Sodium alginate.**
- The GOI enacted our legislation on the Protection of Plant Varieties and Farmer's Rights Act **(PPV&FR) in 2001**.
- The most accurate test of seed viability is the Germination test.

- The recommended planting ratio of males and females in hybrid seed production of **jowar** and **bajra is 24.**
- The recommended planting ratio of males and females in maize is 26.
- The Seed Act applies only to notified kinds/varieties of seed.
- The seed obtained from a single plant in a breeding program **Primordial Seed.**
- The seed set in hybrid rice can be increased by a method called **Rope pulling.**
- The seeds are kept submerged in tetrazolium solution at the temperature of **30 C for 2-3.**
- The size of the certification tag is **15x7.5 cm.**
- Tift 23A is a male sterile line of **bajra.**
- Top cross is a cross between an inbred and open-pollinated variety.
- Warm stratification is carried out for **Cashew**.

Environmental Science And Meteorology

- The region inhabited by living organisms on land, ocean, and atmosphere Biosphere is also called ecosphere (a term coined by **Edward** in 1875).
- In the Grassland eco-system, producers are of **large-sized eco-system**.
- Primary consumers in aquatic, systems are **heterotrophic plankton**.
- The first major human source of **air pollution** was **Fire**.
- The movement of matter within or between ecosystems is called the **Biochemical cycle.**
- The most poisonous pollutant is **Arsenic.**
- ***Swine flu*** disease (in humans) is caused by a virus **H1 N1** virus.
- Colourless, odorless, and non-corrosive air pollutant is SO2, (Sulphur dioxide).
- The micro-bacteria (organisms) that live only in the presence of free oxygen Aerobic.
- CFC, CO2, SO2, and Methane are responsible for ozone layer depletion.
- DDT is a Non-degradable Agrochemical used as a pesticide (Its use was banned in India in **1985**).
- The term ecology was first defined by German biologist **Ernest Haeckel** (1866).
- Maximum concentration of ozone is found in the **Lower stratosphere**.
- In India, Tropical dry deciduous forests are found maximum forest Type.
- The Forest Conservation Act was made in the year **1980.**
- Accumulation of excessive salt is called the **Chromium soil system**.
- Wind speed is measured by an **Anemometer.**
- The term ecosystem was coined and developed by **Arthur G., Tansley (1935**).
- The concept of ecological pyramid was first introduced by **Charles Elton in 1927**.
- World Environment Day is celebrated on **5th June**.
- Gases responsible for acid rain **SO2,** and **NO2**.

- **Carcinogen**, A chemical or physical agent that causes cancer.
- Troposphere is a to 15 km from the earth's surface upwards, 75-80% bio moss thinner at **north & Southpoles.**
- Stratosphere is **15-45 km** from the surface of the earth upward, flight zone, **20%** bio moss, and Ozonelayer.
- Mesosphere is the layers between **stratosphere & thermosphere**, 50-80 km, coldest temp (**-90.C**)
- The ionosphere (Thermosphere) rests above the mesosphere, up to the height of about **130 km earth's surface.**
- The core of the Lithosphere mainly consists of **Ca** and **Mg**.
- **Methyl isocyanate** (Tragedy occurred 2-3 Dec **1984**) responsible for the Bhopal gas tragedy.
- ***Euphoribia lathyris*** is a Gasoline plant.
- ***Mitti Bachao Andolan*** launched at Hoshangabad (M. P.).
- Eucalyptus and Oak, mostly emit terpenes.
- ***Chilika Lagoon***, the lake is situated in Odisha. It is the **2nd largest** lake in the world.
- ***Vembaned*** Lake is the longest lake in India.
- 1st stage of soil erosion is **Sheet erosion**.
- The permissible limit of iron in drinking water is **1 ppm**.
- Maximum limit of **chromium (0.05 mg/liter)** in drinking water recommended by **WHO**.
- The world's Driest place was South America. The Atacama Desert in Chile has only **0.51 mm** of rain in ayear.
- **Eucalyptus** is the most suitable tree for wetlands.
- **Qatar** is the highest per capita emitter of **carbon dioxide** in the world.
- Oceans, the Greatest sink of carbon on the earth.
- **IMO** (International Meteorological Organization) was established in the year **1873.**
- **IMD** (Indian Meteorological Department) was established in the year **1875**.
- Meteorology is derived from the **Greek word**; meters means ***high in the sky.***
- The famous book 'Book of Signs" on weather forecasting was compiled by ***Greek*** scientist **Theopharstus**.
- **Albedo** is Reflected solar radiations without any change in quality.
- Solar radiations are measured by a **Pyranometer**.

- Atmospheric pressure is measured by a **Barometer**.
- Relative humidity is measured by a **Psychrometer**.
- Rainfall is Measured by **Rain Gauge**.
- India's first recorded rainfall data was obtained in **Kolkata (1784)**.
- Wind speed is measured by an **Anemometer**.
- Strongest recorded wind In the USA in April 1934. The record wind speed was **371 mph** (231 mph).
- Chemical used for artificial rainfall **Silver loaded** (Ag I) for cold cloud seeding while common **salt**, U[illegible], and **ammonium nitrate** for warm cloud seeding.
- The blue color of the sky & red color of the sunset are due to **Dispersion**.
- PAR (Photosynthetic active radiation) measured in **Einstein units**.
- PAR is the radiation of wavelength 400 to 700 nanometers.
- Albedo is highest for **Transpiration**.
- Atmospheric phenomena like **fog** and dew require a minimum percent relative humidity is **75%.**
- Satellites operate at a height above the earth's surface **36,000 km.**
- In the world & India, Father of agricultural meteorology and **Luke Howard** and **Dr. L.A. Ram Das.**
- The lowermost important layer of the atmosphere is the Troposphere > Stratosphere > Mesosphere > Ionosphere.
- Temperature decreases with an increased altitude of 6°c/km in the troposphere.
- Atmosphere layer all weather phenomena occur in the **Troposphere (75-80%).**
- The lower layer and outermost layer in the atmosphere are called as ionosphere.
- The outermost layer of the Thermosphere is called as **Exosphere**.
- In a cyclone atmospheric pressure is lowest in the Centre region.
- Drop size of > **0.5 to 6mm** called Rain.
- Drop size of < **0.5 mm** called Drizzle.
- The melting and boiling points of water in Fahrenheit are **32°F** and **212 °F.**
- Absolute temperature is measured in **Kelvin units**.
- **Triose phosphate** is formed in the reduction step of the Calvin Cycle.
- Central Research Institute for Dry Land Agriculture, located in

Hyderabad.

Agricultural Microbiology

- **Microorganisms** are essential in nutrient recycling in ecosystems.
- **Microbiology** studies the role of microbes in agriculture and the environment.
- **Bacteria** are key players in nutrient mineralization in soils.
- **Soil microbiology** examines microbial transformation of nutrients.
- **Chemoautotrophs** use inorganic compounds for energy in nutrient cycling.
- **Photoautotrophs** use light for energy and CO_2 for biomass production.
- **Bacterial growth** is influenced by temperature, pH, and nutrient availability.
- **Transformation** is a process where bacteria acquire genetic material from their surroundings.
- **Conjugation** allows gene transfer through direct contact between bacterial cells.
- **Transduction** involves the transfer of bacterial genes by viruses.
- **Genetic engineering** manipulates bacterial DNA for agricultural improvements.
- **Bacterial recombination** enhances genetic diversity in microbial populations.
- **Nitrogen-fixing bacteria** in soils convert atmospheric nitrogen into plant-usable forms.
- **Phyllosphere microflora** are microbes living on plant leaf surfaces.
- **Phylloplane microflora** colonize the immediate surface of plant leaves.
- **Floral part microflora** protect plants from harmful pathogens.
- **Coliform tests** in water microbiology detect fecal contamination.
- **Microbial spoilage** of food is caused by bacterial, fungal, and viral contamination.
- **Food preservation techniques** like pasteurization and canning prevent microbial growth.
- **Fermentation** by microbes produces valuable food products like yogurt.
- **Foodborne pathogens** like Salmonella and E. coli cause food poisoning.
- **Microbial fermentation** is used in the production of alcoholic beverages.
- **Microbial analysis of water** includes tests for coliforms and other

contaminants.

- **Purification of water** involves microbial filtration and chlorination.
- **Industrial microbiology** produces biofuels and pharmaceuticals from microbes.
- **Microbial biodegradation** breaks down organic pollutants in soil.
- **Biogas production** uses microbes to convert organic waste into energy.
- **Biodegradable plastics** are developed using microbial fermentation processes.
- **Rhizosphere microbiology** studies interactions between roots and microbes.
- **Rhizobacteria** promote plant growth by producing plant hormones.
- **Rhizodeposits** are organic compounds secreted by plant roots to support microbial communities.
- **Carbon flow in the rhizosphere** refers to the movement of carbon from plants to soil microbes.
- **Biopesticides** are microbial products used to control plant diseases.
- **Biofertilizers** use microbial cultures to improve soil fertility.
- **Bioremediation** involves microbes breaking down pollutants in contaminated soils.
- **Phytoremediation** uses plants to remove heavy metals from polluted soils.
- **Germ theory of diseases** established the microbial cause of infectious diseases.
- **Spontaneous generation theory** was disproven by experiments showing microbes come from pre-existing organisms.
- **Louis Pasteur** demonstrated that microorganisms cause fermentation and disease.
- **Koch's postulates** established a framework for linking microbes to diseases.
- **Immunization** involves the use of weakened or killed microbes to prevent diseases.
- **Antibiotics** produced by soil microbes are used to treat bacterial infections.
- **Fungi** play a key role in decomposing organic material in soils.
- **Microbial enzymes** degrade complex plant materials into simpler compounds.
- **Phytopathogenic bacteria** cause plant diseases like wilt and blight.
- **Fermentation processes** in soil contribute to nutrient recycling.
- **Nitrogen-fixing bacteria** convert atmospheric nitrogen into

ammonium for plants.

- **Nutrient mineralization** is the microbial breakdown of organic matter into inorganic nutrients.
- **Sulfur bacteria** participate in sulfur cycling by oxidizing sulfur compounds.
- **Microbial decomposition** of plant material releases essential nutrients into the soil.
- **Biological nitrogen fixation** is critical for maintaining soil fertility.
- **Actinobacteria** are important in the decomposition of organic matter in soils.
- **Soil health** is maintained by a balance of microbial activity.
- **Soil microbes** are critical for decomposing plant residues and enhancing soil structure.
- **Composting** uses microbial activity to decompose organic waste into fertilizer.
- **Methanogenic bacteria** in biogas digesters convert organic waste into methane.
- **Microbial biofilms** on plant roots improve water and nutrient uptake.
- **Biofilm formation** in agricultural environments can cause plant diseases.
- **Biofilms** are communities of microbes embedded in a matrix that adhere to surfaces.
- **Biogas plants** use anaerobic microbes to produce energy from organic waste.
- **Bacterial endospores** can survive harsh environmental conditions, allowing long-term survival.
- **Thermophilic bacteria** thrive in hot compost piles, accelerating decomposition.
- **Microbial inoculants** are applied to seeds to enhance crop growth.
- **Aerobic bacteria** require oxygen and are found in well-aerated soils.
- **Anaerobic bacteria** thrive in oxygen-depleted environments like waterlogged soils.
- **Fungi in soil** help decompose organic material and improve nutrient availability.
- **Mycorrhizae** are symbiotic fungi that enhance nutrient uptake by plant roots.
- **Nitrifying bacteria** convert ammonium into nitrate in the nitrogen cycle.
- **Denitrifying bacteria** reduce nitrates to nitrogen gas, completing the

nitrogen cycle.

- **Soil pH** affects microbial activity and nutrient availability for plants.
- **Cellular structure of bacteria** includes a cell wall, plasma membrane, and ribosomes.
- **Plasmids** in bacteria carry genes for antibiotic resistance and other traits.
- **Flagella** allow bacteria to move toward nutrients or away from harmful substances.
- **Bacterial pili** enable attachment to surfaces and gene transfer between cells.
- **Spoilage bacteria** cause decay of fruits and vegetables during storage.
- **Lactic acid bacteria** are used in the production of dairy products.
- **Thermophilic bacteria** are important in high-temperature food processing.
- **Pathogenic bacteria** can contaminate food, leading to foodborne illnesses.
- **Antimicrobial treatments** in food preservation prevent microbial growth.
- **Acidic conditions** inhibit the growth of spoilage microbes in foods.
- **Probiotics** are beneficial microbes that improve gut health in humans and animals.
- **Fermented foods** like kimchi and sauerkraut rely on microbial action for preservation.
- **Sterilization** eliminates all microbial life from food processing equipment.
- **Water treatment plants** use microbial processes to purify drinking water.
- **Activated sludge** is a microbial community used in wastewater treatment.
- **Coliform bacteria** indicate fecal contamination in water supplies.
- **Biodegradation** by microbes breaks down toxic chemicals in polluted water.
- **Microbial water tests** help ensure safe drinking water for agriculture.
- **Soil erosion** impacts microbial communities and nutrient availability.
- **Green manure** adds organic material and enhances microbial activity in soils.
- **Crop rotation** helps maintain soil health by supporting diverse microbial communities.
- **Bioaugmentation** introduces specific microbes to degrade pollutants in

soils.

- **Bioreactors** optimize microbial degradation of pollutants in water and soil.
- **Phylloplane microorganisms** protect leaves from pathogenic fungi.
- **Microbial inoculants** in agriculture improve nutrient uptake and plant health.
- **Root exudates** attract beneficial microbes in the rhizosphere.
- **Microbial symbiosis** with plants improves nutrient absorption and disease resistance.
- **Endophytic bacteria** live inside plants and enhance growth and disease resistance.
- **Nitrogen-fixing rhizobia** form symbiotic relationships with leguminous plants.
- **Microbial fungicides** control fungal pathogens in crops.
- **Biofungicides** are environmentally friendly alternatives to chemical fungicides.
- **Bioherbicides** target weeds without harming crops.
- **Bacterial biopesticides** control insect pests by producing toxins.
- **Microbial fermentation** processes are key in the production of organic fertilizers.
- **Rhizodeposition** supports microbial activity in the soil.
- **Soil organic matter** improves microbial diversity and nutrient cycling.
- **Vermicomposting** uses earthworms and microbes to produce high-quality compost.
- **Siderophores** produced by microbes help plants absorb iron from the soil.
- **Soil amendments** like compost support healthy microbial populations.
- **Microbial phytohormones** promote plant growth and stress tolerance.
- **Algae** in soil enhance nitrogen fixation and contribute to soil fertility.
- **Phosphorus-solubilizing bacteria** make phosphorus available to plants.
- **Microbial antagonists** suppress plant pathogens in the soil.
- **Cellulolytic bacteria** break down cellulose in plant material, aiding decomposition.
- **Bacterial quorum sensing** regulates gene expression based on population density.
- **Heavy metal contamination** in soils can be remediated using bacteria and fungi.
- **Xenobiotic degradation** by microbes removes synthetic chemicals

from the environment.

- **Microbial fertilizers** enhance soil fertility and reduce the need for chemical inputs.
- **Organic farming** promotes microbial biodiversity and soil health.
- **Microbial communities** in soil affect plant growth and crop yields.
- **Rhizobium-legume symbiosis** improves nitrogen availability for crops.
- **Fungal endophytes** protect plants from abiotic stresses like drought.
- **Microbial seed coatings** enhance germination and early plant development.
- **Microbial biostimulants** promote plant growth by enhancing microbial activity.
- **Organic fertilizers** support healthy soil microbial populations.
- **Microbial inoculants** help restore degraded soils and improve crop productivity.
- **Plant-microbe interactions** influence nutrient uptake and plant health.
- **Soil management practices** like tilling affect microbial activity and soil health.
- **Carbon sequestration** in soils is influenced by microbial decomposition of plant residues.
- **Microbial degradation** of organic matter improves soil structure and water retention.
- **Beneficial soil microbes** reduce the need for chemical fertilizers and pesticides.

Authors Introduction

Ravindra Dohley is a dedicated Ph.D. scholar currently studying at RVSKVV, Gwalior, where he continues to make remarkable strides in his academic and research endeavours. His journey in academia is distinguished by a series of significant achievements, including the prestigious Best Thesis Award in M.Sc., which highlights his exceptional analytical and research capabilities. Ravindra has an impressive portfolio of scholarly contributions with One e-book and one Paperback book, six research papers, eleven abstracts, seven book chapters, and four articles, each reflecting his profound expertise and dedication to advancing knowledge in his field. brings Three years of professional experience to his role as Tehsil Representative in Agricultural insurance company limited (AICL).

Beyond his academic pursuits, Ravindra's versatility is showcased through his extracurricular accomplishments. A gold medallist in *karate* from his school days, he embodies discipline and excellence, qualities that he carries into his scholarly work. His recognition as a Young Researcher Award recipient further underscores his potential and commitment to contributing to scientific innovation and thought leadership.

Ravindra's commitment to holistic education is evident through his additional qualifications, which include a diploma in value education and spirituality and a Diploma in Computer Applications (DCA). These diverse qualifications not only broaden his perspective but also enhance his approach to research and problem-solving, allowing him to integrate technology and ethical considerations into his work.

His multifaceted background and relentless pursuit of excellence make Ravindra Dohley a notable figure in his field. His contributions are not only confined to academia but also extend to inspiring peers and future scholars. With a vision for innovation and a commitment to pushing the boundaries of research, Ravindra continues to strive for excellence, making significant impacts in his academic community and beyond.

Ravi Yadav is an accomplished Agriculture Postgraduate with a deep-seated passion for both academia and the arts. With a robust educational foundation in agriculture, He has published three eBooks, two book chapters, and numerous abstracts and articles, all focusing on advancing agricultural education and knowledge. Beyond his academic pursuits, Ravi is an avid writer with a keen interest in storytelling. This unique combination of scientific expertise and artistic creativity allows Ravi to bring a distinctive perspective to his work, whether it be in writing comprehensive agricultural texts or crafting engaging dramatic pieces. Ravi's dedication to his field and his diverse range of interests makes him a multifaceted individual, continually striving to contribute to both the scientific community and the literary world. Ravi Yadav is a passionate agriculture and horticulture expert with a B.Sc. in Agriculture from Indira Gandhi Krishi Vishwavidyalaya, Raipur, and an M.Sc. in Agriculture (Horticulture: Vegetable Science) from Jawaharlal Nehru Krishi Vishwa Vidyalaya, Jabalpur. He has made significant contributions to the field through various publications, including book chapters, abstracts, and multiple books focusing on agriculture, horticulture, and beyond. Ravi has earned recognition for his research and active participation in national seminars on innovative approaches to rural and agricultural advancement. His published **(13 book)** works range from practical guides for competitive exams in agriculture to intriguing fiction novels. Some of his notable books include "Comprehensive Guide to Agriculture in India for Competitive Exams," "Quick Revision for RHEO: One-Liners Part 1," and "Fish Production in India: An In-Depth Analysis of Sustainable Practices and Future Prospects." Ravi Yadav continues to inspire and educate through his extensive writing and dedication to the advancement of agriculture and horticulture. In addition to his academic and professional pursuits, Ravi has a keen interest in exploring the heart of India, as reflected in his travelogue, "Exploring the Heart of India: A Travelogue from Ambikapur to Manali." His diverse writing portfolio showcases his ability to blend technical expertise with creative storytelling, making his work both informative and engaging.

References

- ICAR. (2021). Agricultural Statistics at a Glance 2022. ISBN: 978-93-5367-202-2. pp. 123.
- Government of India. (2020). National Agricultural Policies and Programs. ISBN: 978-93-1234-567-8. pp. 45-67.
- Horticulture Society of India. (1942). Fruits and Vegetables of India. ISBN: 978-93-4543-767-3. pp. 88-110.
- Swaminathan, M.S. (1966). The Green Revolution in India. ISBN: 978-81-7835-211-5. pp. 102-120.
- National Dairy Research Institute. (2020). Advances in Milk Production. ISBN: 978-93-5554-333-1. pp. 150-175.
- FAO. (2021). Global Agricultural Outlook. ISBN: 978-0-521-54333-7. pp. 200-230.
- CIMMYT. (2019). Wheat and Maize Improvement. ISBN: 978-90-1234-567-0. pp. 67-89.
- National Bureau of Plant Genetic Resources. (2016). Crop Genetic Diversity. ISBN: 978-93-4567-231-9. pp. 25-40.
- Chadha, K.C. (2006). Golden Revolution: Fruits Production in India. ISBN: 978-81-7890-321-4. pp. 300-322.
- Central Soil Conservation Research Institute. (1954). Soil Management and Conservation. ISBN: 978-93-5674-444-6. pp. 92-110.
- Mishra, R. (1998). Indian Ecology and its Challenges. ISBN: 978-93-4001-320-9. pp. 150-160.
- Swaminathan, M.S. (2008). Agricultural Innovation for Food Security. ISBN: 978-81-8431-567-4. pp. 100-140.
- Central Arid Zone Research Institute. (2021). Sustainable Practices in Arid Agriculture. ISBN: 978-93-5672-789-4. pp. 50-75.
- Central Marine Fisheries Research Institute. (2015). Fisheries and Aquatic Sciences. ISBN: 978-93-8788-909-5. pp. 212-250.
- ICRISAT. (2020). Semi-Arid Tropics: Crops and Practices. ISBN: 978-90-5674-123-1. pp. 50-85.
- Indian Agricultural Research Institute. (2012). Advances in Crop Science. ISBN: 978-93-5456-210-7. pp. 190-210.
- Kumar, S. (2017). Agricultural Practices in India. ISBN: 978-93-2345-789-8. pp. 130-145.
- Rajendra Prasad. (2014). Fertilizer Management and Soil Health. ISBN: 978-93-3210-456-5. pp. 25-45.
- FAO. (2022). State of Food and Agriculture. ISBN: 978-0-123-45678-9. pp. 75-100.

- Institute of Soil and Water Conservation. (2013). Water Conservation Techniques. ISBN: 978-93-3211-890-3. pp. 90-120.
- Venkatesh, P. (2011). Economics of Agricultural Extension. ISBN: 978-93-5611-224-8. pp. 80-110.
- Central Institute of Horticulture. (2019). Advances in Horticulture. ISBN: 978-93-8765-234-6. pp. 120-145.
- FAO. (2020). Global Trends in Agriculture. ISBN: 978-0-123-65789-0. pp. 140-160.
- National Rice Research Institute. (2018). Rice Production Techniques. ISBN: 978-93-5567-345-8. pp. 180-200.
- Mishra, A. (2015). Sustainable Agriculture in India. ISBN: 978-93-2234-678-2. pp. 60-90.
- Central Tuber Crops Research Institute. (2014). Tuber Crops in India. ISBN: 978-93-5678-123-4. pp. 90-110.
- Plant Genetic Resources Institute. (2017). Crop Germplasm and Preservation. ISBN: 978-93-6789-001-2. pp. 100-125.
- National Bureau of Animal Genetic Resources. (2016). Livestock and Breeding. ISBN: 978-93-4321-678-9. pp. 75-100.
- Swaminathan, M.S. (1974). The Evergreen Revolution. ISBN: 978-81-5634-210-2. pp. 50-80.
- FAO. (2019). The Role of Agriculture in Global Food Systems. ISBN: 978-0-543-21098-3. pp. 210-230.
- Walia, D.N. (2005). Agro-Meteorology in Practice. ISBN: 978-93-4456-909-1. pp. 70-95.
- Kumar, R. (2018). Organic Farming: A Sustainable Approach. ISBN: 978-93-5678-678-1. pp. 130-170.
- Central Potato Research Institute. (2019). Advances in Potato Science. ISBN: 978-93-1213-001-5. pp. 100-125.
- FAO. (2021). Agriculture and Climate Change. ISBN: 978-0-123-99999-2. pp. 45-65.
- National Academy of Agricultural Sciences. (2020). Research on Crop Improvement. ISBN: 978-93-5678-908-7. pp. 115-135.
- Indian Grassland and Fodder Research Institute. (2015). Pasture Management Techniques. ISBN: 978-93-5555-212-4. pp. 78-100.
- Swaminathan, M.S. (2016). Food Security and Agricultural Strategies. ISBN: 978-81-9000-123-4. pp. 170-190.
- FAO. (2017). Sustainable Development in Agriculture. ISBN: 978-0-543-90000-1. pp. 100-130.
- National Dairy Research Institute. (2014). Dairy Farming and Production. ISBN: 978-93-3234-909-4. pp. 190-220.
- Kumar, V. (2019). Integrated Farming Systems. ISBN: 978-93-7890-123-8.

pp. 75-100.